The Gardening Book

Monty Don

An Accessible Guide to Growing Houseplants, Flowers,
and Vegetables for Your Ideal Garden

PHOTOGRAPHY BY MARSHA ARNOLD

Gardeners' World

CLARKSON POTTER/PUBLISHERS
New York

CONTENTS

INTRODUCTION

If you are new to gardening it can seem a bit daunting. There is an awful lot to learn, a whole load of Latin names and a world of pests, diseases and seasonal imperatives waiting to scupper your best horticultural intentions.

But don't worry about any of that. It is not an exam. No one is judging you. The only point in gardening is to try and make something beautiful whilst working in tandem with nature. As a by-product you will experience intense and lasting satisfaction. That is not a bad deal.

A garden is no more random than a meal. When you select food from a menu or a shop you are editing based upon inclination, experience and circumstance. Making a garden uses exactly the same processes.

So the most important question to ask yourself before you start any kind of garden project, is what do you want from it? How can it best serve your needs and desires?

Challenge some of the preconceptions of a 'good garden'. Do you really want a lawn? If you have children then it is almost certainly a good idea but in a small garden lawns are hard to look after and keep looking good. Their function as an open space can often be better performed by a paved area, which will have the advantage of being a firm, dry surface all year round.

You do not have to have flowers. I have seen stunning gardens that are entirely green all year round. You do not even have to have any plants. A garden is whatever you want it to be. No one else can dream your dreams for you.

Although gardens often serve different functions for different occasions and users, no garden can do everything. The more specific you are about what you want from a garden, the more likely you are to create a space that works well for you.

Of course, your lifestyle will evolve and change with time – but so can gardens. In fact, one of the first things to understand about any garden is that light, the seasons, weather and the rhythm of plant growth mean that it is constantly changing. It cannot be fixed at one perfect moment in the way that a built space can be fixed.

Gardens are only alive when they are interactive. Passively admiring a show garden might be pleasurable and informative but nothing is actually happening. In effect such gardens would perform just as effectively as pictures – which is perhaps why they work so well on television.

Every garden needs a gardener to come alive. The gardener, however inexperienced (or frankly, bewildered), is always directly part of the process of the garden itself. It is a relationship between mankind and the natural world. The way that you walk around it, the effect of footfall on the soil, the way that colours, textures and fragrances impact you all shape that relationship.

Anybody who has had the good fortune to enjoy a lovely garden will testify to the extent that it enriches and adds to their lives, and the profound beneficial effect it has on physical and mental health.

This works with all kinds of gardens, of every type and situation. We are conditioned to think that there are archetypal gardens that are 'better' than others, and feel pressure from media of all kinds to aspire or conform to those paradigms. I am sure that I have been guilty of being party to this at times. But it is not true and not helpful to anyone trying to make a garden that is relevant to them and their life.

The truth is, a garden is a creative process. It can be whatever you want or need it to be.

No garden can please everybody. But every garden can be a delight for those that use and live in it. The key to making your garden right for you and the way you live your life is this process of editing and decision making.

To help focus how you can channel your garden, however big or small, to best complement and enrich your particular lifestyle and needs, I think that most gardens can be whittled down to six main areas of focus. There is obviously overlap between them, but each has its own distinct characteristics and horticultural drivers that will affect the significant initial decisions you make.

A GARDEN TO ENTERTAIN IN

This garden is focused around the desire to have somewhere to sit, eat, drink and share with friends and family when the weather is good.

That does not exclude having beautiful plants, attracting wildlife or having a sanctuary to relax in, but those things will be secondary considerations and unless you have a large space will inevitably be subject to compromise.

The first thing to do is follow the sun. Find out where, and even more importantly, when, it shines on the garden. Wherever that might be is where the active heart of the garden is and the centre around which everything else will turn.

This will be where you create a paved area with table, seats, perhaps a full-blown outdoor kitchen or simple barbecue, pots with fragrant flowers, culinary herbs and also – not least – a sense of sufficient privacy, although that will mean different things to different people.

Having found where the sun shines, you need to decide at what time of day you are most likely to use this space. For most people it will be in the evening, so you need to go where the last of the daylight falls. But it may be that lunchtime at weekends is the big moment, so midday sun is important, or perhaps midday shade. We have an eating area that is ideal in the morning and for lunch in spring and autumn but too hot in summer. Everything melts.

The central point is that the ideal spot might be at the far end of the plot or might be just outside the back door. But follow the sun. Even in a small garden it might be most practical to have more than one entertaining space. In our small London garden in the 1980s we had a seating space by the house that got the morning sun, and a path that led down the garden to another paved area with a table that had the best of the evening's light and warmth.

Take into account your likely seasonal use. Are you likely to use the garden to entertain yourself and others in winter? In which case you will definitely need plenty of paved/hard-surfaced area – because grass is muddy in winter – and space for a fire-pit or similar heating. But inevitably most use will be between April and October so the planting must reflect that. It needs to have fragrance, seasonal colour and an uncluttered, strong but stylish design. The majority of this will come from containers on the paved area and easy-to-maintain shrubs and perennials in the borders.

It is likely that the maintenance of the garden is focused on keeping it looking as you want it, rather than as a fulfilling pastime in itself, so keep it simple. Consider clipped, simple topiary shapes for structure, especially in winter, and plants like rosemary and lavender for summer fragrance and tactility. Use annuals for summer colour. Herbs you can use daily for cooking – grown in containers or a raised bed – will be both practical and can look very stylish. However complex, mixed borders are unlikely to be a main priority.

AN EDIBLE GARDEN

If you have a garden of any kind then it can be a source of delicious, seasonal produce that will be free from chemicals, ecologically damaging growing practices and travel miles, do you good and give the real added satisfaction of having been raised with your own hands.

But above all, I have yet to meet a single person who does not agree that anything grown at home, picked when ready and in its due season and eaten absolutely fresh does not taste better than anything, however glossily packaged, from any shop.

We have all grown to expect to have access to exactly the same food in the middle of winter as we do in summer, almost as a right. But this comes at a high cost, financially, environmentally and to a deeper connection to life's seasonal rhythms. More and more people are growing up completely unaware that vegetables and fruits have seasons and meanings that are connected to the rhythm of life.

You really do not need a lot of space, although deep shade can be a problem. As long as you have sunshine for half the day, most vegetables, fruits and herbs can be grown well.

Raised beds are excellent for vegetables and herbs and can be created on a rooftop or concrete yard as well as a conventional back garden. Many vegetables can be raised in a variety of containers, and many herbs do especially well in pots.

Fruit trees can be trained and pruned to grow and bear lots of fruit against walls, fences or as free-standing espaliers or step-overs (see page 240) that take up very little space and look really good.

Unless you are lucky enough to have an allotment or a big garden it is best to edit expectations by growing a few things that you love, so that you can eat them at their very best. Modern storage and transport means that produce like pears, strawberries, sweetcorn or new potatoes are very hard to find when truly ripe and ready.

It is also possible to supply yourself with herbs like basil or parsley in the kind of generous quantities that open up a whole range of culinary opportunities.

You might want to focus your efforts on bringing the produce to a crescendo for a few special occasions, like a summer birthday or pumpkins for Halloween. Perhaps – as I do – you want the freshness that salad leaves can give you for as much of the year as possible and make that your priority.

It really does not matter what your aim is. But by focusing it a little you will maximise the potential of your space and time. Make somewhere to eat outside and capitalise on the beauty of edible plants as well as their productivity.

The secret is to keep it simple. Grow what you like to eat. Whatever that may be, harvest it at its perfect moment, prepare it as simply as possible and share it with friends and family. Few things in life give or create more pleasure.

A WILDLIFE GARDEN

Throughout the twentieth century, many gardeners were indoctrinated with the belief that nature was full of 'pests' existing with the sole intention of destroying your prize plants. However, you can create a haven for wildlife whilst also creating and maintaining a beautiful and productive garden. The two are certainly not mutually exclusive. An increasing number of gardeners now (at last!) realise that as well as giving us a huge amount of pleasure, a rich and diverse wildlife is one of the best ways to ensure that your garden is healthy.

We are still a culture that associates 'good' and 'interesting' wildlife with the remote and rare, fed by amazing footage of creatures in the Himalayas, rainforests, frozen wastes or depths of the sea. Although this informs and entertains us hugely it also has the effect of distancing us from the wildlife on our doorstep. However this is changing a little. Over recent years – not least due to enforced familiarity resulting from lockdowns during the Covid 19 pandemic – enforced containment meant that people could take their time, and a new delight was discovered in the ordinary and local. They discovered that the natural world outside their back door is as rich and fascinating as anywhere on this planet. If you maximise the opportunities for wildlife to thrive in your garden, nature ceases to be something separate from us, permanently on the other side of a screen, but instead part of our everyday lives.

As well as the pleasure that this is giving, it has made garden owners aware of the importance that their gardens – and they as gardeners – have in conserving and protecting our wildlife. Gardens are not just at the cutting edge of climate change but the front line of the natural world too.

There is also the growing awareness that our gardens are increasingly a vital habitat for a wide range of life. For example, hedgehogs are now much more common in gardens than in the agricultural countryside and songbirds such as blackbirds, thrushes and robins also thrive in back gardens but struggle to survive on modern farmland.

For far too long gardeners have categorised too many things as 'pests'. Inevitably, some creatures are more attractive than others – we are all susceptible to the Fluffy Bunny syndrome to some extent – but the goal is to create a balance of predator and prey that can sustain itself without destroying our garden. This invariably means increasing the range of species rather than the number of any one species.

A healthy, balanced wildlife population in a garden is a pyramid. The broader the base, the higher the pyramid can rise. The base is invariably formed of insects and invertebrates, and anything you can do to increase them will directly improve conditions for birds, bats, many mammals, amphibians and reptiles – as well as improving pollination for your plants.

Long grass; flowers that are nectar and pollen filled and accessible to a wide range of insects; a pond, however small; shrubs; and cover for nesting birds are all essential ingredients of a garden, maximising the wildlife that a garden can nurture and that the gardener can enjoy.

After the indiscriminate use of pesticides, nothing is more detrimental to wildlife than officious tidiness. Leave fallen leaves, windfall fruit, rotting wood, piles of twigs, patches of weeds, grass growing in the cracks, moss on the stone. These are all important habitats and there is no reason why they cannot be gently tweaked to look beautiful as well as be useful.

A GARDEN WITH SMALL CHILDREN

Children from babes in arms to about twelve years old are going to influence how you garden in a dramatic way – whether you like it or not!

From a safe place for toddlers to play to a garden that will absorb the footballs, bikes, camps and general mayhem of normal outdoor fun, you want a garden that is good for them and yet also looks good for you.

The biggest mistake I made when my children were small was to make a play area for them too far from the house. Until a child is about five or six they will want to play right outside the back door, preferably with it open all the time so they can run in and out freely. Go with that. Make a safe, fun space as close to the house as possible and they will use it.

Children need a soft surface to play on, and a lawn – again, near the house – fits this purpose better than anything else. Forget the horticulturally immaculate sward and go for a hard-wearing green lawn that will be compacted, divoted, rutted and generally trashed but make small people very happy. A paddling pool will kill the grass beneath it and a trampoline do nearly as much damage. No matter, a lawn is ideal for both. Plant around the lawn with tough shrubs like cotoneaster, kerria or buddleja that will withstand being trampled over as balls are being retrieved. If you must have a border at the edge of the lawn, protect it with a low hedge that will act as a crash barrier and is resilient enough to recover from a spot of roughhousing.

Try not to have spiny, spiky or sharp-leaved plants within reach. Avoid all poisonous plants altogether. There are not many of these but laburnum and monkshood should not be grown and the sap of all euphorbias can burn tender skin badly. Yew is very poisonous, and although most children seem to resist chewing on it, it is best kept away from small toddlers.

Children need their own special space. Their own 'garden' is not going to do the trick. It is too much a mini-version of the grown-up garden. Some sort of building is ideal, and a tree house best of all. If you have no trees then a house constructed on stilts will do. There is something about being up in the air that is magical, and earthbound adults ignore this at their children's peril.

Once their space is created, they might want a garden attached. Don't be precious about this. Remember, this is playing at gardening, not an apprenticeship for your horticultural world. Plant sunflowers, marigolds, beans, peas, nasturtiums and poppies. Keep your finer sensibilities out of it and the planting bright, vulgar, big and brash.

Finally, make somewhere that is good for you, where you can keep an eye on the children as well as eat and entertain and have plants you love out of reach of destructive childish hands. The obvious way to do this is to have a paved seating area with raised beds or large containers that cannot be knocked or pulled over, all butting directly onto the lawn.

A PEACEFUL OASIS

A garden can be created to be the perfect oasis, where batteries can be recharged and a sense of proportion and healing returned to even the most stressful life.

A garden like this is a place to retreat to and even hide from the world. It is somewhere private and intimate that you only share with those you invite into your domain.

So the most important thing to establish is privacy. This is not always practical for the whole garden but can nearly always be achieved with some part of it, even if it only extends to a single seat where you can relax completely, knowing that you are not overlooked or watched by anyone.

Walls, fences or hedges – or all three in their place – are essential, especially around the perimeter of the garden. Fences can be heightened by the addition of trellises, and these covered with climbers such as roses, wisteria, clematis and honeysuckle will not only screen your garden from the outside gaze but also enrich your space with colour and fragrance in season.

Rather than having the central area dominated by a lawn, it is better for this type of garden to have a path. Often winding, this path can move through borders to arrive at a seating area, however short the path or modest the destination, that is itself planted around to screen it from unwanted view.

Fragrance is essential to create the sense of peace and luxury that inculcates true relaxation. This can come from a wide range of plants, from herbs that release their scent as you brush past them to roses hanging in swags over a hidden bower. Night-scented plants like tobacco plants or stocks make sitting outside as darkness falls a sensual delight.

As with any seating area, it is essential to work out at what time of day you are going to use it most before investing time, energy and money into creating it exactly as you want it to be. If it is somewhere to sit with a drink in the evening then it will need to face west and catch the evening light. If life is hectic all week and you use the garden mostly during the day at weekends then midday sun – along with some shade – will determine its place in the garden, even if that only amounts to which direction you face.

This is not the place for pared-back minimalism. To create an atmosphere of ease and relaxation, the planting should have a softness and fullness. In my experience, to become a place where you can truly unwind, there also needs to be active involvement – i.e., some gardening – to be done, even if it is just dead heading roses or watering containers.

Softness and fullness comes in many guises. Gardens of this kind can work superbly well with exotic and quite dramatically transformative plants such as palms, yuccas, bananas, cannas, tree ferns or whatever takes your fancy. The important thing is that the planting takes you reliably and swiftly away from the strains of daily life.

GARDENING WITHOUT A GARDEN

Without doubt the biggest change to gardening over the past decade or so has been the rise in interest and love for plants that can be grown and nurtured indoors. A generation of gardeners has emerged that has less access to a garden than any in living memory and yet has creatively made green spaces indoors that are every bit as beautiful, inspiring and, perhaps most critically, good for mind and body as any outdoor garden. This has certainly made me reassess my own relationship with houseplants and rekindle what was a distinctly fading interest.

Houseplants need designing as much as any other component of a living space. The way that you display and use them will depend upon a mixture of aesthetic and horticultural imperatives. Whilst the former is always subjective, the horticultural needs of a plant will determine its health and thus how it looks.

Whilst it is certainly true to say that there are houseplants that you can grow indoors in any conceivable living situation, one of the basic rules of gardening still applies, which is choosing the right plant for the right place. So position plants where they grow best. As soon as you start collecting more than a handful of plants they will become a strong determinant of how any room looks and feels – after all, that is their main virtue – so as well as exercising your own design aesthetic, let them dictate a little how you arrange things, by giving them the very best opportunity and situation to thrive in.

Plants that originate from tropical jungles will need year-round warmth, surprisingly high levels of humidity and ample shade. However, cacti and most succulents, although needing much less watering, coping well with central heating and dry air and also managing with quite low night-time temperatures, will need as much bright light as they can get all year round. Of course, they look completely different and lend a totally different atmosphere and feel to any room, so rarely look good grown together. In short, decisions of style and horticultural imperatives are always going to go hand in hand to get the best from your plants, regardless of where or how you live.

As well as those that have no outdoor space at all in which to grow plants, there are also lots of people whose gardening is necessarily restricted to a balcony, roof, or small paved yard. In these cases there are still lots of plants, both decorative and edible, that can be grown in pots or containers of any kind.

A whole garden, with a range of plants, mood and impact, can be created entirely from containers, including ponds, wildlife plants, good culinary plants, climbers and even trees. They have the advantage of being moveable so the space can be altered and adjusted according to what is looking good in its season or given extra protection from cold and wind.

There are two big considerations with growing plants in containers. The first applies to all plants grown in a pot, wherever they are, and this is that they will need regular watering. Unlike plants grown in the soil, whose roots can grow out to find moisture, plants in containers can very easily dry out, especially in hot weather or if they are exposed to drying winds, even when it is otherwise cool.

The second consideration is weight. A large pot with watered compost is heavy and it is always important to check that there is ample load-bearing provision for plants grown on a balcony or roof.

PREPARING A PLAN OF ACTION

Before you can begin to plan what you want your garden to become, you must first take stock of what it is.

Part of making changes is to sort the wheat from the chaff and analyse carefully what you want to keep. So go out into your garden and consciously look at it as though it is the first time you have ever laid eyes upon it.

Then take lots of pictures of it from every aspect and look at them. A camera often shows you things that your brain glides over or focuses too hard upon.

Measure your garden (you can simply pace it) and draw an accurate scale plan of the site, marking in everything that is there. This can be daunting but I strongly urge you to try because even the process of doing it is very revealing. Inevitably things will be spaced in a way that surprises you. There will be much more or less space in an area than you have been taking for granted, or the garden may actually be much longer and thinner or more rectangular than you have assumed. Only mapping it out on paper will reveal this.

Then, once you have an accurate scale plan of your garden as it is now – even if it is apparently 'empty' of all but an old shed, a couple of scruffy shrubs and some bad lawn – then you can start to plot in your ideas and dreams. It is a good idea to use tracing paper for these so that the original plan remains unmarked and is always there to refer to. This also means you can have many different tracing paper versions until you are satisfied that you have got it exactly right.

Once you are happy with what is on paper you can then transfer the plan onto the ground using canes and thick white string or line marking spray paint that can be bought from any builders' merchant.

When you have done this, look down at it from an upstairs window and live with it for a few days. The chances are that what seemed a good idea on paper does not quite transfer onto the ground. Paths might need widening, or curves and angles adjusting. Make the changes and look again.

Remove everything that you are sure you do not like or want. Never give anything the benefit of the doubt. If you like it then keep it but you do not have to include anything just because it is there. At this stage the right plant – i.e., one you like – in the wrong place is wrong. Buy some pots (or even better, plant bags that will store flat and have handles which make moving plants much easier) and dig up all the plants you think you might want to keep, plant them up in good compost and set them to one side. They can then be replanted in the right place when you are ready.

Most gardens fail because they try to do too much rather than too little. There has to be some compromise and a lot of editing. The secret is to keep the heart of the garden strong and clear and dispense with all the peripheries. Decide on the one thing that you want most from your garden and make it the central, dominant element, even if that means excluding other desirable aspects.

Grow what wants to grow. Choose the plants that will thrive in your particular situation. If you are not sure what they might be, look around. See what is growing well in your immediate neighbourhood. It will not be happening by chance.

When we think of our dream garden it is usually high summer and perfect weather. Design your garden for all seasons and all weather. How you do it will depend upon your chosen style of garden, but always plan from the outset for winter, as well as your favourite flower-filled season.

Do not be frightened of being generous with scale. Most flower borders are too small. Make them as big as possible. A few large plants make a space seem bigger whereas lots of small ones make it feel crowded.

Finally, it is worth reiterating the most important rule of garden design for any but the largest gardens, namely that it is far better to do one thing well than try and make the garden do or be too many different things. Keep it simple.

ASPECT

The direction that your garden faces – or its aspect – will be a huge influence on how you use it and what you can grow.

In principle, gardens have four compass faces – north, south, east and west – although most gardens will align slightly off neat compass divisions and face northeast, southwest, etc. Each of the four aspects create very different growing conditions, and most plants are adapted to growing best in one of them. If the first rule of gardening is not to fight nature then the second is to try and make every plant feel at home, rather than forcing it to grow and perform where it is uncomfortable.

So before you make any planting decisions, establish the compass points of your garden and pay close attention to just how much light they get throughout the year. Aspect will also strongly affect how cold, warm, wet and dry these different areas are.

In practical terms, this means knowing where the sun rises, where it is in the middle of the day and where it sets for every week of the year. Unless you have paid particular attention to it you will be amazed at how much the sun moves round the horizon. In my own garden, the sun rises against the front of the house in midwinter, never climbs above the roof of the house and barely reaches round the western side before it sets around half past four in the afternoon. But in midsummer the sun rises far along the eastern side, moves round the front, filling the entire garden with light, and moves on round the western side of the house whilst still high in the sky. It then sets at around 10pm with its beams shining directly through the windows at the rear of the building – not so very far from where it rose eighteen hours earlier.

When we speak of a south or north wall it means, of course, that they face south or north. If you stand with your back to your front door and the sun is setting to your right then the house faces south – and by implication the part of your back garden nearest the house will be shady and rather cold – making it a bad place to sit and eat, save if you want shade in very hot weather.

But if you sit on your back doorstep cradling your morning coffee whilst the sunlight streams in from your left (the east) then you are facing south and where you are sitting will get more and more sun throughout the day until evening when it will fall into shade. This was the case with our first long, thin garden in London in the 1980s, so we made a place to sit and eat in the evenings at the far end of the garden (even though it meant carrying food and drink down on trays) because it caught all the evening light.

SOUTH

A south-facing garden is going to get the full force of the sun from mid-morning until early evening. In the UK's mild climate this is the best possible aspect for any garden with the greatest range of plants that can be grown. It means that when designing a garden you can create a space to relax and eat near the house, knowing that it will be sunny but will not catch the last of the evening rays.

Because the garden is sunny for much of the day it is likely to be a good place to grow vegetables, herbs and fruit as well as plants that respond primarily to heat rather than day length. If the drainage is good it will be ideal for Mediterranean plants of all kinds but woodland plants and those that need lots of moisture to thrive will struggle more.

A sheltered south-facing wall will grow a huge range of tender climbers. However, quite a few climbers and wall shrubs find a south-facing wall too hot and dry, and the base of a south-facing wall, even after quite heavy rain, is a dry place.

Shade will be important, particularly for the middle of the day, so a bower or somewhere to sit at the opposite end of the garden, facing north, is likely to be welcome on hot days.

WEST

In many ways a west-facing aspect is the best of the lot for gardens. The afternoon and evening sun is always warmer than the morning so means that the garden is likely to be a pleasant place to sit in as the sun goes down – which is when most people have time and opportunity to sit in their garden. So plan your seating and outdoor eating area around this.

The quality of light as the sun is sinking in the west makes rich colours look especially good in the evening.

Camellias, magnolias and very early flowering fruit, such as apricots and plums, will all do well, protected from the cold of an early spring morning but with enough light from the afternoon and evening sun.

A west-facing wall has all day to absorb heat, and almost all climbing roses, late-flowering clematis and indeed any summer-flowering climber will thrive.

A vegetable plot sheltered from the east but open to the west will always do well. The soil will warm up quicker and there will be more moisture and enough light and heat for all to do well and most to thrive.

When planting hedges or trees or erecting fences that may be necessary for privacy or to provide shelter from the wind, take stock of where the sun will be in the western sky in the evening and be careful not to screen it out. The setting sun should always be allowed into any garden.

EAST

An east-facing garden has one big disadvantage – it will be cold. The early morning sun, however bright, has not had time to warm up the air. An easterly wind is also cold. Some kind of windbreak of trees, shrubs or a fence with a trellis attached, which can in turn be clothed with climbers, will make a big difference.

But the quality of this coolish morning light can be exquisitely beautiful. It has a delicacy, even fragility, that gives a spring and summer garden an ethereal quality and is by far the best light in which to view pinks, pale blues and other pastel colours. It makes sense to work with this and choose colour schemes accordingly, even if it is only for a small section of your garden that catches the morning light.

However, there are a few plants that should never be planted against an east wall. Camellias are the best known but it also applies to apricots, peaches, a few ornamental cherries or any of the very early-flowering trees and shrubs. This is because a clear spring day is often followed by frost overnight and the frosted buds and blooms are exposed to the full glare of the rising sun. The flowers then defrost too fast and are irreversibly damaged.

Not all plants are afflicted. For example, flowering quinces shrug off any combination of ice and sun. Many clematis, especially spring flowering, do well on an east wall.

NORTH

If your garden faces north it is going to be shady. But many plants do surprisingly well – most green looks better in shade, and flowers that tolerate shade draw the eye in to linger.

But even if you have permanent dank shade, you can grow ferns, ivies, hostas, bergenias, mahonias, alchemillas, cyclamens and hardy geraniums like G. phaeum. The effect can be rich and dramatically gothic.

Many plants with white flowers have adapted to shade so they attract insects both at dusk and in gloom. White flowering plants also often have a strong scent at night so make a heady evening combination. This selection includes the tobacco plant nicotiana sylvestris, lily of the valley, hydrangeas, impatiens and hostas.

Nearly all clematis – especially those that flower in spring and summer – do very well in shade as long as they do not get too dry, as do honeysuckles. Do not be put off growing roses in shade either. 'Souvenir du Dr Jamain', which has rich burgundy flowers, dislikes full sun as does the more frothy pink of 'Madame Alfred Carriere' and 'Zephirine Drouhin', which is also pink but thornless, so good for placing near a path.

Finally, all fragrances smell better in shade after a warm day, when the air is still warm and the flowers gently release their scents to attract moths to pollinate them.

SOIL

No element of your garden is as important or influential as its soil. It is earth, the goddess Gaia, and she shall not be mocked. All good gardening begins with the realisation that the earth is a living entity working with your plants rather than an inert medium in which to raise them under your bidding. Sustaining that largely invisible life and nurturing its relationship with your plants is the secret to a healthy, thriving garden.

Twenty five per cent of all life on this planet lives in the soil – yet we have so far only identified one per cent of these organisms. We do not yet know enough to know how much we know. One small teaspoon of soil will contain billions of microbes divided amongst around 5,000 types. There will be thousands of species of fungi, nematodes and protozoa as well as the mites, ants, beetles and, of course, earthworms. All of these will be working to create a healthy root zone, ensuring air, nutrients and water are available to plants either inadvertently or in exchange for its own food or benefit given up by the plant.

Subsoil is the basic type of soil that forms a layer above the underlying rock. Whilst it does contain water and nutrients for plants, these are often not easily available, and most plants grown in subsoil will be stunted and unhealthy. However, the addition of air, organic material and microorganic activity can gradually convert subsoil into topsoil.

Topsoil is the layer of soil that has been enriched by the constant addition of organic material, and the resulting humus is incorporated into the soil to make loam. The deeper the topsoil, the easier it will be for roots to grow and take up nutrients. Also, the better it will both drain and retain water and – not least – the easier it will be for you to work.

In an old garden that has been cultivated for hundreds of years, the topsoil can be up to 3 feet/1 metre deep. In new gardens on uncultivated ground it can scarcely exist and has to be made or imported. But it is never too late to begin improving the soil that you plant into.

Loam describes soil that is rich in organic matter and is the ideal that every gardener aspires to. Regardless of the basic type of soil, loam can be created if you grow lots of plants and mulch or dig in plenty of organic goodness each year. So when we talk about a 'clay loam' or a 'sandy loam' it means a good, rich soil of a predominate characteristic. You can improve your soil but cannot change its fundamental character.

Soil is complicated, and the relationship between plants and the soil is subtle. However, the received horticultural wisdom is that there are four basic types of soil – clay, chalk, sand and peat. The average garden is likely to be dominated by one of these types (although as a natural peat-based garden soil is very rare in the UK, I have omitted it from the following pages) and this determines the range of plants you can comfortably grow.

You can do a simple pH test to establish whether your soil is alkaline or acidic or – as most of our gardens are – roughly neutral. This is useful insomuch that soil with a pH at either extreme will not be able to support plants that have adapted to the opposite end of the pH spectrum. Limestone and chalk are alkaline, and sandy soil tends to be acidic. Clay lies in the middle. But it is simplest to check the plants growing in your neighbourhood. If you see rhododendrons, camellias and heathers growing happily then the soil is acidic. If, on the other hand, all these are absent, but weigelia, lilac, ceanothus and lavender are common, then the soil will most likely be alkaline.

The structure of soil is as important as its nutritional components, and the two are inextricably entwined. Often the simplest way to ensure maximum uptake of a plant's needs is to improve the texture of the soil. The best way to do this is to add organic matter, and the very best organic matter is home-made compost. There is no need to dig this in. Spread it on the surface as a mulch and let worms do the work for you.

But whatever soil you have, however apparently good or bad, there is no absolute ideal. Plants adapt and there will be a wide range of plants that thrive in your specific soil. Look after it as best you can, choose your plants appropriately, and the soil will look after you and your garden.

CHALK

I grew up on this soil – chalk is my geological memory and its flora flowers across my childhood. It is dry and dusty in summer, making even good soil milky, and occasionally it lies above a belt of clay, with the result that although the chalk drains quickly, rain sits on top of the clay and makes the chalk above it into a sticky paste.

Chalk itself is fast draining, which makes it quick to warm up in spring, and easy to work. But it is thin and you need to add as much heavy organic material as possible to beef it up so it will retain moisture and nutrients. Because the high lime content breaks humus down very fast, it is best to mulch any ground to be dug as thickly as possible in autumn so it can slowly be incorporated into the soil over winter.

Chalk is very alkaline with a pH of 7 and above, so ericaceous (see glossary) plants will never be happy growing in it. It is not possible to make alkaline soil significantly more acid (or vice versa) so the best approach is to entirely eliminate all acid-loving plants and to make the most of the huge range of plants that relish chalky soil. Roses, however, never do as well in chalk as in clay soil. It is, for example, ideal for all clematis. Lavender loves it, as does rosemary, and it has exactly the right balance between good drainage and hot, stony resilience for Mediterranean herbs like rosemary, lavender and thyme. Yew and box prefer it to all other soils. Wildflowers love it and it is the best of all soils for making a wildflower meadow.

Sometimes, seemingly similar plants will react very differently to soil types. So beech grows very much better in chalk than hornbeam. Grass on the other hand prefers more acidic conditions and quickly turns yellow in drought.

Plants that will relish chalk:

Trees: beech, yew, maples (just not Japanese maples), horse chestnut, hawthorn, sorbus, Japanese cherries, mulberry

Shrubs: berberis, buddleja, box, ceanothus, cotoneaster, cornus, deutzia, euonymus, forsythia, fuchsia, hebe, philadelphus, potentilla, sambucus, senecio, lilac, weigela

Perennials: acanthus spinosa, anchusa, bergenia, cowslip, campanula, dianthus, eremurus, bearded iris, geranium pratense, gypsophila, hellebores, heuchera, linaria, peonies, salvias, verbascum, veronica

Annuals: wallflower, snapdragon, dianthus, linaria, convolvulus, echium

Climbers: honeysuckle, all clematis, eccremocarpus, ivy, hydrangea petiolaris, jasmine, sweetpeas, vines, wisteria

Herbs: most, but particularly all the Mediterranean herbs like rosemary, lavender and thyme

Vegetables: all brassicas (cabbage, brussels sprouts, cauliflower, etc.)

Fruit: most, but not blueberries, raspberries or pears

SAND

Although my childhood home was on chalk, I went to school in an area of intensely sandy soil. It was gritty grey stuff, quick to infiltrate socks, pockets and hair. There were woods of pine and birch trees with an understory of rhododendrons, bracken and gorse. Heather grew in the headmaster's garden, and the football pitches shone emerald green. Sand is in fact ideal for grass, especially winter grass like football pitches. It drains fast, never gets too muddy and roots can easily grow down into it.

Take a spoonful of your garden soil and shake it up in a jar of water. After an hour it should have settled into strata. Any sand will be at the bottom with a layer of silt over it and whatever clay there might be on the top. If the soil is predominately sand there will be little clay and a fat wedge of relatively huge grains.

Sandy soil is always described as 'hungry', meaning that it takes and demands regular large amounts of organic matter to be added to it. But a rich, sandy loam is great stuff to garden in. Sandy soil is ridiculously easy to dig, warms up quickly and never gets waterlogged. These are huge advantages. Although you cannot make a sandy soil unsandy, organic matter will clog the pores between the grains of sand, slowing the leaching down so that plants have a chance to draw on the available food – which, in the main, they can only do when dissolved in water.

Sandy soil will dry out quicker than any other so is more prone to drought. A really thick mulch is the best solution and in time this will incorporate deeper and deeper into the soil structure so roots can reach moisture further down below ground which will be less prone to drying out. Deep and strong root growth will also alleviate root-rock, which is a common problem on sandy soils where the anchorage of surface-rooting plants is not secure enough and they get damaged by wind. As long as there is a good water supply, anything that grows fast is going to flourish in a sandy loam. Any vegetables with long tapering roots, such as carrots and parsnips, will love it.

The following plants are likely to feel happy in sandy soil:

Trees: birch, sweet chestnut, Judas tree, holly, robinia, pines, juniper

Shrubs: berberis, buddleja, heathers, rock rose, cotoneaster, eleagnus, escallonia, broom, kerria, burnet rose, gorse, santolina, senecio, yucca

Perennials: acanthus, yarrow, anthemis, wormwood, cornflower, cardoon, cushion spurge, cat mint, evening primrose, oriental poppies, salvia, sedum, lamb's ear

Climbers: ceanothus, ivy, honeysuckle, ipomoea, parthenocissus

Vegetables & fruit: carrot, parsnip, potato, onion, early lettuce, tomato, asparagus, French beans, New Zealand spinach, peaches, apricots

Bulbs: most, but especially tulips, irises, crocus, daffodils, muscari, scilla and nerines

CLAY

Clay is the most naturally fertile of all soils. It takes harder work and some skill and timing to manage, but returns this input with a dividend of great fecundity. If you are not sure whether you have clay soil, pick up a handful and squeeze it. If it holds together it has clay in it. If it can be moulded and hold its shape then it is mostly clay. Clay particles are tiny, less than 0.002mm in diameter. To put that in some context, particles of sand are a thousand times bigger. These tiny bits of clay can pack tightly together, leaving little space for air, microorganisms and roots to move through them. This compressed characteristic is also its greatest strength, because it holds on to nutrients and there is a large surface area for roots to come into contact with to absorb the goodness, ensuring high fertility.

The downside of clay soil is that it can become baked into hard, brick-like clumps as it dries or equally unworkable sticky putty as it gets wet. It is also slower to warm up in spring than other soils.

The solution is to add as much organic matter as possible every year. Because it is so often too dry or too wet and also compacts so easily, the best way to do this is with a thick mulch in autumn and spring. Horse manure is better at lightening the soil than cow manure, and garden compost always the best thing possible. You can also add horticultural grit to improve drainage and root-run. This is very effective but you will need to incorporate a layer at least 2 to 4in/5 to 10cm deep, which works out at about 35 cubic feet/1 cubic metre or ton for every 30 to 40 square feet/3 or 4 square metres covered, so can be expensive albeit an excellent investment.

Plants that do particularly well in a clay soil:

Trees: Japanese maples, chestnuts, alders, birches, hornbeam, hawthorn, ash, holly, crab apple, oak, cherry, willow, lime, firs, larch, juniper, pine, thuja

Shrubs: berberis, chaenomeles, choisya, cornus, corylus, cotinus, cotoneaster, deutzia, escallonia, forsythia, genista, hydrangea, hypericum, mahonia, magnolia, osmanthus, philadelphus, potentilla, pyracantha, ribes, roses, skimmia, spiraea, viburnum, weigela

Perennials: acanthus, ajuga, aruncus dioicus, astilbe, caltha, filipendula, hardy geraniums, hemerocallis, hosta, inula, ligularia, lythrum, phormium, polygonum, rheum, rodgersia, troillus

Climbers: clematis, golden hop, sweet pea, honeysuckle, passion flower, vitis coignetiae, wisteria

Annuals: love-lies-bleeding, foxglove, sunflower, impatiens, lobelia, mimulus, forget-me-not, ornamental maize

Bulbs: (despite the adaptability of the following, plant these with extra grit) snowdrops, fritillaries, camassia, crocosomia, eranthis

POTTING COMPOST

If you are raising any plants, whether propagated yourself from seed, cuttings or division, or growing any bought plants in one of your own containers, you will need to use potting compost.

For many years, peat was the main component of branded potting compost (until the 1970s most potting compost was home-made) with devastating environmental and ecological consequences. Over 95 per cent of British peat bogs, which are essential for a whole range of birds and plants, have been lost over the past hundred years. But peat bogs are a unique and specialised ecosystem that cannot be replicated anywhere else. If that was not enough, peat sequesters carbon so extracting it from the ground is on a par with cutting down the rainforest or ploughing meadows. It is out-and-out eco-vandalism and no garden – not mine, not yours, nor any other garden on this earth – is worth that.

As it happens, peat is completely unnecessary in any garden. There are excellent alternatives. In my experience a variety of commercial composts made from bark, wood chip, coir, bracken and wool all work well as general-purpose potting compost. It is worth trying different brands and components to see what suits you – we now use a coir-based one as our basic compost. For acid-loving plants like camellias, rhododendrons and heathers, composted bracken and pine needles make an excellent ericaceous alternative to peat.

A general-purpose peat-free compost will serve for almost any plant at any stage of its growth, from seed to a small tree in a large pot. Everything else is fine-tuning.

But if you want to get the best from your plants, fine-tuning can make a significant difference. So I have slightly different mixes for seeds and for potting. This is because seed compost needs less nutrition – the seedlings are not going to be in it for long, but they do need the right texture to encourage good early root growth. Adding vermiculite to open out the compost helps a lot.

Compost for potting on or long-term containers, on the other hand, has to feed plants, sometimes for months, as well as having the right structure for roots to develop fully. To that end I add sieved garden compost and horticultural grit or perlite to create an open yet water-retentive structure. I also add sieved leaf mould to create a nice loose mix for both seed and potting compost – however, I appreciate that first you have to have the leaf mould to sieve.

Bulbs need extra drainage, and Mediterranean herbs positively thrive in poor conditions. This is where horticultural grit is invaluable. For bulbs like tulips, and herbs like lavender or thyme, I mix an equal volume of grit with potting compost. The result is gritty, not very nutritious and very free-draining – which is exactly how these plants like it.

Many cuttings will grow roots perfectly well in pure perlite and all need a very free draining mix, so to improve the chances of success with any cuttings, mix at least 50 per cent in volume of perlite or grit to the standard potting compost.

If you really want to finesse your potting mix, add some sieved garden compost from your own garden plus some sieved topsoil. Both of these will provide your plot's unique blend of bacteria and fungi so the roots of the growing plant can establish a symbiotic relationship from an early stage and therefore grow quicker and better when transplanted into your flower or vegetable beds.

But don't get bogged down in detail. Keep it simple. Most plants want to grow, often despite your best intentions. Use a peat-free compost, try different brands to see which suits you best and give it a go.

GARDEN TOOLS

Good tools foster a kind of respect and sensuous pleasure that inevitably improves your experience of gardening. They should also make your work easier and more effective.

In my experience you tend to get what you pay for. Good tools that are well made, do the job you want from them well and easily, and last despite much use will inevitably cost more than ones that look similar but have none of those qualities. Always get the best tools you can afford, although you do not need to spend a fortune.

Despite there being a wide range of fine tools to be had, you actually only need a basic kit to garden perfectly well.

To start with you must have a good **digging spade**. A good spade will feel light and easy to use yet be robust enough to dig all day and versatile enough to dig a hole for a large tree or gently chop an herbaceous plant into new sections. I like stainless steel because it is less inclined to clog with heavy clay. I also prefer wooden handles of ash or hickory. A smaller **border spade** should have the same virtues and is useful for lifting or planting within the confines of a border.

You also need at least one **fork**. I prefer square tines (as opposed to round or flat), not too long, not too curved, made of stainless steel and robust enough to serve arduous use. A small **border fork** is also useful for lifting a plant without damaging its neighbours. It is worth stressing that digging is always best done with a spade. Keep the fork for breaking up the soil once dug or for lifting plants.

Perhaps the single most useful and important tool for any gardener is a pair of **secateurs**. As with any cutting tool, they are only as good as the steel that the blades are made from. The shape, colour or detail of design is a matter of subjective taste, but high-quality steel holds an edge and makes pruning easy. Try them before buying – they should feel comfortable and easy in the hand.

A pair of **long-handled loppers** is really useful for pruning trees, shrubs and climbers and I increasingly use **Japanese saws** which come in many shapes and sizes. They are frighteningly sharp but incredibly useful.

One **rake** will do but three is a counsel of perfection. For general preparation of a seedbed a round-tined **flathead rake** is best. A **spring-tine rake** doubles as a grass scratcher and leaf collector and **rubber rakes** are invaluable for gathering up leaves from borders without damaging plants and seedlings.

You do need a good **trowel** or two for planting – one big and one small. Cheap trowels just do not last and are uncomfortable so get the best you can. If you are planting a lot of bulbs in grass, a **long-handled bulb planter** helps hugely.

If you grow vegetables you must have a **hoe**. The design of a hoe depends upon whether you push the cutting edge through the soil or pull it back towards you. I think that for smaller, annual weeds it is best to push, cutting through the roots of weeds just below the surface of the soil. It is a mistake to try and save time by using a big-bladed hoe. A small one is twice as useful.

Bigger weeds are best chopped out with a **swan-neck or draw hoe**. If you find a good **mattock** it can be very useful for rough digging as well as weeding.

In a very small garden you can manage without a **wheelbarrow**, with **plastic trugs** taking its place, but it does make life a lot easier and is essential in anything bigger. Plastic bodies are light and very durable but metal is even stronger.

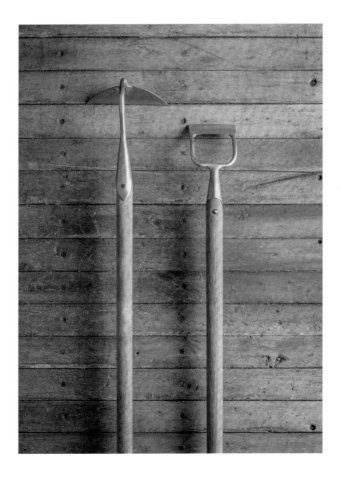

FLOWERS

BULBS

Bulbs are little flower bombs fully primed to explode into colour. A bulb will begin to shoot whilst still unplanted, and will flower when rooted in pure water rather than soil. The leaves and the roots convert sunlight, air, nutrition from the soil and water into developing next year's bulb and flower. That is why you must never cut off the leaves from a bulb after it has flowered. Leave them until they die back of their own accord before tidying them up or else you may find that there will not be enough food stored in the bulb and the plant will be 'blind' in a year's time.

The rule of thumb when planting bulbs is to allow at least twice their own depth of soil above them and to put them pointy end up. That's it. Everything else is fine-tuning whether growing them in a container, border or long grass.

Most bulbs come from mountainous, almost alpine conditions so extreme cold is rarely a problem in winter nor extreme heat in summer. However, good drainage, especially in winter, is essential for most spring-flowering bulbs (although a few, such as snowdrops, fritillaries, and camassias, do well in damper conditions). Some summer bulbs like bearded iris and alliums love full, hot sunshine whereas many lilies like cooler, slightly damper, slightly shady conditions as long as they have a loose root-run and do not become waterlogged.

We tend to call anything that is bulbous a 'bulb', whereas there are a number of bulbous roots that have different characteristics. A true bulb is a reduced root stem which grows fresh roots each year. Daffodils, tulips and lilies are all true bulbs. Each year new bulbs are made from the 'mother' bulb and these may take a few years to become big enough to make a flower and become mother bulbs themselves. Most bulbs need good drainage and space in which to fully develop their roots to flower successfully year after year, so they should either be treated like annuals, like tulips in pots, or, like daffodils in grass, be lifted and divided every few years.

Bulbs are one type of storage organ adapted to help plants survive but there are others, like corms, tubers and rhizomes, which are scientifically different but to the gardener equally important to bulbs and just as useful:

CORMS are replaced by new corms every year and are made from the swollen base of the stem. Crocuses, gladioli and crocosmia are all corms.

TUBERS are swollen roots and stems that are used for food storage – unlike most roots and stems which are solely a medium for conveying food around the plant. Dahlias, daylilies and cyclamen all have tuberous roots.

RHIZOMES are swollen stems, usually horizontal, and the best-known examples are bearded irises, whose rhizomes are above ground, and lily of the valley.

DIVIDING SNOWDROPS

Snowdrops never grow very well from dry bulbs. They spread naturally by seed and by clumps, slowly increasing by generating new bulbs. By far the best way for a gardener to increase their display of snowdrops is to lift and divide existing ones.

The time to do this is either whilst they are in flower or just after the flowers have finished, which in my garden is around the end of February. This then leaves time for new bulbs to be fed by the foliage before it slowly dies back in subsequent weeks and months, ensuring they flower well the following winter.

Snowdrops are woodland flowers that thrive in slightly damp light shade. Under the canopy of deciduous trees or shrubs, where the trees are not competing for light or moisture whilst the snowdrops are flowering, is ideal.

By the time that leaves appear in the woody canopy in April and May and the demand for water increases, the snowdrops will have finished flowering, set seed, the foliage will have died right back and next year's flowers will be prepared and ready for the following year's display.

The technique and process for dividing snowdrops is the same and as effective whether they are growing in a border or in grass.

METHOD

1. Snowdrops naturally form clumps that in time become large drifts, so choose a clump that has reached at least 6in/15cm across and carefully dig it up, trying to preserve as much root as possible and ideally keeping plenty of soil attached to them.

2. Gently pull the clump apart so you have 2 to 4 sections, each the size of the palm of your hand. Return one of them to the original hole and fill the space around the roots with the extra potting or garden compost or topsoil from elsewhere in the garden.

3. The remaining sections can either be planted separately to extend the spread of the snowdrops or used to fill in gaps of the existing plants to thicken it up. In both cases, plant each new clump about 8 to 12in/20 to 30cm apart and in time they will join to form a drift.

4. Water them in well.

5. This process can – and should – be repeated every year. Not only will it dramatically increase the spread of snowdrops in your garden but also keep the plants reinvigorated.

YOU WILL NEED

Small spade or trowel

Trug

Some potting compost, topsoil or ideally garden compost

Water

BULBS IN POTS

There are very good reasons for growing spring-flowering bulbs in pots as well as planting them into the ground. The first is that it means you can create exactly the right growing conditions by adjusting the compost mix and this is very important if you have heavy clay soil, especially for bulbs such as tulips, iris, muscari or the autumn-flowering nerine.

The second is that you can position them where they will be most appreciated. For very early bulbs like iris, crocus and the first daffodils, place them where they can be seen from the house and in as much sunshine as possible in late winter. For later bulbs like tulips you can use their dramatic display as part of the design and performance of the whole garden in spring by judiciously placing larger containers where they make the biggest floral statement.

The third is that when they have finished flowering you can move them to a less prominent spot to quietly die back, or, in the case of larger pots, remove them to a plastic container to die back so you can make the most of the expensive pot with a fresh summer display.

METHOD

1. Choose a suitable container for your bulbs. Tiny, jewel-like iris or crocus are lost in a big pot whereas daffodils or tulips need something more substantial both to contain them and balance their display.

2. Put crocks (keep any broken pots for this but pebbles or polystyrene packing chips will work as well) in the base of the pot so that the potting compost neither falls out of the drainage holes nor blocks them.

3. Mix your compost with at least 33% volume of grit. Half and half is ideal. The result should be a very gritty, free-draining growing medium.

4. Fill the container at least a third full with the compost mix and set the bulbs onto the surface, pointy end up, packing them in as tightly as you can but ensuring that none are touching.

5. Cover the bulbs over with a good 1 to 2in/3 to 4cm of compost (this will dictate the size of pot), leaving .39in/1cm or so from the brim. Sprinkle a layer of pure grit over this (which will help drainage and stop the emerging petals being splashed by wet compost) and label the pot clearly.

6. Water well. The bulbs are completely hardy and need a spell of cold weather to trigger flowering but good drainage at all stages is absolutely essential so put them somewhere where they will not get sodden. Water once a month if it is very dry and bring them to their final position once the first signs of flower buds appear. This will be late January for irises, February for daffodils, crocus and muscari, and April for tulips.

7. A tip – we recycle our tulips that we grow in pots by planting the dried bulbs into grass the November after flowering, buying fresh bulbs for the very best display in the pots.

YOU WILL NEED

A container – any will serve as long as it has good drainage, although terracotta always looks good

Crocks to stop drainage holes blocking

Peat-free potting compost

Horticultural grit or perlite (grit is preferable)

Your choice of tulip, daffodil, crocus, iris, muscari or scilla bulbs

Water

BULB LASAGNE

You can create a long flowering season by planting layers of bulbs on top of each other in a container to create a flowering 'lasagne'. This works well with different varieties of the same kind of flower, such as daffodils or tulips, using varieties that flower early, middle and late in spring and merge and blend as they overlap.

It is also a way of creating real variety and combinations by using different species all within one pot, combining bulbs such as tulips, daffodils, muscari, scillas, irises and crocuses.

As a rule, three or four layers is enough and I often combine just two kinds of bulbs. This can be done at any time between late August and Christmas for flowering in spring.

METHOD

1. Mix the grit or perlite with the compost so that it is very free-draining. Half and half as a ratio is fine. Put a crock or two in the bottom of the pot so the compost does not fall out or get clogged up and put in the first layer of about 6in/15cm of your own mixed compost.

2. Place a layer of tulips on this, fitting in as many as you can without any of the bulbs touching. Cover them over with 3 to 4in/8 to 10cm of more compost and cover that with a layer of daffodils with a similar density. Don't worry about blocking the growth of the bulbs below – they always find a way up and through the bulbs above them.

3. Add another layer of soil and plant this with a smaller bulb such as muscari, scillas or irises. If the pot is deep enough you can add a fourth layer of very small bulbs or corms such as crocuses (don't bother with snowdrops – they are famously difficult to grow from bulbs but in a very large pot you can plant pansies or wallflowers as a final floral carpet). In any event cover the final bulb layer with at least 2in/5cm of compost topped with a generous layer of grit. The grit stops 'capping' where the surface of the compost can develop a hard crust (preventing new growth from pushing through) and also helps drainage.

4. Water until liquid runs out of the bottom of the pot and put the container aside (it can be in a dark, dry place) until the first shoots appear and then place it in full sun where it should flower from late February through to mid-May.

YOU WILL NEED

A deep container with crocks to ensure the drainage hole(s) do not clog up

Peat-free potting compost

Horticultural grit or perlite to mix with the compost. Grit for dressing the surface (see page 50)

Different spring bulbs (I am using tulips, daffodils, muscari and crocuses in this example)

PLANTING LILIES

No flower signifies the paradoxical but seductive combination of purity and voluptuousness so vividly as the lily. Also, no plant has such a rich and delicious fragrance.

The key to growing lilies successfully is to keep the roots shaded and moist and the flowers sunny and warm. When growing in pots this can be done by using suitable compost and placing them facing west where they will make the most of the afternoon and evening sun.

Most lilies are essentially woodland plants so ideally you try to recreate a 'woodland' soil, namely one that is loose, open and yet moisture retentive. The best way to achieve that at home is to use home-made leaf mould as the base with some added bark-based compost and perlite or grit.

Unlike other bulbs, lilies don't have a protective outer coat, and the scaly bulbs – looking rather like an artichoke – are very prone to drying out. So when you buy them, look for plump bulbs and plant them as soon as possible.

Most lilies prefer an acidic soil so leaf mould or a potting mix using composted bracken or pine bark is ideal. However the Madonna lily prefers dry, limey soil, and whereas most other lily bulbs are best planted about 6in/15cm deep, it should be planted shallowly, just covered with soil. Again, whereas most lilies can happily be planted in early spring, Madonna lilies should be planted along with the spring-flowering bulbs in early autumn.

METHOD

1. Make sure that your chosen container has good drainage holes and use crocks to stop them being blocked by the compost. (You can get specialised trumpet-shaped lily pots that show off the plants to best advantage.)

2. Mix the grit, leaf mould and compost in equal quantities and fill the pot half full. Place the bulbs pointy end up, 6in/15cm apart. Three per 24in/60cm diameter pot is about right. Cover the bulbs with at least 4in/10cm of compost above the crown, leaving 1 to 2in/3 to 5cm from the rim to water into.

3. Give them a soak and put them somewhere lightly shaded to grow. Keep them well watered – a soak once a week should suffice – and move them to their final flowering position when the buds develop in May and June.

4. The bright red lily beetle is becoming an increasing problem, munching all parts of the plant. However they are very easy to see and by far the best way of controlling them is to simply remove them by hand.

5. When the lilies have finished flowering, remove the seed heads (they snap off) but leave the stems and allow all top growth to die back naturally. The pots with the bulbs in can be stored outside and out of the way all winter and brought back out in spring. They should need repotting with fresh compost every 3 to 4 years.

YOU WILL NEED

Terracotta pots

Crocks

Bark-based compost

Lily bulbs

Perlite or grit

Ideally leaf mould

Water

BULBS IN GRASS

Making a true wildflower meadow is fashionable and a lovely thing but can actually be quite tricky and not very practical for a smaller garden. However, there is a compromise that looks stunning, is wonderful for insects and is much easier to make and – critically – sustain. This is to plant spring bulbs into grass.

By having a wide mixture of bulbs, you can create a bejewelled display from February through to late May. The grass then remains long for at least six weeks after the last flower, which creates the perfect conditions for insects and – I think – looks very beautiful.

I suggest using more delicate daffodils, such as pseudonarcissus or 'pheasant's eye', rather than some of the bigger, more strident varieties. Conversely, strong tulip colours can look very good growing in grass. In damper ground, snowdrops, snakeshead fritillaries and camassias all look best in grass rather than a border.

Whatever you choose, once flowering has finished (the last camassia will fade by the end of May) do not cut the grass until every scrap of bulb foliage has died back, as this feeds next year's bulbs. Cut too soon and next year's flowers will be diminished. As a rule of thumb, leave the grass uncut until July – and even August.

Once you have cut the grass, gather it all up and add to the compost heap. It can then be mown regularly short as lawn right through to winter and the grass should be very short by the end of January when the first crocuses start to appear.

METHOD

1. Make sure that the grass is cut short before you plant – it makes life a lot easier.

2. Take a handful of bulbs and throw them at random onto the grass.

3. Plant them wherever they land, including any tight groups or extra-wide spacing. Trust me – this always looks more natural than any attempt to move them into position to be 'natural'.

4. A robust bulb planter – preferably long-handled – makes life a lot easier if you have any more than a hundred bulbs to plant, but a sturdy trowel will do if the ground is not too hard.

YOU WILL NEED

An area of grass that you are prepared to leave uncut until at least the end of June

Spring-flowering bulbs: crocuses, daffodils, tulips and alliums are best for ground with good drainage. Snowdrops, fritillaries and camassias are more likely to thrive in heavier soil and damper conditions.

Bulb planter or strong trowel

5. With a bulb planter, take out a plug of turf and soil and pop a bulb, pointy end up, into the hole. In the process of making the next hole, the first plug will be pushed out and can be used to fill back over the first bulb. If using a trowel it is easiest to lever the soil just wide enough to squidge the bulb into the slit you have opened and then push it closed.

6. Whatever you use, make the hole as deep as possible – in principle the deeper the better, although in practice as long as the tip of the bulb is at least 1in/2cm below the surface it will be OK.

7. A counsel of perfection is to plant bulbs into grass in September (except tulips, which should be planted in November and December). However, you may well have to wait until there is enough rain to sufficiently soften the turf and soil. No harm is done by leaving it as late as November but in any event this has to be completed by Christmas at the latest.

DAHLIAS

Despite flowering robustly from mid-summer deep into autumn, dahlias, which originate from Mexico, are tender plants, and any new shoots will be killed by a late spring frost and this will delay flowering by weeks. It is best then to plant them after all risk of frost has passed, which in my garden is mid-May.

But if you buy them earlier in spring or have been storing your own plants, they can be potted up and grown on with some protection so that when the weather turns warmer they can be planted outside already growing strongly.

METHOD

1. Take the tubers out of their protection, either from their wrapping if new or however you have stored them if already your own. Check them over, feeling them for firmness and discarding any that are either rotten or shrivelled.

2. Then pot up these tubers in a recycled plastic pot. When planting dahlias permanently in the ground they should be buried as deeply as possible with good drainage, but grown like this they can just be covered by a little compost and fitted quite tightly into the pots.

3. Make sure that they are labelled clearly, give them a soak and put them somewhere frost-free but where they will get at least half a day's light. Cold frames or a greenhouse are ideal but a windowsill or porch work well.

4. They can then grow on, developing strong shoots, until you are certain there is no chance of frost. They can then be planted out into the garden or potted into a more attractive container. If they get a bit lanky, cut the shoots back by half, to just above a leaf. This will encourage side shoots and a stronger, bushier plant that will bear more flowers. To keep new flower buds coming it is essential to dead head them increasingly regularly as summer moves into autumn.

5. Dahlias may be semi-tropical but they flower much better when kept moist, so in a dry summer they should have a really good soak at least weekly and almost daily if they are in a pot.

YOU WILL NEED

Dahlia tubers

Plastic pots

Peat-free potting compost

Labels

Water

A frost-free but sunny place

DAHLIA CUTTINGS

When dahlias are taken out of storage or newly purchased in spring, it is too early to plant them into the garden if there is still a risk of frost. But if you pot them up and put them somewhere warm and light they will quickly sprout new shoots, which make excellent material for cuttings which develop into young plants for late summer. These cuttings are easy to grow and tend to be exceptionally healthy and floriferous, albeit a little later in the season than the parent plant, thus extending their vivid flowering season well into October.

METHOD

1. Pot up tubers so that the tops are only just covered by the compost. Water well and place the pot on a heated surface – if you do not have a heated mat (and I can thoroughly recommend investing in one to aid propagation of all kinds) a windowsill above a radiator will do fine.

2. Keep the dahlia watered and warm, and in a week or two it will produce strong young shoots. When these are about 4in/10cm high, use a very sharp knife to cut the strongest where they join the tuber, which is why you do not want to bury the tubers too deep. Taking a slither of tuber with the stem will help the cutting root. Immediately put the cuttings into a polythene bag to slow down evaporation.

3. The parent plant can then be put somewhere frost free and light to grow on, ready to plant out as soon as the risk of frost has passed.

4. Fill a pot (3in/7cm is ideal) with a mix of an equal volume of perlite and potting compost, make a hole and place the cutting in (up to 4 cuttings, one in each corner or a single in the centre). Place somewhere light and warm but not in direct hot sunlight or else they will dry out.

5. Water well and spray with a mister at least once a day. As with all cuttings it is a race between new roots forming and sustaining growth whilst the old stem dries out, so the more humid and warmer the air, the quicker it will root.

6. Dahlias root easily and you can expect at least a 50% success rate within a few weeks. You will know when they have rooted because there will be new, healthy growth and roots will begin to poke through the bottom of the pot. When you see this they can be potted on individually into a richer compost mix (75% compost and 25% perlite or grit) and then grown on as young plants to provide flowers from late summer and healthy new plants to replenish your stock for years to come.

YOU WILL NEED

3in/7cm plastic pot(s)

Plump, healthy dahlia tubers

Peat-free potting compost

Perlite or grit

Water

A sharp knife

Polythene bag(s)

STORING DAHLIA TUBERS

Dahlias will continue flowering until the first sharp frost shrivels the leaves – the timing of which will vary across the country – and that will stop all flowering.

At this point, if you live in a part of the country where the temperature rarely drops below 23°F/−5°C AND you have free-draining soil, then you can simply cut back all top growth and mulch the dahlias thickly to provide an insulating blanket against winter cold. The chances are very high that they will reappear next spring without any problems.

But if it is ever likely to be colder or you have – as I do – clay soil, then the combination of even mild winter cold and wet will often rot the tubers, so in this case it is best to dig them all up and bring them indoors over the winter months.

METHOD

1. Cut back all material above the ground, leaving just 2in/5cm of stem. Carefully lift the tubers with a fork, avoiding damaging them if at all possible.

2. Clean off all soil, checking to remove any slugs, and then place the tubers upside down in a dry place under cover for a day to drain any water from the stems, which would in turn increase the chances of rot when they are stored.

3. Pack the tubers in a tray or pot packed with old potting compost, vermiculite, sand or even old newspapers. Be sure to label them at this point very clearly and securely – it is almost impossible to know a variety from the tubers alone!

4. The idea is to keep them cool but frost-free, dark and fundamentally dry but not to let them dry out completely or else the tubers will shrivel. Humid air, such as in a cellar or frost-free outdoor shed, should be fine.

5. Check them around the New Year to see if any are mouldy or shrivelling up and lightly water them if they appear very dry.

6. Take them out of storage at some point in March and go through them all, discarding any rotten tubers, before potting them up with the tubers just buried beneath the compost. Put them somewhere frost-free and light to trigger them into growth. A greenhouse, porch or windowsill is ideal.

7. Grow them on until the risk of frost is passed and then put them in a sunny place outside for at least 2 weeks to harden off before planting into their final position in the garden. They should start to flower around the middle of July.

YOU WILL NEED

Secateurs

Fork

Tap or hose

Flowerpots, crates or strong cardboard boxes

Sand, vermiculite, perlite, old potting compost or scrunched-up newspapers

Somewhere dark, cool but frost free

DIVIDING
BEARDED IRISES

DIVIDE: EARLY SUMMER (AFTER FLOWERING)
FLOWER: FOLLOWING YEAR IN SPRING

Bearded irises have an intensity of rich velvety colour that few other plants begin to match. There are thousands of varieties in every shade from white through to almost black, which means that you are bound to find ones that will fit in and enhance your chosen colour schemes. However, they are particular in their growing conditions, needing as much sun as possible and really sharp drainage. In heavy clay soil they soon rot. I get round this by growing them in a raised bed that has had a lot of grit added to it to improve the drainage.

If they are happy then the rhizomes – that look like lumpy fingers of ginger – will grow and spread quite rapidly and can form an almost continuous mat. This will result in congestion and a reduction in flowering, so they need lifting and dividing regularly and the best time to do that is immediately after flowering – usually sometime in July.

METHOD

1. Using a fork, carefully lift a group of rhizomes, gently levering the roots from the soil, trying not to damage the roots that are growing from them.

2. Brush off the soil and cut them with a sharp knife so that there is a visible bud on each section. Discard the oldest, woodiest part (which always occurs nearer the centre of the clump of the rhizome) and replant your new sections either in small groups or individually. Trim any very straggling lengths of roots and plant them so the remaining roots are buried below the soil but the rhizome itself remains above the soil level so it can be fully baked by the sun. The more it is baked, the better next year's display will be, so I always align the length of the rhizome with the south so it gets the full arc of the sun's movement across the sky.

3. Cut the leaves back to 6in/15cm to stop them catching the wind and rocking the plant before the roots have a chance to grow and act as an anchor. Any irises that you do not lift do not need their leaves cut back and should be left to die back naturally, feeding goodness into the rhizome.

4. Water the divided plants in well and then let the sun do its work. They will then hit their peak performance after growing and spreading for a couple of years and be ready for dividing again a couple of years after that.

YOU WILL NEED

A fork

Brush

A sharp knife

Secateurs or scissors

Water

ANNUALS

Annuals are easy to grow from seed and the best way of adding a wide range of colour and interest from spring through to late autumn.

An annual is any plant that germinates, grows, flowers and sets seed in the same growing season – usually between March and October in the UK. All annuals can be broken into two camps – hardy and tender – those that can withstand frost and those that cannot. This dictates how and when they are grown.

Hardy annuals are 'long-day' plants which often originate from the northern hemisphere and have their growth pattern triggered mainly through changing light levels. As the days lengthen throughout spring they grow and produce their flowers and then, as the days shorten after midsummer, there is an increasing urgency to set seed before winter begins and they die. Their seed will then lie dormant (some, like field poppies, can remain viable for years) until the ground is disturbed and the conditions, light and moisture are right for germination again.

So plants such as cornflowers, annual poppies and nigella grow in response to light and can cope with cold – although none enjoy it. As a result it is often best to sow hardy annuals directly where they are to grow, knowing that the seedlings will survive a late cold snap.

Tender annuals are 'short-day' plants – which come from closer to the equator – and are more influenced by heat than light. This is because the light on the equator is more or less constant throughout the year. They tend to grow and flower later in the year than hardy annuals. As the days get shorter and nights get longer and warmer from June 21st, hardy annuals start their inevitable movement towards producing fewer flowers and more seed as a race to provide new plants for next year, whereas tender annuals start flowering in earnest and will stay flowering until the weather cools down, regardless of falling light levels.

Tender annuals like sunflowers, tithonias, zinnias or petunias cannot be safely planted outside until after the last risk of a spring frost has passed, which for many gardens in the UK is May.

Coming from warmer climates, tender annuals also need heat in order to germinate so must be raised indoors and then hardened off outside before planting. At the end of the year, tender annuals will be hit by the first frost or period of cold, which will kill them off.

Biennials like foxgloves, forget-me-nots and honesty differ from annuals in that they grow fast from seed and develop strong roots and foliage in one season and then flower in the next. This means that they germinate and grow without flowering in summer and autumn, remain dormant over winter, then have another burst of growth before flowering in spring and early summer. They then set seed and die.

The great advantage of biennials over annuals is that they are hardy enough to withstand a cold winter and quickly produce flowers in spring without having to wait for the plant to grow first. Just make sure you know what they look like in their first year of growth so you don't accidentally weed them out.

HARDY ANNUALS

Hardy annuals are, as their name indicates, tough enough to cope with cold weather. Exactly how cold varies from plant to plant, but all are good down to at least 23°F/–5°C.

Their growth habits are controlled more by light than heat once the soil has warmed sufficiently to trigger germination (and some need vernalisation, or a period of cold, for germination to happen at all). The seedlings grow fast as the days lengthen, hitting full vigour in May and June when the days are longest and then increasingly forming seed as the days shorten from the beginning of July.

However, although they can withstand cold weather, if it is too warm or too dry, this will trigger the emergency response of setting seed earlier.

METHOD

1. Hardy annuals can be raised like tender annuals but with less protection, and then planted out as and when the plants are large enough and you are ready.

2. They are also tough enough to be sown directly where you wish them to flower. This is obviously much easier and quicker than raising the plants indoors and then planting them out individually. You simply scatter seed into a border and let them germinate and grow where they fall. Job done.

3. Try to do this in spring as soon as the soil is no longer cold to touch. (A few hardy annuals, like ammi and sweet peas, do much better if sown in early autumn and overwintered as young plants.)

4. However, with simply scattering the seed there is a risk that they will be swamped by weeds, weeded out by mistake or disturbed as and when you add new perennial plants. The way to minimise this collateral damage is to scratch shapes such as zig-zags, crosses or circles in the soil with a stick or your finger and sprinkle the seed in the resulting drills.

5. Close the soil over above them and put a label or stick where these marks are in the soil to ensure that they are not disturbed before you can clearly see them. Water them and, if the weather is very dry, keep the soil moist until the plants are growing strongly.

6. They will quickly become evident as a rash of seedlings marking out the shapes you have drawn in the border. This might look odd for a day or two but the artificiality of these shapes will disappear as they grow and as you thin the seedlings.

7. Thinning is important to allow each individual plant to grow strongly and involves a degree of ruthlessness that is essential. Remove all seedlings to leave at least 4in/10cm between the individual plants, and the lack of competition will mean they flower better and for longer.

YOU WILL NEED

An area of bare, cultivated, unmulched soil

Seeds such as: poppies, nigella, sweet peas, cornflowers, orlaya, ammi, poached egg plants, pot marigolds

A stick or cane

Labels

Water

TENDER ANNUALS

Tender annuals grow and flower in response to heat as their main trigger, rather than light. Most will be killed by any frost and none will survive temperatures below 23°F/–5°C. However, the nature of annuals is that they germinate, grow, flower and set seed in one season, so there is no need for them to cope with even the mildest British winter.

The greatest risk to them are late spring frosts when the plants are still young and have not begun to produce flowers, so if you are buying them as young plants, even though they are often on sale at Easter time, keep them under cover and frost-free, and resist planting them out until all risk of frost has passed – which is mid or even late May in my own garden.

But if you sow them yourself in mid-spring – and the choice of plants from seed is tenfold what you can buy in any garden centre – the seedlings will be ready to be planted into the garden or outside in a container by early June just as the weather warms up. As long as they have enough water, the hotter it gets, the better they will flower.

METHOD

1. Fill a seed tray with potting compost and ideally sit it for 10 to 15 minutes in a tray or sink filled with water so the compost can thoroughly absorb the water. This ensures the compost will be damp, which will encourage germination.

2. In the case of large seeds like sunflowers, either sow them individually into a small pot or, for smaller sunflower seeds, into plugs. Push the seeds on their edge into the compost.

3. For smaller seeds, sprinkle them thinly onto the surface of the compost. The ideal is to have them equidistant about .39in/1cm apart. There is really nothing gained by doing this too thickly – the more space each seed has, the better the roots of the young seedlings will grow.

4. Cover the seeds lightly with vermiculite or a thin sprinkling of compost. If you have not soaked the compost, water it well and put somewhere warm to germinate. A heated mat makes this very easy but a windowsill above a radiator is good.

YOU WILL NEED

Seed trays

Peat-free potting compost

Plugs or small pots

Water

Vermiculite

Somewhere warm for germination and raising seedlings

Seeds such as: sunflowers, zinnias, cosmos, petunias, tithonias, French marigolds, nasturtiums, tobacco plants

5. When the seedlings have true leaves, lift them gently by a leaf and ease the roots from the compost, transplanting them to individual pots or plugs. Grow these on under cover until they are large enough to plant out. Before you do so, put them outside to acclimatise and harden off for at least a week before planting into their growing position.

6. Plant the seedlings into the garden so they get as much sun as possible and water them in.

7. Larger plants like sunflowers and tithonias will need staking. Remember that some sunflowers can grow 6ft/2m or more, so the support needs to be able to hold that size stem with large, top-heavy flowers.

8. After the first frost these plants can all be pulled up and put on the compost heap.

BIENNIALS

SOW: LATE SPRING TO MID-SUMMER
FLOWER: FOLLOWING SPRING/SUMMER

You can buy biennial plants in autumn and spring and put them into your garden and they will duly flower. That is an easy and very straightforward way of growing them and you will not need me to tell you how to do that.

But a much cheaper and, I think, more rewarding method is to grow them yourself from seed.

This takes some planning because biennials, by definition, span two growing seasons. They germinate and start to grow roots and foliage in the summer of one year and then produce their flowers the following spring or summer. This means that the seeds you sow in early and midsummer will not bear their floral harvest for up to another year. You will either find that frustrating or an intriguing part of the seasonal flow of gardening, according to your mindset.

METHOD

1. Prepare a seed tray with peat-free compost. Sit it in a tray or sink of water for 15 minutes to absorb moisture like blotting paper. This will aid germination and mean you do not have to water the seeds for a few days and thus avoid the risk of the water spray moving the fine seeds to the edge of the seed tray.

2. Sprinkle the seeds thinly over the surface of the damp compost. In the case of foxgloves, these seeds are absolutely tiny so just a few pinches of seed will do.

3. Put them somewhere protected to germinate, away from cats and dogs and heavy rain. This need not be a greenhouse or windowsill.

4. When the seedlings – which will be very small – have a pair of 'true' leaves, they can be carefully pricked out into plugs or spaced equidistantly in another seed tray. Grow them on for another month or so until they are about 5cm tall.

5. These small plants can be planted out in late summer or autumn where they are to flower next year, be potted into individual pots to grow larger ready for planting in spring, or, if you have space, be planted out in a row on a spare patch of ground and then transplanted in spring.

6. Foxgloves should grow strongly as the days lengthen and warm up and flower in May and June. They will then produce thousands of seeds that can be left to fall and produce new plants around the parent plant, shaken from the seed cases. The seeds can then be sown in July and August for next year's display in other parts of the garden.

YOU WILL NEED

Seed tray

Peat-free potting compost

Biennial seed such as: foxgloves, honesty, sweet rocket, wallflowers, forget-me-nots, sweet william, columbines or granny's bonnets, evening primrose

Plugs or small pots

Water

72 | FLOWERS

PERENNIALS

Perennials are defined as having no woody growth or permanent structure. There are two types, herbaceous perennials whose top growth dies back completely at the end of the season, and evergreen ones that keep their foliage.

Herbaceous perennials make up the vast majority and although all their growth above ground dies back completely in autumn, the roots remain perfectly healthy, if largely dormant, below ground.

Because its growing season is short, the plant has to grow with tremendous vigour in order to flower and set seed before autumn, hence the dramatic transformation in the herbaceous border in the months from April to July. There is always something wonderful about the sheer volume of growth an herbaceous plant can make in a season. Added to their vigour is their hardiness and longevity: some herbaceous plants last for decades and survive the worst of winter weather.

Although in principle a perennial goes on living from year to year, in practice there is a huge range of life expectancy, from three or four years for the average lupin to scores of years for a healthy peony. However long-lived, most are extremely tolerant of being dug up, split, moved around and generally manhandled and this adaptability makes the design and assembly of a border infinitely flexible. Short-lived perennials will also invariably make new plants from offsets, suckers and seeds so the display instigated by the parent plant can continue indefinitely.

Spring perennials, such as pulmonaria, primroses and periwinkles, tend to originate from woodland and flower before the leaf canopy shades them out. In summer they are dormant and start growing again in early autumn as the leaves begin to fall. Some perennials, like many alpines, catmint and sedums, come from high up on mountainsides where trees and shrubs cannot survive and are adapted to hot, dry summers. Others, like echinacea and rudbeckia, come from prairies and love open, sunny conditions, surviving fire and extreme winter cold. Finally, there are a range of superb perennials, like ligularia, candelabra primulas and rogersias, that thrive in very damp and even boggy conditions. Add to these specialisations that most perennials are adaptable and forgiving, and as a result there are perennial plants for every conceivable situation.

Because herbaceous perennials grow so much so fast, they will often need support, particularly if the soil is good or rainfall high, so they grow extra lush (as they do in my garden). The secret of effective plant supports is to prevent damage rather than repair it. The best way to do this in a border is to establish a system of supports that you put into place in mid to late spring, just as the herbaceous plants are starting to grow really strongly. By doing this, within a few weeks the supports will be hidden but quietly doing their work, with the tender new growth contained within their gentle, protective embrace.

HELLEBORES

There are twenty species of hellebore with two – H. viridis and H. foetidus – native to Britain, but the most widely grown are varieties of H. orientalis, the Lenten rose, and increasingly, relatively new hybrids that are more upright, flower earlier – often before Christmas – and hold their flowers for longer. The downside of these newer hybrids is that they lack the elegance and charm of the Lenten rose. But there is room for both in most gardens.

The best way to enjoy the details of the often exquisite speckled flower variations of the Lenten rose is not on the plant itself, because the flowers hang down (to make it easier for the bumblebees that pollinate them to get at their pollen). Instead, carefully cut a selection on short stems and then float them in a bowl filled with water like tabletop water lilies. They last a surprisingly long time like this and make the most beautiful centrepiece for any table.

The flower buds are formed six months or so before they appear from mid to late summer. This is effectively the start of their growing season so I always give mine a mulch of good compost in late August. Sometimes flowers do appear in summer but it is much more common from plants that have been moved or divided or perhaps stressed in some way. Having done it once, they usually hit their winter-flowering rhythm the next season.

Hellebores live a long time and do not like being moved, so it is worth taking some trouble when you plant them. They flourish in a situation that has some degree of shade, shelter and rich, well-drained soil.

METHOD

1. Hellebores keep their rather leathery leaves for a year until they are replaced by the new ones, and these old leaves do slowly biodegrade. However, the leaves can obscure the flowers or even suppress them as well as carry the fungal disease of hellebore blight, Coniothryium hellebori. This manifests itself as chocolate splotches on the leaves, which will then wither and die and spread to the stem and flowers. So it is a good idea to remove all the leaves in the new year which not only tidies away the old foliage but also increases ventilation, which in turn reduces the chance of the fungus spreading.

2. When I plant a hellebore I dig a hole deeper than the pot they are in and add a good amount of garden compost. This extra goodness gives them a good start and improves drainage.

3. Cut the leaf stems as low down as possible, being very careful not to cut off any growing flowers in the process – it is easily done!

4. Any affected leaves should not be added to the compost heap but burnt. They rot so slowly there is a real chance of the fungus surviving the composting process and reinfecting otherwise healthy plants if it is spread as a mulch around them.

YOU WILL NEED

Oriental hybrid hellebores (Lenten roses)

Secateurs

Peat-free potting compost

DIVIDING HERBACEOUS PERENNIALS – SPLITTING

SPLIT: AUTUMN OR SPRING
FLOWER: SPRING TO SUMMER

Herbaceous perennials tend to grow outwards in a concentric ring, with the newest, healthiest growth on the outside and the oldest growth in the middle. After a few years, this old growth dies back completely, leaving a doughnut or expanding circle of plants with an empty centre.

To keep plants refreshed and their display as fulsome and good as possible it is necessary to regularly lift and divide them before replanting the divisions around your borders to make new plants. Even if there is no pressing need to divide a clump, dividing healthy herbaceous perennials is the quickest, easiest and cheapest way to make new plants that will grow quickly and should flower in their first year.

Depending on the way that the roots grow, there are two ways of doing this division. For plants that have a core of fleshy root, such as astilbe, hostas, delphiniums, hellebores and red-hot pokers, the best method is to cut them into sections with a spade or a knife.

METHOD

1. Dig the entire plant from the ground with a fork. The best time to do this is in spring when you see the first signs of new growth (March and April in my garden).

2. If there is little space, put the plant in a trug and take it to a flat area where you can work freely. Paving is fine and smaller plants can be divided on a tabletop.

3. If the inner part is very old and starting to separate from the newer, outer growth, separate it and add it to the compost heap. Otherwise cut the roots into sections so that each separate new piece has visible growth. If you use a spade, be bold and chop down straight. The plant will not be damaged. I find that dividing the plant into quarters is ideal as it means that the outer part of each quarter section is bigger than the inner and thus there is more new growth than old in each segment, but as long as each piece has visible signs of growth you can divide it into as many pieces as you wish.

4. Replant each section either singly or in groups of 3 or 5 spaced 2 to 3in/5 to 7cm apart so that they grow to form one large clump. Water them in well and they will grow far more strongly than if they had not been divided.

YOU WILL NEED

Garden fork

Trug

Sharp spade or robust knife (an old bread knife is ideal)

Watering can

Water

DIVIDING HERBACEOUS PERENNIALS – SEPARATING

Many herbaceous perennials have loose, fibrous roots. These will need dividing every few years to maintain the quality of their display as, like all herbaceous perennials, the best display comes from new growth around the spreading outer edges and, in time, the plant will develop an empty centre. Because of the nature of the fibrous root system, these plants can be more easily pulled or teased apart than cut with a spade or knife.

As with all perennials, division or moving is best done in early spring when you see new growth. It can also be done in autumn, in which case the top growth will have to be cut back. However, this is not a job to do in summer when the plant is in full display.

METHOD

1. Dig up the selected plant with a fork, trying to remove as much soil as possible as you do so, without damaging the roots.

2. Many plants, such as ajuga, heuchera, rudbeckia, epimediums and hardy geraniums, can be teased into sections with your fingers. These sections can be good-sized clumps in their own right or very small, as long as each one has a visible growing shoot and healthy root system. Some plants, like hemerocallis, are a little tougher to separate and the traditional method is to put two forks back-to-back down into the centre of the plant and pull them away from each other so they act like scissors and force the roots apart without damaging them.

3. If there is a more woody inner core to the plant, remove it and add it to the compost heap. The new, fibrous rooted shoots, although small, will grow much faster and healthier.

4. Replant each section, either singly or in groups, and water them in very well. If you do not have space or want to plant them later, they can be potted up and grown on before planting out when you are ready.

YOU WILL NEED

2 forks of a similar size

Watering can

Water

MULCHING

Mulch describes a layer of organic material spread over bare ground and left as a surface blanket. To be effective it should be thick and dense enough to block light from the earth beneath and to slow down evaporation.

Mulch suppresses weeds by denying them light so some, like groundsel or shepherd's purse that need light to trigger germination, will simply not grow and others might germinate but the seedlings will not have enough light to survive. Perennial weeds such as nettles or couch grass will be dramatically weakened and those that do make it through the mulch are much easier to pull out.

With climate change making our summer gardens drier – when the demand for water is at its peak – mulch is becoming increasingly important to slow down evaporation and retain moisture. The majority of feeding roots are near the surface and in response to drought a plant will push its roots even closer to the surface to try and get what moisture it can – and thus dry out even quicker. Mulching breaks this cycle. The thicker the mulch is, the more effectively it resists drought.

Finally, a mulch of organic material will be worked into the soil by earthworms and improve the soil structure as well as the fertility, which in turn enables and encourages roots to delve deeper for water and therefore be better equipped to cope with drought.

METHOD

1. The best time to mulch is just as the new growth of borders is appearing – usually early to late March. But you can also mulch in autumn after tidying the borders and this can be a good idea if you have a lot of bulbs in your borders whose new shoots you do not want to suppress by an application in spring.

2. Before mulching remove as many weeds as you can so you are spreading the mulch onto bare soil. It is also not a good idea to mulch onto very dry soil, although this is unlikely in spring.

3. If you buy mulch in bags it is easiest to pour it straight from the bag onto the border and then manipulate it around the plants with a rake or by hand. Try not to cover emerging growth but do not be too precious about it.

4. If your mulch is loose – such as your own garden compost or shredded material – fill a barrow or trug and ladle it into place with a shovel, spreading it evenly with a rake.

5. In my experience a layer at least 2in/5cm – and ideally 4in/10cm – thick is needed to work well as a combined weed suppressant, moisture retainer and soil improver. If you have a lot of soil to mulch, it is much more effective to mulch part of your garden thickly, rotating it every year, than to do the whole garden with too thin a layer.

YOU WILL NEED

Organic mulching material such as garden compost, mushroom compost, bark chips or council compost. You can use an inorganic mulch such as gravel, pebbles or slate for individual plants or dry, herb or alpine gardens where soil fertility is kept deliberately low.

Barrow or trug

Shovel

Rake

PLANTING HERBACEOUS PERENNIALS

Herbaceous perennials, by definition, live a long time and are tough. In fact, they vary hugely. Some, like lupins or echinacea, can be relatively short-lived, lasting only for a few years, whilst others, like peonies, can last for generations. But all will perform at their best with a good start.

It really is worth the effort to prepare the ground well before planting. Dig over the whole bed or border, removing any trace of weeds that you come across. Don't stint on this: the more thoroughly you do this before you plant anything, the more time and trouble you will save yourself later on.

Traditionally you would double-dig or trench the ground, incorporating as much manure as you could get hold of. It was hard graft – and I did years of it. But there is no need to do that beyond a macho satisfaction. However, it is really important to break up any compaction that may be below the surface, especially on a new-build plot where heavy machinery has run over during construction. So turn the soil over as deeply as you can to loosen the structure of the soil.

A surface layer of compost or manure lightly worked in with a fork or a rake will help. Ideally the ground should be friable enough to plant easily with a trowel, spade or even your bare hands. You are then ready to go.

METHOD

1. If you are planting more than one individual plant – and, if it is a new border, I strongly recommend that you buy or raise enough plants until you have the basis for your planting group or the whole border – place them where you want them to grow before you put anything in the ground. Think in terms of drifts or groups, how the colours of flower and foliage will interrelate and harmonise, how different heights and rate of growth will affect each other and how the planting will span the seasons. All this should be considered before you put anything in the ground.

2. But, having said that, plants can and inevitably will be moved around, so don't worry about it too much.

3. When planting in groups, odd numbers tend to look better than even. Do not plant too close together because small plants quickly get bigger. By and large leave 8 to 10in/20 to 25cm between plants within a clump of the same plant and twice that between different plants.

4. Planting itself is easy. Make a hole, take the plant out of its plastic pot and pop it in the ground, firming the soil back around it.

5. Water it in well and mulch around the plants, being sure not to cover the young growth with mulching material.

YOU WILL NEED

Your chosen perennial plants

Spade and/or planting trowel

Water

Mulch

EARLY PERENNIAL PLANTS

Perennial plants in the first half of summer, from late May through to mid-July, have a freshness and vivacity that is not weighed down by the fullness of burgeoning growth. So it makes sense to plant to capture and celebrate that. This means creating clumps and drifts of colour, using different heights and rates of growth to add form and texture to the border, above all being generous with plants and colour. It is much more effective to have a smaller border that is crammed with plants than a larger one with the same quantity rattling around in too large a space. The light in June is bright and still has a freshness, so use colours that respond to that best. Blues, lemon yellows, whites, pink – all shades of pastel in fact look best in this first half of the season. Foliage plants like cardoons with their great silvery grey leaves are the perfect foil for this colour palette.

METHOD

1. When planting for best effect in early summer, try and plant in uneven numbers to create groups or drifts of colour, or let the plants drift through a border, picking up colour notes and foliage shapes and textures. This works especially well in long borders.

2. Whilst it makes sense to have lower-growing plants like big-root cranesbill or dusky cranesbill, lady's mantle or aquilegias near the front of a border, it is also a good idea to stagger heights so that the border is not rigidly tiered, rising up to the back like football stands. You need to look through plants and have glimpses that are only fully revealed by moving along or round the border. Plants like knautia macedonica are superb for providing a fragile foreground (although there is nothing fragile about these plants as long as they have really good drainage), enhancing all that lies beyond their burgundy flowers held on slender, even thin stems.

3. Blue is rare in plants but this is their best season. Bellflowers, knapweed, catmint, Siberian iris and bugloss 'Loddon Royalist' are all good blue perennials. Delphiniums are a must, and the Elatum Group hybrids are perhaps easiest to grow.

4. Oriental poppies have intense blood reds like 'Beauty of Livermere' and 'Allegro' but are also beautiful in subtler shades like 'Prinzessin Victoria Louise' or 'Cedric Morris', which have pink flowers. Like delphiniums and hardy geraniums these should be cut right back when they have finished flowering and this will give them the chance to regrow and flower again later in summer.

YOU WILL NEED

Selection of plants such as:

Lupins

Delphiniums

Hardy geraniums

Lady's mantle

Oriental poppies

Peonies

Astrantias

Euphorbia palustris

Gillenia

Monarda

Thalictrum

Persicaria

Siberian irises

Knautia macedonica

Bleeding hearts

LATE PERENNIAL PLANTS

As summer moves into August and September the whole palette and range of perennial plants changes. Oranges, caramels, purples, burgundies, magentas, coppers and golds run like velvet threads through our borders. The quality of the light changes too, with the sun lower in the sky and picking up the richness of the new shades.

At the same time the exuberance of June and early July has gone. The fullness of high summer starts to hang heavy and the brilliance of new spring green has become tired, ready to start turning autumnal.

The skill here is to use all this to make the most of your garden and select those plants that are happiest at this time of year and look really good.

METHOD

1. Many of these are vigorous plants and are best in the middle or back of a border where their growing foliage and stems make a good backdrop and fill for the earlier-flowering perennials. Plant them in spring in cooler areas and autumn if you live in a sheltered, milder part of the country.

2. Plants like rudbeckia, inula, helianthus, crocosmia and some heleniums can make substantial clumps, so give them room but also be prepared to lift and divide and redistribute them every few years – which will also invigorate them and make them grow even more strongly. Because these plants grow tall, most will need support and this should be – like all garden supports – put into place before they need it rather than as a recovery action.

3. For the front of a border or along a path, sedums (many are now called Hylotelephium) like 'Voodoo' or 'Purple Emperor' are dramatic, very tough (they thrive in poor soil with very good drainage) and attract butterflies like no other plant.

4. The coneflowers – rudbeckia and echinacea – are prairie plants that like to be out in the open in full sunshine and make superb companions for grasses.

5. Heleniums – also coneflowers and also from North America – originate from the banks of rivers and like sunshine but dampish soil. Dry shade is hopeless for them whereas, once established, Japanese anemones are remarkably tolerant of dry, slightly shady conditions, and penstemons positively hate sitting in wet soil. Asters like moist but well-drained soil in sun and light shade. Trying to find the ideal spot for every plant in a garden, especially in one border, is impossible, but if you can please some and particularly the more fussy ones like heleniums or penstemons, then so much the better.

YOU WILL NEED

Selection of plants such as:

Rudbeckia

Heleniums

Echinacea

Aster

Helianthus 'Lemon Queen'

Japanese anemone

Agastache

Inula

Penstemon

Crocosmia

Red-hot poker

Anchusa

Cardinal flower

Geranium 'Ann Folkard'

Sedums

Patrinia

A BOWL OF
WINTER PANSIES

PLANT: AUTUMN TO WINTER
FLOWER: WINTER TO SPRING

Even in the harshest winter weather the delicate petals of pansies (which are a type of hybrid viola) still retain their colour and poise, and brighten the darkest midwinter day. There are many different kinds of pansies in colours ranging from pure white to almost black. True pansies have one downward-facing petal whereas violas have two, but essentially they are all very similar, despite differences in colour and size.

METHOD

1. Put a layer of compost in the bottom of the pot, having first put a crock over the drainage hole(s) to ensure they do not get clogged.

2. Remove the plants from their plastic trays and place them directly onto the compost.

3. For an instant display that will look dramatic from the outset and last for 2 or 3 months, cram as many of the plants into the container as will fit. However, if you want the plants to last longer – and they are perennials so potentially will last for a few years – then they will need more room for the roots to grow. If you leave sufficient room, dribble extra compost between the individual plants.

4. Water them in and place them where you can see them from the house. A sunny position will ensure that they flower more freely, although they will tolerate quite a lot of shade. They should not be allowed to dry out but also do not like being waterlogged.

5. The trick to keeping them flowering right through winter is to dead head the spent flowers as soon as they are over. In spring, as the plants start to become leggy, cut the whole plant back hard. Keep them watered and fed throughout summer and they should be good for at least one more year's winter display.

YOU WILL NEED

A container (which can be fairly shallow) with drainage hole(s) and crocks to ensure they do not get blocked

Peat-free potting compost

A generous amount of young plants, which are invariably sold in trays

Water

TENDER PLANTS
IN A CONTAINER

Tender plants, such as bananas, cannas, dahlias and salvias, although large, can be grown in containers and look really dramatic from midsummer to autumn.

If you have a large container, it can have a winter and spring display based around dramatic bulbs, such as daffodils and tulips, with perhaps wallflowers to complement them. These can then be removed when finished in May and the pot used for the tender plants to last until cold weather in autumn – at which point it will be the correct time to plant bulbs. This keeps a permanent display and makes the most of an expensive pot (and all large terracotta pots are expensive!).

In principle the choice of plants and their arrangement is wide and subjective. However this is a recipe for a tried-and-tested combination that I have used for many years.

Whatever plants you use, it is always a good idea for any large container to have a pillar, a filler and a spiller. The pillar is placed in the centre of the pot and gives height. The filler gives body and colour, and the spiller spills over the edge of the pot, hanging down to the ground.

METHOD

1. Put crocks in the bottom of the pot and half fill with the compost mix. A large container packed with this number of plants performing at full bent for months needs a good compost mix to grow in. A bag of standard potting compost, however good, is not going to do the job for more than a month or two. So add soil improver or your own garden compost at a ratio of 33% volume. Also add grit at about 12% volume. The result should be a rich mix that drains well.

2. Position the central 'pillar' so the surface of its compost is about 4in/10cm below the rim of the pot. Fill around it so your 'filler' plants can fit equidistant apart at the same height.

3. Fill around these so the compost is up to the full height and then plant the 'spillers' at equidistant space between the 'fillers'.

4. Finally cram – and I mean squeeze in tightly – as many annuals, such as the cosmos, zinnias, petunias or whatever you choose, into the remaining available space.

5. Water it all in until the water is flowing out of the bottom of the pot.

6. This will need a weekly soak and daily watering in extreme heat and drought. Feed with liquid seaweed weekly. I combine this with the weekly soak.

YOU WILL NEED

A large pot, preferably terracotta

Crocks

Peat-free compost

Garden compost or soil improver

Grit

Pillar plants – canna 'Wyoming', standard fuchsia, phormium, or banana ensete

Filler plants – dahlia 'Grenadier' x 3 or 'David Howard', salvia 'Amista' and bush fuchsia, cosmos 'Dazzler' x 8 or zinnia 'Hero Mix' or calendula

Spiller plants – licorice plant, nasturtiums, bacopa, trailing fuchsias or petunias

Water

Liquid seaweed

PELARGONIUMS

As a general rule, the harder a pelargonium is treated, the better it will flower. However, you can make it grow rapidly by repotting it annually into a slightly larger container before it starts to flower. If you keep doing this, the plant will continue to grow vigorously until its roots become constricted. Then, when it is as big as you want it, leave it in the pot it is in and it will flower profusely thereafter.

Pelargonium cuttings take easily, and many people start anew every year from cuttings, discarding the old plants. However, I rather like the unruly, winding extravagance of an old, mature specimen. Species pelargoniums, like all species plants, tend to be tougher and less showy. So for example, P. sidoides has small glaucous leaves and tiny flowers carried on long wispy stems, but these are the colour of the deepest, plummiest wine and it has real charm.

Quite a few of the species have scented leaves, especially when handled, and are worth growing for this tactile fragrance, regardless of their flowers.

METHOD

1. Pelargoniums should be kept in a cool, frost-free bright place over winter. Keep them dry all winter.

2. Once growth is underway in spring, cut back old growth, using this for cuttings.

3. Cuttings are best taken from non-flowering, straight shoots 2 to 4in/5 to 10cm long. Strip off the lower leaves and insert into a 50:50 perlite and compost mix or pure perlite. Do not put the cuttings in a polythene bag, but water them in and then keep the tops dry without letting the compost dry out. When they have rooted, pot them on individually and they will quickly become strong-growing, floriferous plants.

4. Having cut the parent plant back, repot it into a slightly larger pot, using fresh compost with a lot of grit or perlite added to ensure good drainage, and put it somewhere sunny and warm. Start to water regularly (but let it dry out completely between waterings). Pelargoniums respond well to feeding so apply a balanced liquid fertilizer weekly between April and September.

5. Deadhead the spent flowers regularly and pinch out long shoots in summer to encourage more flowering sideshoots.

6. If you have a pelargonium that has become too big and unwieldy and you are not sure how best to prune it, simply remove all top growth 4 to 8in/10 to 20cm from the base in spring, and it will regrow vigorously until it reaches a manageable size.

7. Most problems with pelargoniums are due to overwatering. They need only minimal water, especially over winter. If the leaves start to become tinged with orange or yellow, this is an indication that the plant is being over-watered.

YOU WILL NEED

Pelargonium plants

Secateurs

Peat-free potting compost

Grit or perlite to mix with the compost

Terracotta pots

Crocks

Water

Liquid fertiliser

SHRUBS

A shrub is a multi-stemmed, woody plant. There are a multitude of variations on this theme that range from the enormous rhododendrons billowing across Himalayan hillsides to neat little alpine affairs clinging on to an icy rock face, with hundreds of flowering garden shrubs between – not to mention those that are grown for their foliage.

Shrubs are often used as the middle layer of any border, the fill or backdrop adding texture and substance that allows other more obviously spectacular plants to shine better for their more ephemeral moment in the sun. Many shrubs are exceptionally hardy and adaptable although some have adapted especially well to either acidic soil, such as heathers and rhododendrons, or alkaline soil, like lilacs, ceanothus and lavender.

Shrubs also bear some of the most feted of all flowers. Roses are shrubs, as are lilacs, amelanchier, camellias, rhododendrons, buddlejas, magnolias, philadelphus, hydrangeas and fuchsias, to name but a handful of shrubs grown for their glorious spring and summer floral display. A few shrubs will also flower reliably in the depths of winter, such as the winter-flowering honeysuckle, witch hazel, daphne, a number of viburnums and mahonias.

Then there are shrubs that display their brilliance in their foliage. Many shrubs have purple leaves, such as the smoke bush, purple elder, many acers, purple hazel and purple crab apples. Others have stupendous autumnal foliage including acers, witch hazel, Viburnum plicatum, amelanchiers and sumachs.

There are also shrubs whose fruit – hips and berries – are even more spectacular than the flowers they emerge from; rugosa rose, berberis, pyracantha, callicarpa and the guelder rose all fit that bill.

Because they have a permanent woody structure, shrubs are very responsive to pruning and can be shaped, trained and controlled to serve the purpose you most want for them in your particular garden. Many can be left almost entirely alone whereas others can be coppiced – with all top growth cut right back to the ground – every year or two. This will result in a fresh burst of new stems that will both carry exceptionally large leaves and, in the case of some willows and dogwoods, brightly coloured stems in winter when all the leaves have fallen.

Some shrubs – such as lavender, rosemary or myrtle – are both excellent as individual specimens and make very good softly rounded, even loosely billowing hedges. Quite a few shrubs – such as box, euonymus, elaeagnus, laurels, phillyrea and privet – lend themselves to clipping into sculpted 'cloud pruning' for an evergreen, year-round performance.

ERICACEOUS SHRUBS IN A POT

There are a group of shrubs that need acidic soil to thrive – and in some cases, even survive. Where they are flourishing they tend to dominate, to the exclusion of those more numerous shrubs that need alkaline soil. So rhododendrons, azaleas, camellias, gorse and heathers all thrive but lilacs, ceanothus and clematis struggle. A rhododendron or camellia in soil that is not sufficiently acidic will show its displeasure by a yellowing of its leaves, and if it is in chalk or pure limestone it will surely die.

But by and large we are all hostages to the pH of our soil and there is nothing much we can do to affect that, let alone change it. In practice most of us have soil that is neither very acidic nor very alkaline, so most plants will survive, although some do notably better than others.

However, you can grow plants that need very clear, extreme conditions by raising them in a container and creating the perfect custom conditions for them. This works very well for rhododendrons, azaleas and camellias, most of which are evergreen plants with dramatic spring flowers.

METHOD

1. Choose a pot a bit bigger than the one that the plant is in. Rhododendrons and azaleas have shallow roots so width is more important than depth. Make sure the pot has good drainage holes and cover them with crocks or pebbles to stop them being blocked by the potting compost.

2. The compost must be specifically ericaceous. This used to be peat based but this is now illegal and there are good substitutes available. I have found bracken-based compost to be excellent, as is a pine bark compost. Mix this with some perlite or grit to improve drainage and, ideally, with home-made leaf mould, to make up about a quarter of the mix by volume. This creates the open, loose medium that rhododendrons, camellias and azaleas like.

3. Set the plant so that the surface is at least 2in/5cm below the rim of the pot. This allows sufficient room for generous watering and an annual mulch of ericaceous compost which will protect the shallow roots.

4. Keep the plant well watered, especially in late summer and early autumn, which is when next year's flower buds are forming. Rhododendrons and azaleas like cool, moist air and do best in light shade rather than full sun, so when it is very hot and dry, mist the foliage with water in the evening.

YOU WILL NEED

Rhododendron, azalea or camellia of your choice

A container large enough to allow 4in/10cm of growth both around the sides and bottom

Crocks

Peat-free ericaceous compost

Perlite or grit

Leaf mould if you have it

Water (rainwater if you're in a 'hard' water area)

PRUNING DECIDUOUS SPRING-FLOWERING SHRUBS

The deciduous spring-flowering shrubs such as philadelphus, lilac, forsythia, weigela and ribes all produce their flowers on shoots grown the previous summer. It follows that if you do not prune them, most of the new growth will be on the outer edges of the shrub and most of that at the top, where it gets most sun. This will increasingly shade out the lower part, leaving it not just bare of flowers but also of foliage. The whole thing gets straggly, unbalanced and looking bad.

The flower buds form best on wood that has had a chance to 'ripen' before autumn, i.e., go from being a whippy green shoot to a slightly more woody stem, which in turn means growing early and then being exposed to some hot sun. In other words, the quality of the flowers in spring is strongly influenced by the quality of the previous summer.

Your pruning should adapt to this and be done as early as possible after flowering to encourage new growth either from the very base of the plant or nearer the middle rather than inexorably creeping upwards. This gives those new shoots as much time as possible to grow and do some sunbathing to maximise flowering next spring.

METHOD

1. Young shrubs should have the weakest growth cut back to encourage stronger regrowth, with the remainder pruned just to shape and size and to take out any stems that are crossing or damaged.

2. Mature shrubs should be pruned by cutting back most of the current year's flowering stems by about half to a healthy new bud or side shoot, and taking the oldest growth (but never more than a third of the plant in any one year) right back to the base so it is completely renewed every 3 or 4 years.

3. A very overgrown shrub can be drastically renewed by coppicing it, cutting all growth right back to the ground. This will result in a rash of stems that can then be shaped and thinned the following year. A more measured way is to cut back a third of the growth every year for 3 years.

4. Weed, water and mulch with compost after pruning is done and, if you are feeling adventurous, take semi-ripe cuttings from some of the healthy, straight non-flowering pruned stems.

YOU WILL NEED

Pruning kit: secateurs, loppers, saw

Early Spring:

amelanchier, berberis, chaenomeles, forsythias, kerria, lilac, osmanthus burkwoodii, ribes, viburnum

Late Spring:

ceanothus, cotoneaster, daphne, kolkwitzia, tree peonies, potentilla, pyracantha, philadelphus, weigela

PLANTING ROSES

Most roses are surprisingly tough and adaptable to most soils and situations but it is always worth giving them the best start in life that you can, in order to encourage a healthy, strong plant.

The best time to plant any rose is when it is dormant, during winter, but a pot-grown rose can be planted at any time. Bare-root roses – which are cheaper and usually available from nurseries with a far wider choice – are only available in winter.

METHOD

1. Water roses in pots an hour before planting and put bare-root plants to soak in a bucket of water. Never expose bare roots to the air for a minute longer than necessary – keep them in the bucket of water or wrapped in a bag right up to the last moment to stop them drying out.

2. Dig a hole that is at least twice as wide as the pot and remove every scrap of weed.

3. Loosen any compacted soil at the base and the sides of the hole, but there is no need to add compost as this would only discourage the growing roots from going out into the surrounding soil. A thick mulch on the surface of the soil is much more beneficial.

4. Whilst not essential, mycorrhizal fungi will aid fast root development by acting as a beneficial conduit, trading sugars from the plant's roots in return for nutrients from the soil. It is important that the fungi make direct contact with the roots, so wet the roots and sprinkle the powder directly onto them so it sticks.

5. All roses are grafted onto a rootstock because this is a very cost-effective way of commercial propagation. When you buy a rose in a pot, the graft (a noticeable bump or line where the rootstock [roots] and scion [stem] join) is always 1in/2.5cm or so above the surface, but all roses should be planted so that the graft is 1in/2.5cm or so below the soil surface, so the graft is fully buried. This means that when the soil is backfilled, just the branches are sticking out of the ground. This will secure it firmly.

6. Back-fill the soil, working it in and amongst the roots and firming it carefully with your heel.

7. Water it well and then mulch generously. This will feed the growing roots, suppress weeds and retain moisture.

8. Finally, prune out any long, thin shoots to an outward-facing bud to encourage strong growth right from the base of the plant.

YOU WILL NEED

Bare-root rose plant of your choice

Bucket of water

Spade

Mycorrhizal powder (optional)

Mulch

PRUNING SHRUB ROSES

Too many people are intimidated when confronted by a rose that needs pruning, worried that unless it is absolutely right in every detail you would be absolutely wrong and potentially destroy the rose.

Nothing could be further from the truth. Roses are extraordinarily tough plants and will survive any amount of hacking and snipping. Certainly, you can do a lot worse than simply reducing all rose bushes by half with a pair of shears or a hedgecutter and leaving them to regrow and flower perfectly happily.

However, there is a middle way. Although roses can survive brutality and incompetence, considered pruning will result in a better-looking shrub with maximum performance and health.

Before setting to with a sharp blade, try and establish what kind of rose it is. If it is a Hybrid Tea (a stubby, prickly bush with large, opulent flowers) it should be pruned hard, to 8 to 10in/20 to 25cm each spring, as all the flowers are carried on new growth and old growth is generally bare and not attractive.

If it is a shrub rose – which covers all the old roses such as gallicas, albas, damasks, rugosas and others as well as the modern 'English' roses – pruning will be to maintain the shape and health of the shrub and create the right conditions for flowering. Shaping with garden shears, like cutting a rounded hedge in September, is often enough.

Species roses (which have just Latin names, such as rosa moyesii, r. primula, etc.) have small flowers produced on older shoots, so should either be pruned immediately after flowering or by cutting the oldest growth right back to the ground in spring.

If in doubt, don't prune, but watch and note when your rose bush flowers and what the flowers are like and whether they are produced on old or new growth. That should give you the information you need to help you prune next year.

METHOD

1. Roses can be pruned any time from autumn through to spring but by and large the best time is January and February.

2. When cutting, obey the first rule of all pruning, which is to cut back to something. That will usually be to a side shoot, leaf or bud, but never prune in the middle of a stem as this will die back and at the very least look ugly.

3. Remember that what remains after pruning will not bear any flowers but is the framework for new, flowering shoots.

4. Cut back hard all weak, spindly, curling shoots, and remove any that are crossing and rubbing against each other. Then, when you have a splay of healthy, straight-ish shoots with plenty of air in the centre of the bush, reduce these by a third to a half.

5. Finally, having cleared all the pruned material away, be generous with your mulch around each plant.

YOU WILL NEED

Secateurs (plus loppers and a small pruning saw for older, thicker stems)

Thick gloves so you can hold a floppy stem to cut accurately

Mulch

CLIMBERS

The third dimension is an essential element in any garden and increasingly so in the smaller garden. In fact, many very small gardens have more vertical growing space than horizontal.

A garden with lots of height is always much more interesting – and environmentally rich – than one spread out flat like a carpet. Most houses have at least one face that can be planted against, and most gardens have a wall or fence around the outside. These are all ideal for training climbers against. You can also easily erect fences and walls within and divide the garden, however small it might be, which immediately provides two more vertical planes to grow plants against.

There is a huge range of climbers, from tiny alpine clematis that tip over the edge of a small pot to the famous rambling rose 'Kiftsgate' that will easily cover an entire house – and then some.

Climbers are particularly responsive to aspect. The quality and quantity and timing of the light they receive, as well as the resulting temperature and protection or lack of it from wind, will affect their growth and flowering greatly. Some, like wisteria, some roses, jasmine or grapevines, love sunshine and are ideal for a south-facing surface, although there are many plants that find it too hot and dry. Most clematis, for example, are much happier against a west-facing wall and many do surprisingly well on a shady north wall.

Many climbers are woodland plants that scramble up the support of trees to reach the light. They have evolved to like cool, slightly damp roots but to have their flowers in the sun. Honeysuckle, clematis, climbing hydrangea, ivy and Virginia creeper are all woodland plants that will climb a shady wall. Most green looks better in shade, and many climbers with white flowers have evolved to shine out at dusk to attract nocturnal pollinators. The shadiest wall is always that facing north.

Almost any climber will need support to hold it against a wall. This is best either via a series of wires attached tautly to hooks at 12in/30cm spacings, or on a trellis screwed onto wooden blocks that hold it well away from the surface of the wall or fence so that the plant can have room to grow without being cramped. However, climbers do not necessarily need a fixed vertical surface to grow up. I grow roses and clematis, for example, on wigwams made from bean sticks that I regularly repair and replace for permanent positions and move around for annual climbers.

Some climbers, like sweet peas, are annuals and are replaced each year. Others, like some climbing roses or wisteria, can last healthily for generations. Most climbers respond well to pruning both to contain their size and to encourage maximum flowering. I have climbing roses against walls that are cut back hard each winter as well as rambling roses that grow unpruned using large apple trees as their support.

SWEET PEAS

Sweet peas are annual climbers that produce gloriously beautiful and perfumed flowers from late spring to late summer. They look wonderful in the summer garden and make the best cut flowers, filling a room with their fragrance. They are easy to grow, doing best in mild, damp weather.

Sweet peas should be sown between October and March. The earlier they are sown, the larger the plants will be and the earlier they will flower.

METHOD

1. Fill pots with peat-free compost and press 3 seeds into each pot. Cover lightly with a little more compost and label each pot.

2. Water well and place the pots somewhere warm and protected to germinate. This does not need to be indoors but a greenhouse or windowsill is ideal.

3. Once shoots appear they can be placed into a cold frame or a sheltered spot outside to grow into young plants.

4. When they are about 6in/15cm tall, pinch out the top 1.5in/4cm of each plant to encourage strong, bushy plants that will produce the most flowers for the longest time.

5. Plant them out when the ground starts to warm up, usually in April. I plant each pot of 3 plants at the base of a support. If you are doing so in a wigwam of canes, always plant them inside the canes rather than outside to protect their roots and make watering easier.

6. Sweet peas do best in rich soil with lots of water, so add plenty of compost or manure to the soil and water often if the weather is dry. Drought will make them run to seed very quickly and that process is irreversible. However, if you water well and pick the flowers regularly (once a week is about right) you can delay them running to seed until late summer.

7. When the seed pods become more numerous than the flowers, leave them to ripen (turning tawny brown and drying to a crisp) and gather some to use as next year's seed. Then the plants can be lifted and composted.

YOU WILL NEED

Sweet pea seeds

Peat-free compost

Small (3in/7cm is ideal) flowerpots or root trainers

Plant labels

Watering can

Water

Sheltered place to raise the seeds

Support for the growing plants (canes, sticks, netting, trellis)

PLANTING CLEMATIS

Whenever clematis flowers – and they are gathered into three horticultural groups of early, mid-season and late-flowering – they can all be planted in the same way and at the same time. That time is ideally when they are dormant or just coming into growth in late winter, such as February or March. However, you can buy a clematis at any time of year, in full flower, and plant with confidence, although it may not grow very much until the following season.

Whatever clematis you grow, early, late, evergreen, herbaceous, vigorous or miniature (I have a tiny but lovely Clematis marmoraria that grows about 2in/5cm a year), they all hate drying out. You cannot overdo the organic matter in the soil nor the thickness of mulch in the spring, both of which serve as much to retain moisture as to provide nourishment. If you grow a clematis in a container then be sure to give it a good soak at least weekly – and every day if it is really hot.

METHOD

1. Dig a hole at least twice as wide as the pot the plant is in and twice as deep. Add plenty of compost or manure (it does not have to be well-rotted, and straw-y manure or coarse compost will do perfectly well).

2. Remove the plant from its pot, and if the roots are very entangled or even solid and exposed tight against the edge of the pot, do not try and untangle them but rake them down with your fingers to break them a little. This will stimulate fresh growth that will move outwards into the soil and away from the rootball.

3. Wet the roots and sprinkle them with myccorhizal powder if you have some. This is not essential but it will speed up the symbiotic relationship between the roots and the fungi in the soil and therefore help the plant get established.

4. Place the roots in the hole so that the surface of the compost as it was in the pot is at least 2in/5cm or below ground level. This gives it the best defence against wilt, slug attack or drought as it will grow back most strongly from shoots below the soil surface.

5. Fill the soil back in around the roots and soak it with at least 1.3 gallons/5 litres of water, which will be soaked up by the organic material at the bottom of the hole and provide a sump for the roots to reach.

6. Mulch it very thickly. Garden compost or manure is best, bark is good, but pebbles or slate will also help, as the main purpose is to keep the roots cool and moist.

YOU WILL NEED

Spade

Peat-free potting compost or manure

Clematis plant

Water

Mycorrhizal powder (non-essential)

Mulch (absolutely essential)

PRUNING CLEMATIS

PLANT: AUTUMN TO EARLY SPRING
FLOWER: EARLY SPRING TO LATE
AUTUMN (DEPENDING ON TYPE)

There are three distinct groups of clematis covering the whole flowering season, and each group has different pruning requirements. Group 1 includes all those flowering from March through to late May, distinguished by having lots of small flowers and fairly sprawling growth. These include c. alpina, c. montana and the evergreen clematis, c. armandii.

Group 1 clematis only need pruning to restrict their size, and if necessary the time to do it is immediately after flowering in May or early June. They make their flower buds on growth made the previous summer, so pruning later than mid-summer will limit next year's display.

Group 2 clematis includes all those with big, dramatic flowers that start to open in May and are at their best in June. They include famous varieties like 'Niobe', 'Nelly Moser' and 'Lasurstern'. They will often flower twice, initially with large blooms produced on old wood and then again in late summer with smaller flowers on that season's growth. So they are best either pruned very lightly in spring just to tidy or if very overgrown, cut back hard. However, this will result in no large flowers in early summer.

Group 3 clematis includes all the late-flowering ones like the many hybrids of c. viticella, c. jackmannii and c. tangutica, which typically have a mass of small flowers from July through to autumn. These produce all their flowers on new growth so should be cut back hard – to within 6in/15cm of the ground or a couple of healthy buds – every March. If left unpruned the flowers will appear higher and higher up the growth whilst the base becomes increasingly bare.

If all that sounds complicated, the simple mnemonic 'if it flowers before June don't prune' will cover most bases and do no long-term harm.

METHOD

1. It is very simple but be brave! In principle you remove all last year's growth down to the lowest pair of healthy-looking buds. In practice I find it easiest to do this by degrees. Take off half the top growth, removing all ties and fixings to whatever is supporting it. Then you can see better to cut lower and find the lowest healthy buds. These should be very visible and are often just an inch/a few centimetres above the soil but if they are about a foot/half a metre off the ground, so be it. Check the support system, whether it be trellis, canes or wires, then, having cleared away the pruned matter (which will shred and compost well), give the clematis a really good soak and then mulch it thickly (at least 6in/15cm) with organic material. Garden compost is ideal but bark chips do very well.

YOU WILL NEED

Secateurs

Mulch

Water

PRUNING CLIMBING ROSE

Roses that climb, sprawl and ramble come in two distinct types. There are rambling roses and climbing roses and they must be pruned differently and at different times of year.

Rambling roses tend to sprawl more, with long arching stems and smaller but more plentiful flowers that nearly always only appear once, somewhere between late June and mid-August, with the vast majority doing their stuff around the beginning to middle of July. They produce their flowers on growth made the previous year. This means that any pruning should be done immediately after flowering in late July or August.

Climbing roses have greater variety, with some starting to flower in May and some continuing to do so almost until Christmas. Many will produce a batch of blooms two or even three times throughout summer and autumn. These flowers tend to be noticeably larger than their rambler cousins. All climbers share the same characteristic of producing their flowers on new growth, i.e., made in the spring and summer of flowering.

This means that climbing roses can be pruned any time between the end of flowering and the start of new growth in spring, which normally means between October and the end of March.

METHOD

1. Although climbing roses can be pruned at any time between autumn and spring, they will be much less likely to be damaged by winter storms if pruned and tied in securely before the worst of the winter weather.

2. The goal is to establish a semi-permanent framework of around half a dozen strong shoots that fan out from the base. It is the shoots that grow from this framework in spring (the side shoots) that will carry next year's display.

3. Start by reducing all the long side shoots that have carried this year's flowers back down to a couple of leaves or 2 to 3in/5 to 7cm. Be ruthless about this, as the harder you cut, the greater the regrowth and therefore the more flowers that will be produced next year.

4. Then take stock of what remains. There should be a number of long old and younger shoots.

5. Tie them in and remove all excess, crossing or damaged shoots. If you have a very old stem, it can be cut right to the ground and a new shoot trained in to replace it. It is a good idea to do this to 1 or 2 shoots every year so the rose is constantly but gradually renewed.

6. When you have finished, it should be largely two-dimensional, uncluttered and securely fixed to the supports, ready both for the worst of winter and the best of the next flowering season.

YOU WILL NEED

Secateurs

Loppers

Ladder

Strong (but soft) twine

Gloves

FLOWERING TREES

The whole point of a flowering tree is the scale of it. There is always a sense of wonder that a tree can flower with the ease of a bulb or a bedding plant.

In spring we are spoiled for choice with flowering trees – all the ornamental cherries, plums, apples and pears are one of the main joys of the season. Blossom is a no-brainer for any garden and any garden can feature blossom because so many fruit trees can be trained and pruned to fit anywhere. As well as fruit trees there are hawthorns, paulonia, Judas trees, laburnums, acacias and magnolias amongst others. Depending on your soil and the size of your garden there will be a tree for you that will flower magnificently in spring.

But as we come into summer there are still a few more that put on a dramatic display and which are worth adding to any garden. The biggest and grandest of these is the tulip tree, a large tree from the magnolia family. In its native American homeland it can reach 197 feet/60 metres, smothered in upright yellow flowers that bees adore. It does need space to expand into, so is only for those fortunate enough to have room to relish its full form.

Another American flowering magnolia is the bull bay. In the UK we tend to grow this as a climber on a south-facing wall, but if the climate continues to change I predict we will see more and more of these magnificent evergreen trees growing freely and blessed with enormous, water-lily-like flowers that fill the air with incredible fragrance. Italian gardens are full of them.

For a tree that the average garden can more easily accommodate I would go straight to the dogwoods. There are two branches of the dogwood family, one from America, Cornus florida, and the other from Korea and Japan, Cornus kousa.

The American dogwoods are more or less tender and only thrive in the most sheltered parts of the south. A rich, slightly acidic loam soil suits them best.

The Korean dogwoods are more accommodating and hardy enough to grow anywhere. They tend to flower a little later than their American counterparts. Cornus kousa chinensis is reliably free-flowering and 'China Girl' flowers even more exuberantly. They start out creamy white and gradually fade to pink as they age. I have two growing in my garden and they make a superb display every June and July whilst remaining a modest size.

All flowering trees will perform best with at least half a day's full sun, so should not be tucked away in a shady corner. Early-flowering trees such as camellias or magnolia stellata should be planted out of the early morning sun, which can burn frosted buds.

BERRIES, BARK & FOLIAGE

FOLIAGE

All plants are more leaf than flower or stem, and much of a garden – trees, hedges, grass and about 80 per cent of any plant at any time in a border – is leaves. So it is worth taking trouble to select and nurture foliage as carefully as you will any flowers. Deciduous plants lose all their leaves in autumn (the American word 'fall' is so much more apt) and grow new ones in spring. This is a survival mechanism, enabling them to be better able to survive cold and dry weather, and for the gardener, gives scope for huge changes in colour and size as well as the sheer thrill of new growth returning in spring. But it does mean that for three to four months in winter there is a starkness that can be harsh and, on a grey day, grim.

Evergreen plants either keep their leaves or shed them gradually over a long period. When the whole of the plant kingdom seems to be dying and shrivelling up, they remain clear and strong and a potent symbol of life. The garden needs that life force during these increasingly bleak winter months.

Most evergreens – all the cypresses, larches, cedars, thujas, etc. – have been introduced in the last couple of hundred years and there are only five evergreen trees native to the UK – yew, box, holly, juniper and Scots pine. Their scarcity is why they were so revered and such a powerful symbol when almost all other trees, shrubs and hedges were stripped down to their woody skeletons.

Evergreen plants provide superb year-round structure to a garden. This can be formal with clipped hedges of box, yew, holly, or half a dozen other evergreen shrubs that make good formal hedges. They can be repeated tightly clipped shapes of cones, balls, or informal with trees and shrubs such as mahonia, sweet box, holly, pines, hebe, Mexican orange blossom, Portuguese laurels, viburnum, camellias, phillyrea, skimmia, spindle, and the magnificent holm oak to name but a few.

But in the end, the excitement of new leaves appearing in March and April, the intensity of their green and the lushness of full summer blowsiness, not to mention the shifting radiance of autumnal colour, is a thrill that never wanes. The trick is to plan and harness this, to add it knowingly to your garden as part of its display rather than being an adjunct. So for example, I have hawthorn hedges on the outer sections of my garden because I love the intensity of their new growth, but they are a bit prickly and need cutting too often to provide the main structure. Hornbeam, on the other hand, makes fantastic structural hedges and keeps some of its leaves, having turned tawny brown, all winter. There is then a second leaf-fall in April as they make way for the new ones pushing through.

It does not matter what you plant, but consider the impact of foliage as the most influential factor on how your garden will look in all seasons, and choose carefully.

PURPLE LEAVES

Whilst purple beeches and the ubiquitous dark foliage of a purple leafed cherry plum are landscape or street trees and often very big, the purple foliage from shrubs or heavily pruned trees can add drama and contrast to a border and make an excellent foil for perennial and annual flowers with rich colours, even in tiny gardens. The purple or copper colour is a result of a layer of red pigment over the green of the chlorophyll. In my experience this means that they photosynthesise less efficiently than green-leaved plants and grow slower than their all-green counterparts. In consequence they should never be planted in deep shade but in as sunny a spot as possible, as the plant will lose purple pigment as it struggles to collect enough light, thus revealing more green beneath. 'Forest Pansy' with its purple leaves and pink flowers will cope pretty well with light shade, and the various purple forms of Acer palmatum need some shade and protection from wind – but it is a fine balance. Too much shade and they do not thrive.

The purple Japanese barberry is an excellent border plant in summer because of the depth and contrast that its purple leaves give to surrounding colours, and in autumn it is decorated with red berries, which are rather more striking than the small yellow flowers that made them in spring. It is a really good example of choosing a plant that will work hard for you in every season.

The smoke bush, 'Royal Purple', is a good border shrub with rounded wine-dark leaves. I find the leaves of 'Foliis Purpureis' too matte and brown for my taste, but 'Velvet Cloak' good. A purple-leafed crab apple such as Malus x purpurea has purple leaves and slightly grey plum-coloured fruits preceded by deep red flowers.

Purple works well in large pots too. I have used the long strappy purple and powdery grey flax, Phormium 'Black Adder', to create a melodramatic counterfoil to bright orange and red dahlias, with various dahlias such as 'Bishop of Llandaff' and 'Bishop of Oxford' – the former with red flowers and the latter with orange – having purple foliage of their own.

I really like the purple hazel, 'Purpurea', whose new leaves are a lovely rich burgundy with pink undersides, gradually become greener on the upper surface as summer progresses with the lower sides turning chocolate. The nuts have a lovely pale pinky/purple sheath and dark nuts. To get the biggest and darkest leaves it should be coppiced – i.e., all top growth pruned hard to the ground – every five or six years. Whilst hazel is best left for at least three years between each coppice, other shrubs and trees can be cut back annually, with early spring the best time to do it. The purple elder 'Guincho Purple' and the more finely cut leaves of 'Black Lace' are vigorous enough to take a really hard prune every year, outgrowing the competition for light around it.

COLOURED BARK

From December through to mid-March, when the first new leaves start to appear, all trees and shrubs are a tracery of bare branches and these can be very decorative in themselves. Add to that specific pruning and training, and winter bark can be truly beautiful and brighten the greyest day.

The dogwoods always look spectacularly good in the winter cold. The best known is the Cornus alba, which has brilliant stems in shades of crimson. There are a number of Cornus alba varieties, all with red shoots, except Cornus alba 'Kesselringii', which has melodramatic purple-black stems. Dogwood will grow almost anywhere but is happiest in damp soil in full sun.

If you have damp soil, willow will grow easier than any other tree or shrub. The golden willow has, as its name suggests, brilliant yellow stems, violet willow has wonderful purple stems coated in cottony bloom, and coral bark willow has stems that are bright vermilion. As with dogwood, the trick with willow is to coppice or pollard it right back at least every third year to encourage it to throw up strong, straight, bright shoots.

Lime trees have brilliant colours to their new bark, and when pleached with an annual hard prune of all the previous year's growth, these grow extra long and extra bright. The best are large leafed lime, which have gleaming crimson bark, almost orange at their tips and nearly purple at their base, and 'Winter orange', which has orangey red stems.

Birch trees have especially good winter bark with the silver birch shining out starkly both against the gloom and neighbouring colour. 'Grayswood ghost', a form of Himalayan birch, has particularly white bark, and gold birch has a golden tint. Many birches peel, revealing new bark beneath, and the newer that bark is, the brighter its colouring will be.

The paperbark maple has copper coloured bark that peels off in glorious tatters, and the Tibetan cherry also peels annually but its bark is a shiny, deep chestnut, almost purple colour that shines brighter when you polish it. The coral-bark maple has bark that is bright pinky, orangey red, which looks superb both when the leaves change colour in autumn and after they have fallen. Another maple, one of the snake-bark maples, Acer rufinerve, has vertical stripes. If you have acidic soil, the snow gum has bark that is a patchwork of green, copper and grey.

All these trees will develop better bark colours when grown in full sunshine.

PRUNING DOGWOOD

As the weather gets colder, the colour of the bark of plants like dogwood and willow intensifies so that when all the leaves have fallen – which does not really happen until the end of the year – they can then shine out.

The bark on the previous season's growth, sufficiently hardened to have a polished outer skin but pliable and young enough to shine brightly, is always the most decorative, and after a year or two it dulls and ages. This is why the most decorative barks are those that respond most vigorously to pruning, throwing up long stems in their first spring and summer, and why you must prune either some or all of the plant every year to stimulate this winter display.

METHOD

1. There are 2 approaches to this type of pruning.

2. The first is to cut back all the oldest wood, aiming to remove one third of the shrub each year and thus completely renewing it every 3 years. The advantage of this is that you retain the structure, shape and height as a constant. The disadvantage is that only one third is at its brightest and best at any one time.

3. The alternative method is to cut the whole plant right back to the ground every 3 years. This is obviously more drastic but does result in a better, more vivid display. I suppose a third alternative, if you have 3 or a multiple of 3 plants, is to cut one third of them completely back each year.

4. However you do it, the technique is the same. Cut right down at the base of each stem, leaving just a nub no more than a 1 to 2in/3 to 5cm long. When you have finished, mulch each shrub well with compost or bark to help it grow away strongly, which it will invariably do.

5. Although willows and dogwoods look best in groups, there is hardly any need to buy them in bulk because they all take very easily as hardwood cuttings. Using the stems that you have pruned back, cut them to lengths of new stem 6 to 18in/15 to 45cm long, push them firmly into the soil where you want them to grow and there is every chance that they will root and grow away vigorously. It really is as easy as that!

YOU WILL NEED

Secateurs

Pruning saw

Mulch

BERRIES

We tend to take berries for granted, as though they are an afterthought or a by-product from summer flowers, but some are the best thing about the plant and are worth waiting for all year for their particular display.

There are a number of flowering shrubs that have exceptional fruit (for that is all any berry is, edible or otherwise) and to get fruit you must leave the flower to fade into shaggy maturity. Deadheading roses encourages more flowers but fewer subsequent hips (just a berry by another name).

The fruit need summer sun to ripen, so shrubs that flower in May and June tend to make for better berries than the later-flowering plants. Also, shrubs that produce a mass of flowers are always going to be a better bet for berries than those with a few choice 'blooms'. The more heat and sun that a plant gets, the better the berries will be – which is why ones trained against a brick wall usually display better, as a result of the reflected warmth.

Not all roses produce hips but most do and some almost more spectacularly than they flower. In the main, the species roses are more prolific and interesting hip-bearers than hybrid roses. The range of species hips is huge, from the great tomato-like berries on the rugosas to black gobstoppers on 'Scharlachglut' and oval aniseed balls on the dog roses. Best of all is Rosa moyesii 'Geranium' which has orange flagons, long and waisted like gourds.

Hawthorn, also a member of the Rosacea family, is smothered in haws each autumn although 'Paul's Scarlet', the most commonly grown garden hybrid, hardly ever makes fruit. The birds love the haws and once we get the first batch of really chill weather the trees will be stripped in a matter of days.

Birds tend to go for red berries first and leave the dark blue and black ones alone. Viburnum tinus has midnight-blue berries against its evergreen leaves, making an intensely rich, if sombre, combination. Creeping oregon grape, sweet olive and daphne pontica all have blue-black berries.

Pyracantha is closely related to the hawthorns, and I love the firethorn's spectacular autumn display of brilliant oranges, reds and yellows, especially when grown against a gloomy north-facing wall.

Cotoneaster is slightly more subtle and a little less dramatic, but like pyracantha, it will grow in dry shade, trains well against a wall or fence and has lovely berries, and there are hundreds of different species to choose from.

The most optimistic stand against winter gloom comes from the common holly with its perfect combination of bright green and crimson. When people complain that their holly is failing to produce berries it is usually for faults of gender rather than performance because for holly to have berries it must be female, with a male reasonably near to hand to pollinate with. Many of the variegated cultivars are male and will never bear berries. The names hardly help: 'Golden Queen' is a male, as is 'Silver Queen', but 'Golden King' is female. All very confusing.

GRASSES

However you use them, grasses add a tone and texture that is silkily beautiful. Whether used as the dominant planting as sweeping drifts and groups or in smaller clumps and specimens to support more conventionally floral beds, they are an invaluable weapon in the gardener's planting armoury.

Some grasses, such as miscanthus, moor grass, pampas grass and fountain grass, are slow to become established and grow in spring but are glorious later in the year. These need accompanying planting to cover the gap between the removal of their old foliage and any reasonable display of their own, which can be as late as mid-June for some of the bigger miscanthus. I can recommend cardoons, knautia macedonica, coreopsis, thalictrum, verbena bonariensis, fennel, heleniums, rudbeckias, cirsiums, purple angelica, helianthus salicifolius, inula and plume poppies – all of which I plant in amongst my grasses and all of which complement and are complemented by the association.

Grasses that grow sooner and faster in spring and which produce their flowering display in mid-summer include stipas, deschampsia, carex and calamagrostis. By mixing the two groups in the same borders you can have a display that starts in mid-summer and lasts until the new year.

The best grass flowers arrive in September, ranging from the plum tones of Miscanthus sinensis 'Malepartus' that then turn burnished gold to the wonderfully zigzagged silver plumes of M. sinensis 'Silberfeder'. Fountain grass has glorious bottle-brush plumes as wispy and delicate as thistledown, and tufted hair grass has perhaps my favourite flower heads of all grasses, held on tall straight stems high above the foliage. Moor grass, which also has lovely airy flower heads, is one of the few native UK grasses that crosses the line well from its natural damp, acidic habitat to ordinary garden soil, as long as it does not dry out too much. M. caerulea 'Windspiel' has flower stems 6 feet/1.8 metres tall that move gently in the wind, catching the autumnal sun.

Not the least of grasses' charms is how easy they are to grow and how little attention they need from the gardener.

We mulch every other year with pine bark, directly after cutting back and weeding. Pine bark is slightly acidic, which most grasses prefer, but – unlike garden or council compost – does not increase the fertility, as this would result in growth that is too soft and sappy. The alternate non-mulched years give self-sown plants such as teasels, fennel, thalictrums and pheasant's tail grass the chance to establish.

By mid-June the new green growth of the grasses is appearing vigorously in soft green waves. By July these have become strong strands exploding skywards and any accompanying planting has to be very bold to hold its own. October brings an amazing richness of colour, from the deep plum of the flower heads of Miscanthus 'Malepartus' to the gold of the fading foliage of all the grasses. At this point the grasses are, to my mind, the best and richest players in the garden. They handle winter well, withstanding almost all weather save for very heavy snow and emerging upright and intact albeit increasingly threadbare until it is time to pull and cut all the old stems and foliage and let the cycle begin again.

PLANTING & DIVIDING GRASSES

Whilst I am in favour of confidence and simplicity in planting – make a hole, stick your plant in it, preferably the right way up, and the chances are high that it will grow – some details really can make a difference. With grasses, timing is very important.

No ornamental grass likes being disturbed when it is dormant and will often respond to being lifted and then replanted into cold soil by the roots rotting and the plant ailing or even dying.

The secret is to plant or divide them when they are actively growing – preferably at the beginning of that process. For most of us that means mid to late spring, although in a cold year you may have to wait until early June before you see signs of strong growth. They then adapt very quickly and grow untroubled and thereafter tend to be the least troublesome of plants.

By and large all grasses do best in full sun but miscanthus and deschampsia are the most adaptable at coping with shade. As long as they get at least four hours of good sun a day, most grasses will adapt to most situations and most soil.

METHOD

1. Dig and weed the ground before planting, removing any trace of perennial weeds as otherwise they can become entwined in the grass roots and be impossible to remove.

2. Make a hole so that the grass sits at the same level in the soil as it is in the pot. Backfill around the plant, treading it in firmly but being careful not to plant it into a shallow saucer, especially if your soil is heavy. If you do have clay soil, all stipas – which only thrive when they have very good drainage – should have plenty of grit added to the planting hole. Do not do this by putting in a layer of grit, which can become a sump and have the opposite of the desired effect, but mix it in well with the soil in the base of the hole.

3. If you are dividing a grass, wait until there is new growth and then dig up the whole plant with as much of the roots as possible. Chop or pull it apart so that each section is 8 to 10in/20 to 25cm in diameter (i.e., not too small), replant one in the original position and then distribute the others either singly or, if you need bigger clumps, as an odd-numbered group spaced about 8in/20cm apart so that they will grow together as one larger clump.

4. Give them a good soak and then mulch thickly to suppress weeds. During the first year give new plants a weekly soak in very hot, dry weather. Thereafter they will fend perfectly well for themselves.

YOU WILL NEED

A spade

Old bread knife or saw

Grit (if working in clay soil)

Water

Mulch

CUTTING BACK GRASSES

Although border grasses can and usually do look really good well into the new year, by the end of February most are looking tired and battered by winter weather. It is time to cut them back, tidy up any remaining permanent growth and start again.

The timing is pertinent because this is a job to do either before there are any signs of new green growth or very soon after it appears. Otherwise you find yourself cutting the new growth back too and risk spoiling the appearance of that new growth.

METHOD

1. Using secateurs (or even loppers) for thicker grasses like miscanthus or shears for softer ones like deschampsia, cut back to the ground all the existing growth of deciduous grasses. These are the ones that have made all their growth since the previous spring. (If you are not sure whether a grass in your garden is deciduous or evergreen, wait until you can see new shoots emerging at the base of the plant. As soon as they are there then last year's dried stems should be removed. If these have not appeared by mid March in the south or mid April in the north then it is almost certainly evergreen and should not be cut back.)

2. Although deciduous grasses should all be cut back hard before the new green shoots appear, evergreen species like the stipa and pampas grass families should not be cut but merely combed through with a rake or your hands (I advise wearing stout gloves as grasses can be very sharp), pulling out all dead growth as you go. You will find that very cold or very wet weather and, in the case of pheasant tail grass, time, will kill off too much of the growth to make it worth preserving, so these should then be pulled up and replaced in May.

3. When you have finished clearing and cutting back, leave the cut material on the ground to act as a mulch, either as it falls or chopped up with shears. We do this every other year and then mulch with pine bark on the alternate years. This works well because it is slightly acidic and has low-fertility, both qualities that grasses prefer.

4. Alternatively, you can gather up the cut material and, after chopping it with shears, add it to the compost heap. If you have any amount of this then I suggest doing so incrementally, mixing it with grass clippings or other 'green' waste as you do so.

5. Although now is a good time to cut back, do not divide or move any grasses yet as there is a risk that the replanted sections will rot and die in cold soil. Wait until the plants are regrowing strongly, which can be as late as May or even early June.

YOU WILL NEED

Secateurs

Loppers

Rake

Shears

Mulch

Water

BAMBOOS

Bamboos get a bad press, being characterised as uncontrollably invasive, but they are stately plants, make an excellent windbreak, look good in winter and need very little attention. Bamboos are grasses, albeit ones with exceptionally rigid stems, or culms – which is the botanical word for a bamboo cane.

There are two kinds of bamboo: clumping and running. The latter should be avoided as its rhizomes do spread very widely, especially when warm and damp. But clumping types are largely controllable and are better able to survive drought. Fargesia, thamnocalamus and borinda species are the non-invasive clumping species for most gardens, and phyllostachys, which has some of the best-coloured canes, can spread in very warm, damp conditions but is not a problem in my coolish garden on the Welsh border. If in doubt, sinking a strip of metal sheeting such as corrugated iron at least 24in/60cm below ground level around the roots as a kind of open-bottomed underground pot will form a barrier that the shallow rhizomes will not penetrate, containing their expansion.

All bamboos, even the most vigorous such as phyllostachys, sasa and fargesia, can be grown in a container, which contains any spread. As a general rule, bamboos like damp – but not wet – soil and a sunny site that is sheltered from strong winds. Arrow bamboo, however, copes happily with wind and also makes the best garden canes although any bamboo will make a cane of sorts. They are best cut in late summer when two to three years old and left flat on a rack to dry over winter.

METHOD

1. Bamboos will grow in containers but they are much happier in the ground than a pot. The best time to plant them is as soon as you can prepare the ground in early spring. Always plant a little deeper than they are in the pot you bought the plant in.

2. Give them a thorough soaking and mulch thickly with compost or bark.

3. Even older bamboos are very responsive to a mulch of manure or garden compost and are best watered regularly until they reach the size you want.

4. If growing in a pot allow plenty of room for the roots –10.5 to 13 gallons/ 40 to 50 litres per plant – and be sure to keep them regularly watered throughout the year, although there should be sufficient drainage so that they do not sit in cold, wet soil.

5. Prune by cutting out old culms at the base but do this sparingly, as the starch stored in mature culms feeds the vigorous new growth in spring. Cut too much away and the new culms will be shorter and thinner as a result. As a rule, never remove more than a third of the plant in any one year. The best time to prune is in late summer.

6. Most bamboos can be moved fairly easily. The best time to do this is when the soil is moist and warm, so late spring and early autumn are both ideal.

7. After moving, cut back all but the strongest growth to the ground, water very well and mulch thickly with good garden compost or manure.

8. Most bamboos hate seaweed so do not use this as a fertiliser in any form.

YOU WILL NEED

Spade

Secateurs

Sharp saw

Loppers

Water

Mulch

FERNS

A shady urban back garden is in many ways perfect as a fernery, and the cool, feathery greenness of ferns is a counterbalance against the harshness of modern city life. If your garden is shaded by neighbours' trees or large buildings or is just too small to get sun for much of the day, it could well be that ferns will love growing there and you might well grow to love ferns.

There are ferns for almost every situation, and any shady part of the garden, either dry or damp, acidic or alkaline, will be a good home for some lovely ferns.

The buckler fern, like the male fern (Dryopteris filix-mas), is as good a ferny place to start as any. It will grow almost anywhere, wet or dry, but is perhaps wasted in anything less than rather dry shade, as it is one of the most resplendent of all plants for these tricky conditions, never looking less than regal, sending up croziers nearly 3 feet/1 metre tall. I have an especially tall variety, 'Barnesii', which is superb in a large pot or in a border. Its golden-green relative, the golden shield fern, is slightly more fancy, but certainly no less tough.

The lady ferns, such as the native UK Athyrium filix-femina, originate from damp woodland, and for its very feathery fronds to develop to their best it needs some moisture in the soil. This is even more true for the shuttlecock fern which, given damp soil, is easy to grow and truly dramatic, dying down to a brown knobbly stump in winter like a mini-tree fern, from which sprout fresh 3 feet/1 metre fronds in spring, looking, as its vernacular name implies, like a giant shuttlecock. The royal fern needs damp soil and will grow in a bog but I have also found it will be happy in a border of heavy clay soil.

The soft shield fern will grow untended but happily in the corner of a dry, dark yard, coming back year after year. The hard shield fern is a beautifully strong, pure form, reduced down to an almost elemental ferniness. It gets its 'shield' name from the shape of the spores under the leaves.

The spleenworts, with their seaweed-like flat fronds, come in many different sizes, from the tiny maidenhair spleenwort to the dramatic wavy hart's tongue fern, are superb plants for damp shade and are happy in very alkaline soil. I have them growing in the cracks of the lime mortar of a north-facing stone wall.

Whatever ferns you grow and wherever you grow them, do not mollycoddle them. Most ferns do not need any kind of fertiliser other than a mulch of leaf mould or, if grown in a container, a weak liquid seaweed solution every couple of weeks. Overfeeding will result in lush frond growth but weak roots and consequentially they will suffer badly in windy or dry conditions.

PLANTING & TENDING FERNS

Although much of the attraction and virtue of any fern is its hardiness and willingness to thrive where other plants dare not tread, it is a mistake to treat ferns badly, especially early on in their lives. Once established they can be left entirely to their own devices almost all year, but to get the best from them, it is worth doing best by them.

Most are woodland plants, and dappled shade will help preserve the rich green of the fronds. Ferns growing in full sun can often turn a rather sickly yellow. Use their ability to cope with deep shade and make a feature of their lushness in a dark corner.

Most will grow in all but the most extreme alkaline conditions. In practice, ferns like dryopteris, athyrium and osmunda will do best when the soil is naturally acidic, and others like polystichums and hart's tongues do better in alkaline soils, but most ferns will grow in any kind of soil, but they do like drainage. A shady bank of some kind is ideal for this.

METHOD

1. Dig a hole so the soil at the bottom and edges is well worked and loose. Plant the fern in a slight depression so that the soil does not get washed away from its roots.

2. Water it in well. It is a common misconception that plants that cope with very dry, shady spots do not need water. But 'cope' is the operative word so water them as you would any other plant, especially while they are getting established.

3. All ferns will also grow well in a pot as long as they have good drainage, so put in crocks or pebbles to keep the drainage holes unblocked by the compost and a loose root run. In practice this means lightening potting compost with either grit or perlite and – ideally – lots of leaf mould, although the latter has to be home-made as you cannot buy it. It has, however, the perfect light, loose consistency plus low fertility which ferns like.

4. New fronds will appear in spring but before they do, the old, bedraggled ones should be cut back when they turn brown. Cut right back to the base of each frond, leaving a firm 'fist' from which the new growth will soon appear.

YOU WILL NEED

Ferns

Spade

Garden fork

Water

Pot

Crocks

Bark-based compost

Grit or perlite

Leaf mould if you have it

Secateurs

TREE FERNS

Tree ferns tend to be treated in the northern hemisphere as exotic architectural plants, but in their native Australian, Tasmanian or New Zealand temperate rainforest, the tree ferns grow tall and their canopy of fronds creates a soft spangled light falling gently onto the forest floor. It is as far removed from any kind of architectural, trophy planting as might be imagined. By far the most reliably hardy tree fern is Dicksonia antarctica – although even this needs protection from frost. It has exceptionally long leaf blades if kept sufficiently moist and a thick cinnamon-coloured trunk.

They do grow very slowly indeed – no more than an inch a year – so buy the largest that you can afford and accept that how it looks immediately after planting is, to all intents and purposes, how it will look in ten years' time. They fare best in dappled shade and prefer to be constantly humid. In very hot, dry weather the fronds, crown and trunk should be sprayed with water at least once a day. If the fronds seem to be short it is almost invariably due to lack of water.

METHOD

1. When you buy a tree fern it usually arrives as a seemingly bare log, which is the 'trunk'. At one end there will be a few short roots and at the other the furled fronds looking like green knuckles.

2. The roots that grow from the base are very small indeed and certainly will not be large enough to anchor it into the ground when you plant it.

3. So dig a hole about 6 to 8in/15 to 20cm deep (more if it is over 4.5ft/1.5m tall, but taller tree ferns are very expensive) and bury the end of the trunk with the roots in the ground and tread it in very firmly.

4. Water it in well. In principle there should be no need to water the soil around the plant again, assuming there is reasonable rainfall. Much more important is keeping the air around the plant as humid as possible.

5. The 'trunk' is a bundle of vertical rhizomes surrounded by a bristly padding of roots, exposed to the air. Pour a can of water into the top of the trunk at the point where the fronds grow out and this will soak down like a sponge.

6. Dicksonia antarctica is hardy down to about 23°F/-5°C but killed by severe frost, especially if the water that inevitably collects in the cone at the top of the trunk where the fronds emerge freezes. The best way to protect it is to stuff this cone with straw or shredded cardboard packaging and to fold the existing fronds back over it, tying like a bonnet. Then wrap horticultural fleece around the base of the fronds and the top of the trunk like a bandage.

7. Wait until the risk of frost has passed before unwrapping in spring, removing the material in the cone and cutting back any surviving fronds. New ones will very quickly emerge to replace them.

YOU WILL NEED

Tree fern

Spade

Hosepipe with spray attachment

Straw or shredded cardboard wrapping

Horticultural fleece

String

Water

GROWING
FOOD

VEGETABLES

Anyone with any growing space, from a window box to an allotment, can grow some vegetables.

The kitchen should dictate what is in the garden rather than the garden deciding what is on your plate, so always grow what you love to eat, even if it is for a single special treat. I have always grown new potatoes to celebrate my birthday at the beginning of July – and no other spuds throughout the year ever taste half so good.

We have become addicted to instant gratification whether in purchasing ingredients or ready meals, but vegetables grow to nature's rhythm. The quickest items – whether radishes or rocket leaves – still take at least four weeks to produce anything edible, and most crops three to four months. But there is a deep satisfaction from working with this natural timescale.

Vegetables all need as much sun as possible. Some vegetables, like lettuce, runner beans and root vegetables, will cope with some shade, especially in the full glare of a hot summer, but an open, sunny site is always ideal.

You must also have a water supply. When I plant out young plants that I have raised from seed I always soak them really well, and many crops will need very little water thereafter. But some, like lettuce, spinach, rocket, leeks or Florence fennel, are quick to bolt – i.e., run to seed – if they are stressed by water shortage so it is important to give them a steady water supply. As with all watering, a good soak once a week rather than a daily splash will encourage deep roots, which will in turn mean that they will be able to access more water. It is a virtuous circle.

Succession is the key for a steady supply of fresh vegetables. This means sowing small batches of your favourite vegetables in two or three goes across the growing season so that, rather than having one big harvest or a glut as one batch is coming to the end, another is just ready to be harvested with perhaps a third being sown or grown on.

Some crops, like most most brassicas, chicory or garlic, tie up space for most of the growing year so for the most economical use of available space, you can interplant these with a catch-crop like radish or rocket that can be eaten before they start to compete with the slow-grower.

Plenty of vegetables grow well in containers, but cut-and-come-again crops like saladesi and saladini, or mixes of crops, like rocket, oak-leaf lettuces and spinach, are ideal as they can all be harvested by the leaf and will all regrow to provide second or even third cuttings.

POTATOES
IN A CONTAINER

PLANT: LATE WINTER TO EARLY SUMMER
HARVEST: MID-SUMMER TO AUTUMN

Home-grown potatoes are easy and satisfying to grow and taste so much better than most bought ones. Also the gardener can choose from scores of varieties to fit their personal preference, the way in which they are cooked and the conditions in which they are grown.

Instead of a potato being an anonymous, generic vegetable, it can have as much character and variance as apples, tomatoes or different kinds of lettuce. New potatoes, know as 'first earlies' in horticultural terms, are the sweetest and easiest to grow if you are short of space and are ready after about three months, whereas maincrop varieties will take a month or more longer.

You can have a viable harvest from a few seed potatoes grown in a container even if you only have a small back yard. This is brilliant for children or for a special celebratory meal for anyone of any age.

METHOD

1. Choose the biggest container you can. I like plant bags which are strong, have handles and drainage holes, and can be folded away when not in use, but anything that will give drainage and hold enough growing medium will do the job.

2. Even the biggest container will not take many seed potatoes, and the less crowded they are, the bigger the resulting tubers will be.

3. If you can add some soil improver or garden compost to the potting compost then that will definitely help, not least in retaining moisture.

4. Put a generous layer of the compost mix – 10 to 20in/25 to 50cm according to the size of container – in the base and place the seed potatoes on that, leaving at least 8in/20cm between them.

5. Cover them over with another 10in/25cm of compost, so the container is no more than two thirds full. This leaves room for earthing up.

6. Place in a sunny spot and water well.

7. When the foliage appears above the compost and reaches the top of the container, add enough compost to all but bury it – leaving just 1in/ 2 to 3cm at the top for water. This protects the foliage and the tubers from both late frost and light. It is important that the growing tubers are never exposed to light, otherwise they turn green and are inedible.

8. Water at least weekly – more in hot weather – and especially so, once the flowers appear. A weekly liquid seaweed feed once it starts flowering will help the crop.

9. The potatoes will be ready to harvest 80 days after planting – but will not suffer from being left in the pot.

YOU WILL NEED

A large container, bag, bin – anything that will drain and hold plenty of compost

Peat-free potting compost

Soil improver or garden compost if you have it

2 or 3 first early seed potatoes

Water

Liquid seaweed feed

LETTUCE

Fresh lettuce, picked, washed, dried and eaten within the hour, accompanied only by good olive oil and either balsamic vinegar or lemon juice, salt and pepper, is a dish worthy of anyone. I never tire of it.

There are four kinds of lettuce: cos (or romaine), looseleaf (including oak leaf), butterhead and crisphead (or iceberg).

Cos is my personal favourite. The leaves grow upright and tight and the combination of crispness and rich flavour makes it a must for any garden anywhere. Good varieties include 'Little Gem' for spring, 'Lobjoits' and 'Paris Island' for summer and 'Winter Density' for autumn.

Looseleaf lettuce are all 'cut-and-come-again' varieties, so you can cut some leaves or even the whole head and it will regrow for another harvest or even two. I grow 'Oak leaf' and 'Red Oakleaf' as well as green and red 'Salad Bowl'.

Butterhead lettuces are, as the name suggests, soft and buttery. They include 'Tom Thumb' (hardy, very small and delicious), 'Marvel of Four Seasons' and 'All the Year Round'.

Crisphead or iceberg lettuce have got themselves a bad name because of their watery tastelessness in conjunction with fast food. But I grow 'Webb's Wonderful' and 'Saladin' and both are very good. The secret is to harvest them quite small – the size of a grapefruit – and to eat them within a day of cutting.

METHOD

1. You can always choose to sow lettuce directly outside. Rake the ground until you have a fine tilth, and draw straight drills about 18in/45cm apart (I use a scaffolding board both to stand on and as a straight-edge and divider for the rows).

2. Sprinkle the seeds thinly down the rows, gently cover them over with the rake, label and water them, and they will almost certainly germinate and grow. Thin them as they grow until the individual plants are at least 4in/10cm apart and ready for harvesting.

3. When lettuces are very young seedlings they can be completely devoured by slugs and snails. So I grow all my lettuce the following way:

4. I start by sowing the seed thinly in a seed tray filled with compost, cover the seeds lightly with more compost or vermiculite, water them, and put to germinate in the greenhouse (a cool windowsill or porch is just as good).

5. When the seedlings have true leaves and are large enough to handle (about 2 to 3 weeks) prick them out individually into plugs. Do this by holding the seedlings by a leaf and levering the roots out with a label, lolly stick or knife and transplanting them with as much root as possible.

YOU WILL NEED

Prepared patch of ground

Rake

Lettuce seed of choice

Labels

Water

Seed tray

Peat-free compost

Vermiculite

Plug tray

6. Put the trays of plugs into a cold frame or a protected spot outside where you can check daily for slugs. This ensures that each lettuce grows strongly from the very beginning.

7. When they are big enough to be lifted from the plugs with the roots holding the compost together, plant them out in a grid or rows with each plant spaced about 8in/20cm apart. This is close enough to produce lots of medium-sized lettuce and fill available space but much wider apart than you get when sowing direct. This means you have much less wastage of seed and also that each lettuce grows strongly – which deters slug attacks. The grid means that – like growing in rows – they are easy to hoe and keep weed free.

By using seed sparingly it makes successive small crops more viable and avoids a glut or bolting. The latter is very likely in hot, dry weather, as lettuces grow best in cool conditions, so keep them well watered.

ROCKET

If you taste fresh, home-grown rocket leaves in spring you will always be searching for that melting, peppery succulence that no other season can provide. It is my favourite of all vegetables.

Rocket hates hot, dry weather, which will very quickly make it run to seed, with the leaves becoming sparse and tough and the flower stem long and hairy. Although technically hardy, it is killed by temperatures below about 23°F/-5°C. But cool spring weather with the days getting longer is ideal – and it also grows well when planted in September for picking in autumn.

Most of the rocket that is sold in supermarkets or served in a restaurant is wild rocket, Diplotaxis tenuifolia, which is a perennial with its much tougher, more slender, more finely indented leaves. I do grow it – it is less likely to bolt under stress and stores better (which is why it is grown commercially) but it is not nearly as good as garden rocket, Eruca sativa, which is an annual, so that is the one to grow at home. Both are a brassica, related to cabbages, radishes and turnips.

I make my first sowing in February and then another when I plant that crop out so I can replace it in April. By mid-May it is getting too warm, so the final sowing of the year is in August for autumnal harvest.

METHOD

1. After radish – to which it is closely related – rocket is the easiest of all seeds to germinate. Chuck it out onto any soil or compost and it will grow, but it will still need fierce thinning. This will seem very generous with space but closer spacing does not result in any greater harvest of the leaves, and as the widely spaced plants have lots of nutrition and water they are much healthier and last longer.

2. However, slugs and snails will attack them when young (when mature the mustard taste puts them off) so I sow them under cover and then transplant them to their final position.

3. Rocket seeds are biggish and reasonably easy to handle so I now sprinkle 2 or 3 per plug, wait until at least 2 germinate successfully and then ruthlessly thin down to 1 healthy seedling. This is important as 1 large plant will produce many more good leaves and last longer than 2 small ones.

4. These can then be grown on until the roots fill the plugs (experiment by gently pulling them free – if they come out and hold together then they are ready for transplanting). If the soil falls away then wait for another week or so before planting out at 8in/20cm spacing. Water them well and keep them watered – drying out will cause them to bolt.

5. I start picking leaves as soon as they are large enough to handle, and expect to make 3 or 4 pickings from each plant over as many months.

YOU WILL NEED

Rocket seed

Prepared patch of ground

Plug tray

Peat-free potting compost

Water

Labels

RADISH

Radishes are probably the easiest of all vegetables to grow – great for kids and delicious for everybody. Fresh radish in early May eaten with salted butter and a glass of very dry white wine is an unexpected seasonal treat.

Radishes will run to seed in warm or very dry weather so sow as soon as the soil is warm enough in spring and make a repeat sowing every two or three weeks thereafter. Water regularly but keep in mind that too much moisture will only result in extra foliage and split roots.

Radishes are also a very useful indicator crop, i.e., something which grows quickly to remind you where you've sown other, slower to germinate, crops. I sow mine in with parsnips, on the ridge of potatoes and between slow-growing crops like cabbages. Radishes are a brassica and are prone to flea beetle attack, which leaves tiny holes in the leaves and weakens the plant, making it more likely to bolt. To minimise this, keep them very well watered, thin to a 1in/2 to 3cm spacing between each plant and eat them before they get too big.

METHOD

1. Sprinkle the seed thinly, in a shallow drill .39in/1cm deep, or scatter them thinly within a prescribed area. A good way to do this is to place 2 boards flat on the ground about 3ft/1m apart and scatter the seeds thinly between them. Remove the boards and there will be a clear line defining the edge of the radish patch, so you can weed freely without damaging the young emerging seedlings.

2. The seeds will germinate and start to produce seedlings within a week or so and be ready to start harvesting after about a month.

3. It is important to thin them so that they are at least an inch apart, to allow each root to become juicy and swollen before they get woody. The thinnings can be eaten – leaves, roots and all – when they are the size of peas, although the perfect size for a radish is the size of a marble.

4. As soon as they start to produce a flower stem they will become woody and not good to eat so should be consigned to the compost heap. However – just sow some more!

YOU WILL NEED

Radish seed

Prepared patch of ground

Rake

Water

Labels

RECOMMENDED RADISH VARIETIES:

'Cherry Belle'

'Saxa'

'Scarlet Globe'

'Flamboyant' (Long)

'French Breakfast'

BROAD BEANS

Broad beans are tough, reliable and can be truly delicious. They can also be tough to eat and floury, so are best picked and served young so that the beans themselves are somewhere between the size of a kidney bean and the seeds you sow. If they get any bigger they develop a leathery skin which destroys the freshness and subtlety that is the prime attraction.

In fact we always skin older beans, which is a fiddle but worth the trouble. Raw young broad beans are truly delicious and if you pick them small enough – no bigger than your finger – you can eat them pod and all. The trick is to keep picking them and to have a succession of sowings so you have enough but not a glut, although they freeze well so can be stored.

METHOD

1. Broad beans do not like hot, dry weather and are able to germinate in relatively cold conditions. This means they can be sown in autumn to give an early crop in May, as well as in late winter and again in spring, for successive harvests of small, succulent young beans through to August.

2. Whenever you sow, make double rows with about 10in/25cm between each seed and at least 3ft/1m between the double rows for access. Bury the seeds completely (I just push them in the soil with my fingers, but you can make a drill and then cover them over).

3. 'Aquadulce' are the best variety for an autumn sowing. In spring I grow 'Bunyards Exhibition', 'The Sutton' and 'Red Epicure', which has wonderful garnet-coloured beans and vermilion flowers.

4. They will need temporary support as they grow. The easiest way is to place canes 3ft/1m apart along the outside of each double row and add string support at 12in/30cm intervals as needed, to stop the plants toppling (some varieties grow much taller than others).

5. Black fly can be a problem in late spring, with the aphids clustered on the top of the plants in a black layer, sucking the juices from the tender growing tips. They look bad but do not damage or affect the existing flowers or pods – simply cut off the afflicted parts. The best way to avoid this is to pinch out the tops of the plant in mid-May so that only older and less succulent growth remains.

6. Once the pods start to blacken, pull the plants up and add to the compost heap. Beans have roots that go down 6ft/2m or more, most of which will remain in the soil after you pull them up and add to the organic content of the soil.

7. Dig the plot over and use it for a brassica crop (such as kale on page 190) that will benefit from the nitrogen that all legume crops extract from the air and 'fix' into the soil.

YOU WILL NEED

Broad bean seeds

Rake

Canes and string

Water

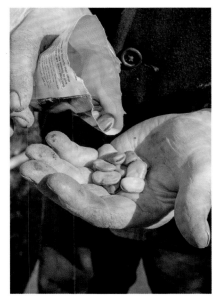

PEAS

Freezing has made peas an everyday vegetable, but fresh peas from the pod are still a treat that adults and children alike (and most dogs too) can enjoy.

Late spring and early summer is their season. They thrive when the days are long and cool but very quickly shrivel up and die when the temperature stays above about 77°F/25°C for long.

'Kelvedon Wonder' is good for small gardens as it is a dwarf variety with good flavour. However, height is the only space peas demand and I like 'Alderman', which grows over 6 feet tall and has really good flavour as does 'Hurst Greenshaft'. 'Carouby de Maussane' is a flat-podded mangetout variety that has a deliciously buttery texture and taste, and 'Nairobi' is a good sugar-snap variety.

Mangetout and sugar snap peas are eaten pods and all. The former never really develop proper peas and retain flat pods and the latter do so slowly, which means that if you do not pick them regularly you can harvest the maturing peas and eat them as a normal variety. There is a lot to be said for growing sugar snap peas if you have limited space and perhaps limited patience for shelling peas.

METHOD

1. Dig the soil over and if you have it add some garden compost, well-rotted manure or soil improver. Peas, like all legumes, respond well to a rich, freshly manured soil. Rake it to a fine tilth – if the soil sticks to the rake or your boots then leave it to dry out a little more.

2. There has been much debate about the most effective and productive formation or arrangement for pea seed, with advocates of single, double and triple rows, but I find twin rows spaced about 6 to 8in/15 to 20cm apart works best, with 2 to 3in/5 to 8cm between the seeds within each row and room to walk between the pairs of rows – so at least 3ft/1m. If you have a draw hoe with a wide blade, use this to draw a very shallow trench .39in/1cm deep, place a double row within it and then cover it over. Otherwise use a board and plant either side of it, standing or kneeling on the board as you go.

3. Water the sown rows.

4. Set up the support for the peas either immediately after planting or as soon as the seedlings appear. I use traditional pea sticks from hazel coppicing but any pruned material will do, as will chicken wire or nylon netting supported by canes. Whatever you use needs to be high enough to support the variety in question.

5. If it is very dry, water the seedlings weekly, but the critical time that they need plenty of water is when they flower and as the seed pods form, which will be about 12 weeks after sowing.

YOU WILL NEED

Fork

Peat-free compost, well-rotted manure or soil improver

Rake

Draw hoe

Water

Support – pea sticks or chicken wire or nylon netting with canes or stakes to hold it

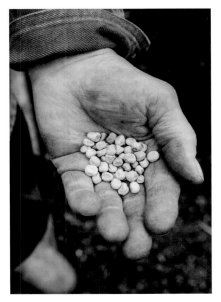

TOMATOES

A good tomato, perfectly ripe, bursting with juice within a thin skin, whether eaten raw and warm straight from the plant, sliced and served with oil, salt and pepper and good mozzarella or made into a sauce, is a luxurious treat – as well as being very good for you.

But you cannot buy a 'good' tomato. Supermarket tomatoes are invariably thick-skinned and more or less tasteless when compared to the intensity of a good home-grown one, so it is always worth the trouble to grow your own – and tomatoes will grow happily in a pot or a bag, with almost entirely vertical growth, so take up very little space.

METHOD

1. The seed can be sown as early as February if you have a greenhouse, or mid-March to mid-April if you are intending to grow the plants outside. I always sow 2 batches to cover possible bad weather in late spring or early summer and to spread the harvesting period.

2. Sow the seed thinly on the surface of the compost in a seed tray and then very lightly cover them either with a layer of more compost or of vermiculite. Water them well and put them in a warm spot to germinate. A windowsill above a radiator is ideal if you do not have a greenhouse.

3. When they develop their first pair of 'true' leaves – that is to say, leaves that are recognisably from a tomato rather than the ones that grow initially, before roots develop – you know that they have roots and should be pricked out into better compost and individual small pots or plugs.

4. Grow them on in a warm, bright place and when they are about 4 to 6in/10 to 15cm tall they should be potted on again into 3.5in/9cm pots. This may sound like a lot of work but it is important that the young growing plant is not checked and the roots have room to grow. The aim at this stage is to produce sturdy plants with a strong root system.

5. The young plants are ready to go out to their final growing position when around 9 to 12in/22 to 30cm tall, by which time they have often developed their first flowering truss. Plant them deeper than the soil level in the pots, burying the stem right to the first leaf. This will hold them steady and encourage new roots to grow from the buried stem. Single-stemmed tomatoes, known as 'cordons', are going to get tall and heavy so they need a good solid support structure or, indoors, strong twine tied to the stem just beneath the soil and fixed to a wire or the roof of the greenhouse and the growing plant gradually twisted round it. Water them in well.

6. Keep a steady supply of water – watering 2 times a week if they are in soil and every other day in pots, or even daily if it is very hot. Too much water results in split fruits that then go mouldy and irregular; erratic watering results in blossom end rot – with one end of the fruits turning black and collapsing inwards. Steady and regular is the secret.

YOU WILL NEED

Tomato seeds

Peat-free potting compost

Seed tray, plug tray, 3.5in/9cm pots, for raising seedlings

Vermiculite

2.6 to 5gal/10 to 30L pots, grow bags or garden soil for growing on

Canes or wires to support each plant

Water

Tomato feed or seaweed solution

7. If you are growing them in soil they will need no extra feed at all until they start to form flower trusses, and then a weak seaweed solution once a week is plenty.

8. If you are using a container of any kind, a general-purpose tomato feed once a week is good or, if you have the resources, home-made comfrey feed works wonders.

9. As the cordons grow, it is necessary to pinch out side shoots. These are the shoots that grow at 45 degrees between the main stem and the leaves. This diagonal growth is very vigorous and diverts energy away from the main cordon. The easiest way to do this when small is to snap them off with a twist of finger and thumb. Otherwise use a sharp knife or secateurs, being careful not to cut the main stem.

10. Outdoor tomatoes will not ripen after the beginning of October and indoor ones by the end of that month. The plants can go to the compost, and any green fruit makes excellent chutney or can be left to ripen in a dark drawer.

GARLIC

Given plenty of sun and reasonably good soil, garlic is reliably easy to grow, stores very well and is delicious both 'green' – the first month after harvest – and stored for use over winter. As well as tasting delicious, garlic may aid digestion, lower blood pressure and boost the immune system.

There are two types: hardneck and softneck. The garlic you buy is almost always softneck because it stores better. But hardneck varieties, which have a rigid stalk, crop earlier, do better in very cold conditions and have a stronger flavour.

Elephant garlic is huge, with cloves the size of an orange segment. However, for all its scale it has a distinctly delicate flavour compared to some of the more powerful garlic varieties.

METHOD

1. Prepare the ground so that it is loose enough to sink your hand into, with an addition of good garden compost if you have it. Finally rake it to a fine tilth (see glossary) ready for planting. Larger cloves make for larger bulbs, so break open the garlic bulbs and sort out the larger cloves for planting. Use the smaller ones in the kitchen.

2. Plant the cloves using a dibber or trowel – making sure you have the pointed end facing up – 2in/5cm deep in rows or a grid about 6in/15cm apart. Water them well.

3. Keep them weed free and make sure they are kept watered in spring if the weather is dry, as the foliage is growing.

4. Break off any (edible) 'scapes' or flower heads as and when they form, and as soon as the foliage starts to turn yellow stop all watering and let the leaves die back.

5. The bulbs should be ready for harvest between the middle of June and the middle of July. Do not pull them out of the ground but dig them up carefully with a fork, trying to keep as much of the roots attached as possible. Clean off the soil but do not remove leaves or roots, and dry them completely in a warm dry place but not in direct sun.

6. When they have completely dried out (usually about 2 weeks) you can trim the leaves and roots ready for storing. I keep ours in a basket in a cool shed and they last well into the following summer.

YOU WILL NEED

A sunny patch of ground or a container at least 10in/25cm deep and big enough for each clove to be 6in/15cm apart

Garden fork

Garden compost

Rake

Seed garlic – you can keep your own cloves as seed but garlic accumulates viruses so fresh seed is advisable at least every other year

A container to sort the individual cloves

Dibber or trowel

Water

COURGETTES

The cucurbit family includes pumpkins, squashes, cucumbers, gherkins, gourds and melons. All thrive in rich soil and warm weather with plenty of water. However, of all members of that family, courgettes are the hardiest and easiest to grow successfully.

Fresh courgettes are always a taste of my summer. I like them sliced and very lightly fried in oil, with a tomato sauce, roasted or made into a creamy sauce for pasta with plenty of parmesan and a dash of lemon, which is an amazingly fresh taste of pure sunshine.

There are many varieties to choose from – green, courgette shaped, yellow, round, scalloped – but whatever variety you grow, harvest them small. Not only will they taste better but this will also stimulate the plant to keep on producing more fruits.

You can also harvest the flowers, which are delicious dipped in a light batter and deep-fried, either just as they are or filled with a cream cheese held in place by twirling the end of the flower over.

METHOD

1. Sow seed in April, May and June but no later than mid-June to give them time to grow and ripen.

2. Put 2 seeds per 3in/7.5cm pot, pushing them into the compost on their edge. Water them well and put them somewhere warm to germinate.

3. Weed out the lesser of the two if both germinate. This might seem wasteful but no family needs more than half a dozen courgette plants to fulfil every possible variation of the most eager courgette consumption!

4. Grow them on, either in a greenhouse or on a windowsill, until the plants are a healthy 6in/15cm, before hardening them off for a week. Then plant outside after any risk of frost has gone.

5. Space the plants at least 3ft/1m apart. I dig a hole and add plenty of compost, back fill it and create a shallow saucer to plant them in which will funnel water to their roots.

6. They are very good grown in combination, either with a quickly harvested crop like lettuce that will have been eaten before the courgettes take up all available space, or with a plant that will rise above them like sweetcorn or climbing beans. Both combinations mean that an otherwise space-consuming vegetable will be worth its place in even a small vegetable plot.

7. They will grow in a container but these are hungry plants with a large root system, so need a large pot and will require watering almost daily once they flower and feeding weekly with liquid seaweed.

YOU WILL NEED

Courgette seed

3in/7.5cm pots

Spade

Peat-free potting compost

Garden compost, well-rotted manure or soil improver

Liquid seaweed (if planting in a pot)

Water

CUCUMBERS

Cucumbers are easy to grow if you can give them the conditions they need: heat, humidity and rich soil. If those three are available there is little stopping them. I find that this needs a greenhouse and daily watering, with lots of garden compost or soil conditioner added to potting compost if you are growing them in a container. If you are growing them outside, add lots of compost or manure to the soil before planting.

Cucumbers grown indoors are susceptible to red spider mite, cucumber mosaic virus and powdery mildew. Red spider mite tends to build up when it is very dry, and damping the floor down and watering regularly should eliminate this. Good ventilation is the best prevention for powdery mildew, and cucumber mosaic virus is carried by aphids and will manifest as yellow and stunted leaves.

METHOD

1. Cucumber seeds should be sown in April, using a peat-free potting compost and putting 2 seeds in a 3in/7cm pot. Experience shows that 3 or 4 plants is plenty for a family of 4 or 5.

2. Put the pots somewhere warm – at least 35°F/2°C – and keep them moist. The seeds should germinate in about a week, and when the 2 seedlings both have 'true' leaves, remove the weaker. If you do this carefully it can be transplanted to its own pot but only do this if 1 of the pots fails to produce either seedling. The second seed is there as insurance, not to double up.

3. Keep the seedlings warm and watered and if you have a greenhouse they can be planted into the soil or a large pot when they start to need support. This support will be very necessary throughout the growing season. I have used a wigwam of bamboo canes, bean sticks or, currently, strong twine fixed to a wire at the top of the greenhouse and dug into the soil beneath each plant. Whatever you use, it needs to be sturdy.

YOU WILL NEED

Cucumber seeds

Peat-free potting compost

3in/7cm pots, 1 for every 2 seeds

Soil improver or garden compost

Water

Canes, trellis or string for strong growing support

A warm and sheltered spot

Liquid seaweed

4. Water them daily and feed with liquid seaweed once a week. Traditionally cucumbers produced male and female flowers. If the male flowers pollinated the female ones, the resulting fruits were bitter, so the male ones had to be pinched off on a daily basis. Today most varieties have all-female flowers, but it is worth checking this when you buy seeds.

5. Once the fruit starts to set and grow, it is important to pick them often, which will stimulate more fruit. If it is happy each plant can produce a dozen or more cucumbers and can quickly become too much of a good thing, although we make tzatziki, cucumber soup and – most deliciously of all – fried cucumbers in a cream sauce.

6. They are annuals, and at some stage in September the plants will be exhausted and can be consigned to the compost heap.

FRENCH BEANS

French beans (which are not remotely French but come from Central and South America) cover both climbing and dwarf versions of themselves. Until the eighteenth century, all French beans were climbing until dwarf varieties were bred from them.

Whereas runner beans are hardier, have flat pods and are normally eaten before the beans mature, French beans can be either eaten when young and the pods tender or allowed to mature and the beans kept for drying.

All French beans are tender, so are very much a summer and early autumn harvest.

For climbing beans you need a structure to support them, but dwarf beans are self supporting and take up much less space and can be grown in a container.

They are available in green, purple (which turns green when cooked) and yellow varieties and are, whatever the colour, invariably very productive.

METHOD

1. I sow my first batch under cover in early May, followed by a second sowing directly into the soil at the same time that I plant the first batch out. This gives a succession of fresh green beans without a glut.

2. To grow your beans under cover, sow the beans either individually into plugs or 2 seeds into each 3in/7.5cm pot, removing the weaker of the two after they germinate. Water them and put them somewhere warm to germinate.

3. Grow them on after germination, putting them outside but protected from frost. They will be ready to plant out as soon as the roots hold together in the compost in the plug or pot – but there is no point in doing so until the nights are reliably warm.

4. Plant them out in a sunny spot with rich, well-drained soil. Add compost or well-rotted manure before planting if you have it – they are plants that respond well to plenty of food and water. Use rows or a grid, allowing 6 to 8in/15 to 20cm between each plant, and if in rows, twice that between the rows for access. If growing in a container, space the plants or seed no closer than 4in/10cm.

5. Water them in well and if there is no rain, water thoroughly weekly and, if in a container, even daily in hot weather.

6. Keep them weeded and start to pick the beans when they are firm enough to snap in your hand.

7. To sow your beans directly, prepare the ground as for beans grown under cover and sow the seed from mid-June onwards in rows or a grid 6in/15cm apart, pushing the seed into the soil. Water them well and they will germinate and appear after about 2 weeks, and the hanging bunches of pods should be ready to harvest after about 8 weeks.

YOU WILL NEED

Dwarf French
bean seed

A sunny, weed-free
site OR large container

Peat-free
potting compost or
well-rotted manure

3in/7cm pots, 1 for
every 2 seeds, or
plug trays

Water

SWEETCORN

Sweetcorn have become so widespread as to be unremarkable but they should be regarded as a buttery, indulgent seasonal treat. The clue to growing them yourself is in the name. They are one of the vegetables (along with new potatoes and asparagus) that very rapidly convert sugar to starch once picked. This means that to enjoy them at their sweetest and best you should eat them as soon as possible after harvest. In fact with sweetcorn, to really get the best of them, the advice is to wait until the water is boiling on the stove or the barbecue ready before going to pick them so the delay is measured in a matter of minutes.

They are not demanding to grow but do need sunshine to ripen and are unlikely to be ready before late summer.

METHOD

1. Sow the seeds in plugs or pots in mid-April. If you sow into pots put 2 seeds per pot. Water them and place somewhere warm to germinate. Remove the weaker of the two plants once they grow.

2. If starting in plugs, transplant the seedlings into an individual 3in/7.5cm pot once the seedlings can be removed from the plug without the soil falling off the roots (you have to carefully test one to see, and if it is not ready, leave it for another week).

3. When the nights have warmed up and the plants are about 10in/ 25cm tall and can be removed from their pot and the roots hold together (but are not rootbound), plant them out into a sunny, weed-free site in a grid formation – not rows – spaced 24in/60cm apart.

4. Sweetcorn is pollinated by wind and not insects. If you plant them in rows and the wind blows from one direction, only those plants downwind of another row will be pollinated. But in a grid they have maximum chance of being pollinated by wind from every direction.

5. Keep them well watered and once they reach 3ft/1m or so tall, support each plant with a cane to keep them upright.

6. The cobs are ready to pick when the tassels at the end of them turn dark brown – which will be 8 to 10 weeks after planting. You can test to see if they are ripe by carefully folding back the surrounding sheaths and squeezing the corn. If they secrete a milky juice then they can be picked.

7. The width of the spacing means that you can grow another crop between them. Traditionally squashes and climbing beans were grown beneath and up them as a mutually beneficial triumvirate. However, I suggest either courgettes or lettuce make an easier combination, with the courgettes having a chance to get established before the sweetcorn shades them too much, and the lettuce will have time to grow and be harvested in the same period.

YOU WILL NEED

Sweetcorn seeds

Peat-free potting compost

Plug trays

3in/7.5cm pots

Water

Area of ground in full sun

Bamboo canes for staking

RECOMMENDED VARIETIES:

'Moonshine'

'Swift'

'Sweet Nugget'

SQUASHES & PUMPKINS

Squashes and pumpkins are very similar, although pumpkins have more robust, solid stems whereas winter squashes, such as the hubbards, butternuts and acorn, have hollow, rather brittle stems. They are members of the cucurbit family along with courgettes (summer squashes), cucumbers, gourds and melons. All thrive when given the combination of heat, water and rich soil.

All are vigorous and some very vigorous indeed. Ideally they should be 10 feet apart in every direction, but few of us have that sort of space to spare. A good alternative is to grow them vertically, and I have often done this, using both stout wigwams with one per structure, as well as home-made trellises, again using really stout wood.

I think that the best eating comes from smaller squashes like hubbards and butternuts. 'Turk's Turban' are very good, as well as Japanese varieties like 'Uchiki Kuri' and 'Green Hokkaido'. But experiment and find your favourites.

METHOD

1. Sow the seeds in April, pushing 2 seeds on their edge into a 3in/7.5cm pot filled with potting compost. Put them somewhere warm – they need to be 69°F/20°C to germinate. If both seeds germinate, remove the weaker, and if neither germinate, use the reject from another pot to replace them.

2. Grow the individual seedlings on in a warm place until they are about 12in/30cm tall, then harden them off outside for a week. This will be about mid-June. Temperatures below 59°F/15°C halt growth and encourage slugs to attack the stems, which happens if they are planted out too early.

3. Plant each seedling in a shallow saucer of soil in ground that has been enriched by compost or manure. These are hungry plants! Give them a really good soak at least weekly.

4. Once there are 3 or 4 good-sized fruits on any plant it is advisable to remove all smaller ones. Far better to consolidate and grow a few really good ones than have lots of small, unripe fruit at the end of the growing season.

5. Around the middle of September I remove all the foliage so that the mature fruits can bask in as much sunshine as possible. This concentrates the sugars which improves taste and hardens the skins so they will store for longer.

6. Pumpkins and squashes should be harvested before any risk of frost and then 'cured' in a sunny place – a greenhouse or porch is ideal – for a week or so. This will finish the hardening process.

7. Despite some pumpkins becoming iconically large, they should all be handled with care to avoid bruising. Never lift them by the stem as, if damaged, this will encourage rot and reduce storage time.

8. They should be stored in a dark place, ideally at a temperature of 50°F/10°C, which is typically that of a garage or well-insulated shed.

YOU WILL NEED

Squash or pumpkin seeds

3in/7.5cm pots

Peat-free potting compost

Water

Plenty of room for the mature plants to grow

If growing vertically, strong support

CHARD

Chard is a very accommodating vegetable. It lasts a long time in the ground, will tolerate hot sun and drought and temperatures down to 14°F/-10°C, and will regrow two or even three times for re-harvesting. It also happens to be delicious and very good for you.

Once established it is very drought resistant but does best in a rich but well-drained soil. Swiss chard (which has no connection to Switzerland at all) has pure white stems and great green leaves and is, to my mind, superior to all other variations, but ruby chard is beautiful enough for any flower border. Rainbow chard is, as the name suggests, multi-coloured, and 'Bright Lights' has brilliant yellow stems.

Chard is related to spinach and beetroot and the leaves are like a slightly coarser spinach. When mixed with any combination of eggs, cream, cheese, anchovy, garlic, or pine nuts, it is exceptionally good. The leaves have a slight metallic edge to their taste, whereas the stems are delicate and subtle. We often cook both together, and with a little bacon, garlic and parmesan they make a superb sauce for pasta.

METHOD

1. I make a first sowing in March and a second in late summer to ensure a continuous supply throughout the year. The seeds can be sown direct in shallow drills about 1in/3cm apart, thinning the seedlings as they grow.

2. However, it is much less wasteful of seed – and a way of limiting slug damage – to sow them in plugs and potting compost, with 1 seed per plug, germinating them under cover (although they do not have to be particularly warm to germinate – an unheated windowsill will do), growing them on and hardening off before planting them out. They make quite large plants so there is no advantage in planting them any closer together than this, and directly sown seeds should be thinned accordingly.

3. Keep the water supply steady, as erratic watering will stress them and induce bolting.

4. Harvest either by taking a few choice leaves from each plant or, as I prefer to do, cut the whole plant and all its leaves flush with the ground which provokes a fresh flush of tender new growth.

5. Being biennials they will only go to seed in the first growing season if they are distressed, so the consistency of water supply is as important as the quantity. If some do start to bolt, cut the central, flowering stem down to the ground and give them a soak.

YOU WILL NEED

Chard seeds

Well-drained weed-free patch of ground

Water

CHILLIES

Chillies are handsome plants, varied enough to be deeply satisfying – there are thousands of varieties and scores that are readily available as seed – but easy enough for anyone to grow. The fruits can be dried and stored for years and, in my humble opinion, almost everything tastes better with some added chilli.

The real secret is in the fruitiness of a fresh chilli. The heat should never obscure this, so start with varieties you know and experiment from this base.

METHOD

1. Fill a seed tray with potting compost, firm it down a little so it's flat and even and then sprinkle seed thinly onto the surface. You can sow them individually straight into plugs, but the seeds are small and this is a bit of a fiddle. Cover the seeds with a thin layer of compost or vermiculite. Water well.

2. Chillies need heat to germinate and I use a heated propagating mat, but a windowsill above a radiator is fine. Be patient – they can take 3 weeks to germinate.

3. Pot on the seedlings into plugs or small pots once 'true' leaves (see glossary) appear and pot them on again in spring until they are about 10in/25cm tall and can go into their final container or bed.

4. Chillies can grow and fruit outside in a sunny spot but a greenhouse, porch or polytunnel is ideal. In any event, throughout every stage of their growth give them as much light and heat as you can whilst making sure they do not dry out.

5. Water them daily and in spring they should be fed weekly with a high-nitrogen fertiliser to encourage new growth. This will help more flowers, and therefore fruit, to develop. Then, as soon as the first flowers appear, switch to a high-potash feed. Any generic tomato fertiliser will do, although I use liquid seaweed or home-made liquid comfrey feed.

6. Ripe fruit look very attractive but inhibit the production of new flowers. So keep picking them as soon as individual chillies ripen. Although you can keep chillies growing for years, I always ditch mine in autumn and start again because as they get older they produce fewer and fewer chillies.

7. I store chillies in 2 ways. The first is simply to freeze them whole, fresh off the plant. They can then be taken out and defrosted individually with most of their fruitiness retained.

8. I also dry and grind them to make chilli flakes. This takes up much less space and retains all heat although inevitably with a loss of their fruity flavour.

YOU WILL NEED

Chilli seed (any capsicum annuum or capsicum baccatum varieties, such as cayenne, jalapeño or any of the aji chillies, are easiest to grow)

Seed tray or plugs

Potting compost or vermiculite

Small (3.5in/9cm) pots for growing on

Final pots – ideally terracotta, 10 to 14in/ 25 to 35cm diameter

High-nitrogen feed in spring

Liquid seaweed or tomato feed once flowers form (home-made comfrey feed is ideal)

Water

CARROTS

SOW: LATE WINTER TO SUMMER
HARVEST: LATE SPRING TO AUTUMN

Carrots will grow quickly and easily in spring on lighter soils, but if you garden on heavy soil then it is worth waiting until the soil is not just not-cold but has actually warmed up. I find that the best crop – and the one that has least trouble from carrot fly – comes from a sowing in late May or early June.

Carrots should be sown outside in ground that has not been freshly enriched by compost or manure, as this causes the roots to split and bifurcate. For this reason, carrots are traditionally grown in a three-way rotation, started by legumes, followed by brassicas and completed by the carrot family – which also includes parsnips, parsley and celery.

They can also be grown perfectly well in a container as long as it is deep enough for the roots to develop – 12in/30cm is a sensible minimum depth.

METHOD

1. Carrots can either be grown in rows about 12in/30cm apart, making a shallow drill and sprinkling the seed as thinly as possible along its length (the ideal is for seeds to be 1in/2cm equidistant from each other – but that is almost impossible to achieve), or broadcast by sprinkling the seed evenly over a defined area. I do this by placing 2 boards 3ft/1m apart and spreading the seed between them so there is a clear demarcation point on either side, where the carrot seed ends.

2. Either way, cover the seed over by raking lightly. Water them and then water weekly if it is very dry; otherwise rain will do the job.

3. The seeds will take 2 to 3 weeks to germinate and then another 10 weeks before the carrots are big enough to be worth pulling. Obviously they will get bigger the longer you leave them in the ground.

4. The biggest problem is carrot fly. This pest is attracted by the scent of carrots – which it can detect up to half a mile away – and lays its eggs just below the surface of the soil where carrots are growing. When the larvae hatch they then tunnel into the growing roots.

5. Traditional advice has always been to put up some kind of physical barrier like fleece so the fly cannot lay its eggs. However I have found that if you do not thin your carrots at all and pull no more than you intend to eat, leaving the other carrots undisturbed, this minimises the scent which draws the flies from far and wide and works as well as erecting a barrier.

YOU WILL NEED

Well-prepared soil that has not been freshly enriched or a container at least 12in/30cm deep

Carrot seed: early sowings are best with a Nantes type, which are shorter. Later sowings can be longer and bigger, for example 'Autumn King Imperator'.

Rake

Water

KALE

Kale is undoubtedly trendy. But despite the loudly proclaimed health benefits of kale chips and kale juices, it has never been glamorous in the horticultural world, not least because it is probably the hardiest and most robust vegetable you can grow. But it is beautiful and can be delicious.

I tend to grow only one kind of kale nowadays – cavolo nero or Black Tuscan kale – but you can get frizzy kale, bright green kale, the plum-coloured 'Redbor' and 'Red Russian', which has grey-green foliage with deep purple stems. However, I think the deep, dark green of cavolo nero outclasses all other varieties in taste.

You can eat it raw when the leaves are very young and it makes an excellent salad with oranges, but the truth is that raw kale is awfully tough on your digestion, however much health gurus will sing its praises. Better to strip the foliage from the central stalk and boil or steam it. This is where kale comes into its own because it will take hours of cooking without becoming mushy or losing taste. This makes it ideal for soups and stews, and for centuries it was an essential ingredient of meals right across Europe. It also makes an excellent sauce for pasta when boiled for about fifteen minutes, drained and then reheated with garlic and cream.

METHOD

1. Kale can be sown as early as January and as late as August but whenever you sow it, unless eaten very young for salads, it will take at least 6 months before harvest. It is a long-term crop.

2. Sow the seeds into a seed tray and put somewhere to germinate – which it will do quickly and easily.

3. When there are 'true' leaves that are big enough to handle, prick the seedlings out individually into plugs. They can be put somewhere sheltered but not especially heated to grow on, and when they have grown to about 2in/5cm and have a good root system, they can be potted on into 3in/7.5cm pots. You can sow direct into plugs but the seeds are quite small and fiddly, so weed out any extra seedlings so that there is only 1 per plug.

4. Plant the growing plants out into the soil when they are about 12in/30cm tall or the roots are filling the pot – whichever is sooner – usually about 8 weeks after sowing. Space them at least 24in/60cm apart and ideally 36in/90cm. Firm the ground before planting and set each plant deep in the soil and firm them in really well so they are well anchored; they become very top-heavy and need a really secure base. Water them in well.

5. Because they have lots of room around their base I always underplant them with a leafy crop, such as lettuce or spinach, that will be cleared away in autumn.

YOU WILL NEED

Cavolo nero seeds

Seed and plug trays

3in/7.5cm pots

Peat-free potting compost

Weed-free ground that has had compost or well-rotted manure recently added to it

Water

Bamboo canes or stakes

BEETROOT

I was brought up in the 1960s knowing beetroot as something that was only ever eaten cold, having been boiled and allowed to cool before being sliced and served, doused in vinegar, with a salad. Despite this abuse it remained good but I love it most when roasted along with generous sprigs of thyme, and served with roast meat or with a hot cream sauce. Beetroot soup is delicious whether made with the full panoply of a proper borscht or a much simpler kitchen soup, and of course beetroot juices sit somewhere between a cocktail and medicine because on top of their deliciousness, beetroots are incredibly good for you, improving blood pressure, digestion and resistance to inflammation.

They are from the same family as sugar beet, spinach, chard and, more surprisingly, quinoa. All like a rich, well-drained soil and are very hardy but, like most vegetables, do best in full sun.

METHOD

1. The seeds are in little nuggety clusters so each seed may produce a number of seedlings. If sowing direct where they are to grow, wait until the soil is no longer cold to touch and sprinkle the seeds as evenly as possible .5in/1 to 2cm apart in shallow drills. However, I usually sow into modules and raise the seedlings under cover, planting them out after about 6 weeks. When sowing in modules I drop 2 or 3 seeds in each module. These will then grow as a little cluster of beets and push each other apart as they grow.

2. The advantage of raising them under cover is that you can make a sowing as early as February so they are ready to plant out as soon as the soil warms up in spring, exactly at the moment when you make your first outdoor sowing.

3. The seedlings grow slowly at first but should have harvestable, golf-to-tennis-ball-sized roots by mid-summer. These will happily sit in the ground all winter although as they age they become large and too woody for eating (but even then they are good for juicing). However, these woody, over-large beets will sprout delicious new leaves in early spring that are very good for eating raw in a salad.

4. The main thing to watch when growing beetroot is running to seed or bolting. This is a response to being too hot, too cold, too wet or too dry, although it may not manifest for a month or two. The answer is to try and ensure a steady, consistent supply of water and hope the weather is not too erratic.

YOU WILL NEED

Beetroot seed

Prepared ground

Seed modules

Peat-free potting compost

Water

CHICORY

Chicory comes in many different shapes, sizes and colours but all share two distinct characteristics. The first is that they all have a bitterness that, if they are grown and harvested correctly, is a delicious counterpoint to the sweetness of other vegetables, in the way that coffee, olives, sherry, green tea and almonds all share.

The second is that chicory plants grow in two distinct phases. The first establishes the root via a heavy growth of leaves, which in most types (with the notable exception of endive which is grown as though it is a slightly bitter lettuce) are inedibly bitter unless they are blanched by stopping access to light. Then, once the long, fleshy root is established, a second growth of leaves follows and it is these that you harvest. This means that they are a much slower, longer-term crop than lettuce.

METHOD

1. I always start chicory off by sowing the seed directly into plugs. Put them somewhere warm to germinate. Try and only sow 1 seed per plug but if there are more, weed out all but the strongest.

2. Once they have 'true' leaves they can be moved outside to a sheltered place to grow on until the roots are sufficiently developed and can be lifted clear from the plug without collapsing but are not in any way rootbound. If in any doubt just gently ease a seedling from its plug and check the roots.

3. Plant them in rows or a grid into well-drained soil in full sun, leaving 8in/20cm between plants. Water them in well and keep them watered and weed-free.

4. They can be sown direct but the vigour of the first flush of foliage means that you end up thinning and discarding nine-tenths of the emerging seedlings.

5. They are very hardy and can take frost down to about 13°F/-10°C, but cold and rain are a bad combination for them so I always cloche as many as I can simply to act as umbrellas to keep them dry.

6. Very hot or very dry weather will cause them to send up flower stems and bolt, and unless these are removed as soon as you see them, the plant is lost for eating purposes.

7. Harvest them in late summer and autumn by cutting the top growth back to a stub with a knife, and new leaves will invariably regrow. Each plant gives at least two harvests.

YOU WILL NEED

Chicory seeds

Plug tray

Peat-free potting compost

A prepared sunny site

Water

ONIONS & SHALLOTS

Onions and shallots grow equally well either from seed or from 'sets', which are immature bulbs. Whereas seeds are slower and more of a fiddle but give you a much greater choice of varieties, growing from sets is easier and quicker.

Shallots are smaller and sweeter than onions and store better. Onion sets will grow to create one larger bulb whereas shallot sets will create a cluster of small bulbs for harvesting as a clump. Onions need a longish growing period – about twenty weeks – if they are to mature into decent sized bulbs. Once the days get shorter after midsummer they are increasingly inclined to go to seed, so it is a good idea to get them going early in the year, aiming for a July harvest.

Both do best in good but light-ish soil and are best grown on ground that has been manured the previous year, following brassicas or legumes.

METHOD

1. Sets can be planted any time the ground is ready after the new year. Although onion and shallot 'sets' are bulbs like a daffodil or tulip, unlike them they should not be planted deeply but just half buried, placed about 8in/20cm apart for onions and 12in/30cm for shallots. Water them in well.

2. Whether you plant in rows or a grid, it is very important to keep them weeded and the easiest way to do this is to hoe regularly.

3. Birds love to pull them out of the ground, especially as the new shoots start to appear, but they can be replanted. However, once they establish good roots they quickly resist any amount of avian tugging.

4. If the soil is too wet or frozen early in the year I suggest planting a batch in plugs, burying just the lower half, and protecting them in a greenhouse or on a cool windowsill where they will establish shoots and roots. They can then be planted into position once the ground is more receptive.

5. Onions like plenty of moisture whilst the foliage is growing which is why it is so important to weed them regularly, so that competition for water is reduced.

6. When the foliage starts to go yellow and die back, stop watering and let the foliage die down until most of the green has gone. They can then be harvested by carefully lifting them with a fork – not yanking them from the ground – so the roots remain undamaged where they attach to the bulb. Dry them completely – a greenhouse is ideal but any airy, dry place will do. The roots and leaves can then be trimmed and the crop stored. Although tradition has them tied in ropes I have found storing in a basket in a cool, dark shed to be best.

YOU WILL NEED

Onion and shallot sets

Rake

Hoe

Well-drained soil

Plugs

Potting compost

Water

Garden fork

Somewhere to dry the harvest

SPINACH

Spinach is rich in iron and vitamin A and has a higher protein content than any other leafy vegetable. Also, somewhat surprisingly, raw spinach has twice the amount of carotenoids compared with raw carrots.

But, over and above its nutritional virtues, it is easy to grow and delicious either eaten raw in salads or cooked. When eaten raw it has a freshness and a slightly metallic taste that seems to me greener than any other vegetable. But when cooked it is literally transformed, its high moisture content meaning that it reduces to a fraction of its leafy bulk whilst having an astonishing ability to absorb butter and, when grated with nutmeg, becomes a very rich, very delicious gooey purée.

METHOD

1. Spinach is a cool-season crop and very quickly runs to seed when the temperature rises or if it gets too dry, so it should be sown in late winter and late summer to avoid growing and harvesting in the hottest months.

2. The seeds are round and fairly large so can easily be sprinkled .5in/1 to 2cm apart direct into shallow drills spaced about 12in/30cm apart, if the soil is dry enough to be raked to a tilth. However, I always make my first spring sowing in a seed tray or plugs, then prick the seedlings out and grow them on so they can be planted out as soon as the soil is manageable.

3. If sowing direct, thin the seedlings until each individual plant is 2 to 4in/6 to 10cm apart. This will give them the room and nutrition to become strong plants that can be cut to the ground and regrow for a second harvest.

4. There are many varieties for growing over winter, like 'Giant Winter' or 'Galaxy' which are better adapted to cold weather. Spring varieties are slightly more tender and better for eating raw.

5. Whatever the variety, it needs really rich soil and lots of water. It can be fitted in anywhere within the rotation and makes a good catch-crop between the rows of longer and slower-growing crops like garlic, brassicas or broad beans.

YOU WILL NEED

Spinach seed

Prepared soil or seed trays and compost

Rake

Water

HERBS

Herbs are relevant to every meal for every kind of eater. Whatever your particular dietary bent, herbs will inevitably be part of it. They are an intrinsic and essential part of every kitchen and so they should be in every garden.

A small selection of fresh herbs is essential for any kind of cooking, and that small selection can be grown in almost any situation, from a window box to some pots outside the back door, to a full-throated, dedicated herb garden with lavender hedges and tall stands of fennel, lovage and dill along with bowers fragrant with aromatic oils.

Lack of space barely need cramp your herb-growing style because most herbs can be grown well and generously in small spaces. They lend themselves to containers of every kind. In fact many herbs grow better in a container than in the soil because Mediterranean herbs like thyme, rosemary or sage need poor soil and extremely good drainage, as well as lots of sunshine, to thrive, which makes life tricky for those of us with heavy or fertile soil. But it means that anyone with a windowsill can grow meaningful herbs – which is more than can be said for vegetables.

It goes without saying that the herbs you grow in your garden and pick absolutely fresh when they are at their best will always taste far better – and be better for you – than anything you can buy.

Herbs lend themselves to generosity, and one of my bugbears is the parsimony with which herbs are treated – all those spindly little plants crammed into plastic pots masquerading as parsley or basil – whereas they are a degraded caricature of what you can so easily grow yourself.

You must be generous with herbs, both in the number of plants you grow and the amount harvested. Handfuls, trugfuls – even wheelbarrowfuls – are what is needed. Given that almost all herbs grow easily from seed or cuttings, this is cheap and easy to achieve. It depends on a state of mind rather than the state of your bank balance.

I like to pick great bunches of parsley so we use it by the handful rather than the pinch. Fresh mint for tea is better both in taste and for healing than dried stuff, and you need an endless supply of peppermint and spearmint for that, at least in its growing season, which is April to October. Roasting lamb should sit on branches of rosemary, and fresh basil can be harvested by the basketful to make a pesto better than anything from the very best Italian store.

So grow herbs. Grow lots. They are easy, essential and life-enhancing – and you do not need lots of space to grow them.

A MEDITERRANEAN
HERB CONTAINER

Mediterranean herbs include some of the most used and useful herbs that you can grow, so a container of these near the kitchen will not only look good but be incredibly convenient.

All these herbs share the same basic growing requirements, which are counter-intuitive to a lot of received horticultural knowledge. They have evolved to thrive in the sunbaked harshness of Mediterranean hillsides, which means that unless you garden on almost pure sand or chalk you will need to dilute your garden soil with grit (ideal) or sharp sand (pretty good), but NOT any kind of organic material (too nutritious).

However, if you have a deep, water-retentive soil that is clay-based or even just good-quality topsoil of any kind it is probably best to grow these plants in a container, where you can give them the kind of limited rations and extreme drainage they need.

METHOD

1. Mix your potting compost with an equal volume of grit. It should feel very gritty and run through your fingers.

2. I grow herbs in a whole range of containers but there is no doubt that terracotta looks great and suits them best as it is porous so drains best. Put plenty of crocks in the bottom of the pot to improve drainage and half fill it with the compost mix.

3. Depending on the size of your pot, plant an upright rosemary ('Miss Jessopp's Upright'), a sage bush or even, if your pot is big enough, a bay tree as a centrepiece.

4. Plant 2 or 3 thyme plants at the front for maximum sun (thyme hates any shade at all), some prostrate rosemary at the edges if you did not use rosemary as the centrepiece and vice versa, and a couple of sage bushes if sage was not in the centre.

5. Oregano plants are slightly less fussy about shade so can be placed round the back of the pot, and, if you have room, add some French tarragon (NOT Russian tarragon which, although hardy, does not taste nearly as good). Otherwise grow this in a separate pot, which can then be brought indoors out of frost in winter.

6. When you have arranged the plants to your satisfaction, infill compost between them and top dress the surface with a layer of grit. This looks good and improves drainage, stopping the surface of the compost forming a crust so water bounces off it.

7. Finally, water well. Just because these are plants that love sun and heat does not mean that they do not need water so give them a weekly drink – but do NOT feed them.

YOU WILL NEED

Peat-free potting compost

Horticultural grit

A generous container – ideally terracotta

Crocks

A selection of herbs such as:

Rosemary ('Miss Jessopp's Upright' and/or prostrate form)

Thyme

Oregano

Sage

Bay

French tarragon

Water

Sunshine!

A HARDY HERB CONTAINER

These culinary herbs will all grow in some shade (as long as they get at least half a day's sun). They are all frost hardy although extreme cold will kill the non-herbaceous plants. They also like better growing conditions and more moisture than Mediterranean herbs, so need less drainage material added to the potting compost, but need watering a little more often.

By growing them as a collection in one container, you can give them the conditions they like best and not compete with the very different needs of Mediterranean herbs.

METHOD

1. The best time to plant this container is in mid-spring, to get the full benefit of their growth which will be vigorous over spring and summer months but die right back in autumn.

2. Mix your potting compost with 25 to 33% grit by volume.

3. Put crocks in the bottom of the pot to improve drainage and half fill it with the compost mix.

4. None of these plants grow very big but sweet cicely is probably the largest when in flower so makes a good centrepiece. It will die back completely over winter and if you cut it back hard when it has finished flowering you will get fresh new – and delicious – growth. Lemon balm spreads inexorably and will need dividing after a year or two.

5. Coriander, chives and parsley are all very easily grown from seed but are otherwise much better bought as individual plants in plugs or small pots rather than as a mass of seedlings in one pot.

6. Chives and sorrel are both completely herbaceous, dying right back in winter, but once they start growing in spring they will take repeated cutting back and are very tough. Chives add a gentle, fresh oniony tang to almost any dish, and sorrel, somewhere between a vegetable and a herb, has a very metallic, sharp taste that is excellent with eggs. It is happy in shade as long as it does not get too dry.

7. Coriander is an annual and if cold or stressed by heat or drought will quickly go to seed. For many who value the seed above the foliage, this is not a problem, and some seed can be resown to create new plants, but in any event for the best leaves, plants can be replaced in mid-summer.

8. Parsley is biennial and although new leaves do regrow at least once, its tendency to develop flowering stems at the expense of leaves after about four months means that plants put out in spring will need replacing with fresh ones in late summer.

9. Water well after planting and give a good weekly soak throughout the summer.

YOU WILL NEED

A generous container – ideally terracotta

Peat-free potting compost

Horticultural grit

Crocks

A selection of herbs such as:

Chives

Parsley

Coriander

Lemon balm

Sorrel

Sweet cicely

Water

BASIL

SOW: MID-SPRING TO EARLY SUMMER
HARVEST: MID-SUMMER TO EARLY AUTUMN

The secrets of growing really good basil are pretty straightforward but need observing.

To start with, basil is not a Mediterranean plant but a tropical one. It hates cold and likes as much heat, water and rich soil as you can give it. Cold turns its leaves leathery and slightly bitter and whilst still very edible, they are never as good again as leaves that have grown in constant warmth. If you have a greenhouse they are much better grown in it.

You must grow it steadily in one continuous process so try and keep the temperature, water supply and root growth as constant and unstressed as possible. It should never stop growing; otherwise the leaves become thick and slightly bitter.

Then – and this is the real key – plant it out with plenty of space: up to 8in/20cm between each individual basil. When you buy a pot of basil from a supermarket it is in fact filled with dozens of small seedlings. But basil wants to be a large plant – almost a sub shrub. Each one of those little supermarket seedlings will grow to 24in/60cm tall or more given the chance. Space your plants out and not only will they get large enough to give you lots of large, aromatic leaves, but they will also have roots established enough to give another good flush of foliage that can be harvested.

METHOD

1. Sow the seed in April, sprinkling them thinly on a seed tray filled with compost. Cover them lightly with vermiculite or compost and water well. They need a warm place to germinate so a heated mat is ideal but at the very least a warm windowsill.

2. They germinate quickly. As soon as they have 2 'true' leaves, prick each seedling individually into a plug or small pot. Grow these individual seedlings on under cover until they are large enough to plant out into the garden or a larger pot.

3. Plant them out after the last frost and when the nights start to warm up – the end of May under cover and mid-June outside – at least 6in/15cm and ideally 8in/20cm apart to give them the room to develop fully.

4. Water them well and never let them dry out completely. They can be harvested at any stage but to maximise the harvest, let them grow into plants 12in/30cm tall (they can reach double that). Pinch out any flower buds as soon as they appear as they will inhibit leaf production.

5. By September they will be flowering and new leaves will become sparse. They can then be pulled up and taken to the compost – but hopefully with a stash of pesto home-made and frozen for a taste of summer in winter.

YOU WILL NEED

Green basil seeds

Seed tray

Peat-free potting compost

Vermiculite

Plug tray or small pots

Heated indoor space

Water

206 | GROWING FOOD

SARAH DON'S PESTO RECIPE

Home-grown basil is not just good with any tomato dish, it also makes the best pesto you have ever tasted. Once the leaves are picked, make your pesto as soon as possible for maximum freshness and enjoy that lovely oily, aromatic, rich green taste that for me sums up summer evenings spent eating outside in the garden as the August light slowly slips away.

METHOD

1. Roughly combine the basil, salt, garlic and pine nuts in a food processor, but not too much.

2. Add the olive oil steadily and combine for few seconds, but again, not too much.

3. Mix in the parmesan.

YOU WILL NEED

4 cups/175g basil leaves

½ tsp sea salt

3 garlic cloves

⅓ cup/45g pine nuts

6.75oz/200ml olive oil

1½ cups/130g grated parmesan

PARSLEY

Parsley is always a treat, whether added liberally to eggs, vegetables, stews and soups, as part of salads or, with walnuts and garlic, as a delicious pesto. It is also rich in antioxidants, vitamins and trace minerals.

It has become commonplace for parsley to be sold in pots as a cluster of stems. But each of the wispy seedlings crammed into the pot is desperate for space. They are like battery hens, producing the goods but for a tiny period and under appalling conditions. But a healthy parsley plant between three and nine months old should be six to twelve inches tall with masses of leaves that can be cut back two or three times with each harvest from each individual plant, providing more delicious growth than an entire mass-produced pot.

Parsley thrives in well-drained but fertile soil, with plenty of moisture. It will also tolerate some shade. It is a biennial so produces its leaves in its first growing season and the flowering stem and seeds in the next. It is a member of the carrot family and will develop a long tap root – not unlike a carrot – and when given the space to develop to its full potential will regrow a new flush of leaves again and again for the first nine months of its life, until the urge to develop its flowers becomes overwhelming and then it has to be dug up and added to the compost heap. When you do this, you will be astonished at the size of the root.

METHOD

1. I make 2 or 3 sowings a year: the first in January, then May and finally August, so I always have fresh leaves to harvest. It takes about 3 months from sowing to harvest and the plants remain productive for another 3 to 6 months.

2. Fill the seed tray to the brim with compost and level off. Sprinkle seed thinly and evenly over the surface. It is always better to sow too thinly rather than too thickly.

3. Cover the seeds very lightly with more compost or a thin layer of vermiculite, water well and put in a warm, light place to germinate.

4. When the seedlings have developed 'true' leaves (those that look like parsley) and are large enough to handle (usually about 3 weeks), transplant them into individual plugs, holding them by the leaves rather than the stems and transferring as much of the roots as possible.

5. Grow them on until the roots fill the plug and can be removed without falling apart – this is usually about another 3 to 4 weeks.

6. Plant outside in rows or a grid, giving each seedling at least 6in/15cm in each direction. Water well and frequently and they should be ready for you to harvest a large bunch of leaves in about a month. It will be the first of many harvests!

YOU WILL NEED

Packet of flat-leafed parsley seeds

Seed tray

Peat-free potting compost

Vermiculite

Tray of plugs

Space to plant out the seedlings 6in/15cm apart, in a position that gets at least 4 hours of sun per day

Water

MINT

Mint is an invaluable herb to grow both for taste and health and is extremely easy to grow, being both tough and reliable. Mint is an herbaceous perennial so dies back in winter, sending up fresh shoots in early spring, and the more you pick or cut it, the more new leaves it will produce.

Like most plants it will always prioritise flower production over foliage, so either keep it cut back or nip off flowers as they appear.

It will grow in full sun, shade, wet or dry, but is healthiest and happiest in well-drained, rich soil in full sun.

However, there is one problem – it has voracious rhizomatous roots that, like bindweed or couch grass, will produce new plants from every tiny section. There are many worse weeds to have in a garden but once mint takes hold, nothing else gets a look in, as it will take over an herb garden or a container shared with other herbs.

The solution is to grow it alone in a container or, if it's growing outside in the ground, to sink an old pot or bucket with the bottom knocked out and plant the mint inside that.

There are many different mints, including eau-de-cologne mint, water mint, Corsican mint, ginger mint and pineapple mint, but the best three to grow for the kitchen are spearmint, peppermint and apple mint. Spearmint is a good all-round culinary mint, peppermint makes the best mint tea and apple mint, which has large downy leaves, has a more delicate taste and is the best for new potatoes.

There is a purist school of thought that says that two different types of mint grown together will muddy each other's taste but I have found growing these mints together produces happy plants with very particular and identifiable flavours.

METHOD

1. Mix the compost with 33% grit by volume to improve drainage.

2. Put crocks in the pot and half fill the pot with the compost.

3. Place the mint according to your artistic eye and fill between the plants with the compost.

4. I like to top the compost with a layer of grit, which looks good and stops the compost splashing onto the leaves when you water.

5. Water in well and keep watered, never letting it dry out completely.

6. Place in the nearest sunny spot to the kitchen door.

YOU WILL NEED

Medium-sized container with ample drainage holes

Peat-free potting compost

Horticultural grit

Crocks

Spearmint plant

Peppermint plant

Apple mint plant

Water

BAY

Bay leaves are a staple ingredient of much Mediterranean and Middle Eastern cuisine, and so should be equally essential as a component of any herb garden.

In the cold of my own garden it can be a struggle to get them through winter unscathed and they will be killed back to the ground when temperatures drop much below 14°F/-10°C, but in the relative warmth of a city they can become large trees and can make solid evergreen hedges when regularly clipped. If frosts are light, some horticultural fleece draped over the leaves is often enough to restrict any real damage. Even if the leaves turn brown and fall so the tree looks stone dead, the tree will very often regrow from the roots, so set it aside in a sheltered spot for at least twelve months and it may well recover.

The thing to remember is that it is a Mediterranean herb and so likes sunshine, relatively poor soil and very good drainage. This means that for those of us with heavy soil or even wetter winters, it is best to grow it in a pot.

METHOD

1. Mix your potting compost and grit well so the grit makes at least one third of the resulting mixture.

2. Put plenty of crocks in the bottom of the pot and enough compost mix in the bottom so the existing level of the soil around the stem of the bay tree is about 2in/5cm below the rim of the pot. This allows room for watering and mulching.

3. Take the bay out of its pot, check the roots, and if they are wrapped around themselves gently break them with your thumb to stimulate new growth which will grow out into the compost rather than stay tightly tangled.

4. Fill the compost around the roots, making sure there are no air pockets.

5. Place the pot in the sunniest spot you have, set upon risers or feet which will ensure the water drains away after watering. These feet can be bought from any garden centre but can also be improvised from broken tiles.

6. Water well. The water should run straight through and out of the bottom of the pot. Water weekly and feed weekly with liquid seaweed between April and August to promote healthy fresh leaves. If the potting mix is sufficiently free-draining it should never be sodden.

7. Bay lends itself to clipping and even topiary so can be shaped into cones, pom-poms or balls and used decoratively, flanking a doorway or path.

YOU WILL NEED

Bay tree

Terracotta pot about twice the size of the pot the tree is sold in

Peat-free potting compost

Horticultural grit
Crocks

Terracotta feet or risers

Water

Liquid seaweed

FRUIT

Historically, fruit was the most prized produce of any garden for the seasonal sweetness it brought, but many modern gardeners relegate it below vegetables or consider it an optional extra. This is a shame as much fruit is very easy to grow and need not, with straightforward pruning, take up much space. Gooseberries, redcurrants, strawberries, raspberries, apples, plums, damsons, quinces, crab apples – these are all fruits that more or less look after themselves. Even some of the more particular fruits, like oranges, peaches or vines, are no more trouble than, say, tomatoes (which are of course a fruit themselves, even though they are conveniently lumped in with vegetables).

Fruit looks good too. Apple and pear trees have magnificent blossom, make superb trees and when hung with ripe fruit are as decorative as anything in the garden. Rhubarb stems glow and fig trees are wonderfully architectural. Red, white and black currants hang with fruity baubles, and crab apples can hold their fruit well into December after all flowers in the garden have faded.

But the main attraction of growing your own fruit is taste. We have grown to accept blandness in fruit that should be luxuriant. However, the perfect ripeness, when all the sugars are at their peak and the taste fully developed, can be fine-tuned in your garden down to a single day or even hour. We all have our favourites but for me, picking a bowl of raspberries and eating them still warm from the sun with a little single cream is a luxury better than anything any restaurant could possibly offer.

An unheralded benefit of growing your own fruit is that you can harvest all shapes and sizes. In an age when all fruit is sold uniform in size, weight and often taste, the sense of variety within a particular fruit is both novel and interesting. It also brings a sense of worth. A criminal amount of perfectly good fruit and veg is rejected by supermarkets because it fails to conform to a certain shape, colour or size, whereas when you grow your own, everything can be used in some form or another.

The key to success with fruit is not to strive after the rare or exotic but to work out what will thrive in your garden and enjoy it at its best. It seems rather pointless to grow a small, tasteless melon with some difficulty whereas you could have a pear as good as any in the land or a quince tree whose fruit are as deliciously fragrant as any flower.

Having said that, if you have a greenhouse or are lucky enough to have a really sunny wall, then the range of fruits that can be grown is greatly extended, and delicious ripe peaches, apricots and figs become very viable.

The important thing is to realise and relish how easy it is to grow a wide variety of fruit that is fresh, seasonal, healthy and completely delicious.

CITRUS

Perhaps the easiest citrus to grow in a pot are lemons. These are pretty hardy, vigorous and spiny and have the great virtue of holding three crops at once. So at any one time there will be flowers, young green fruits and ripening yellow ones all together on the same tree.

They need a dormant period over winter when they should be kept cool but not cold, and humid but not wet. Although citrus should be watered very sparingly in winter – once a month is usually plenty – they do like the air to be quite moist. A good rule of thumb is that if it is dry enough for soft furnishings then it will be too dry for any citrus to be happy for very long.

METHOD

1. The time to prune is spring when they start producing vigorous new shoots – I do this when I put them outside for summer, around the end of April. Begin by thinning the centre of the plant out so light and air can get right into it.

2. Take away the branches that have produced any fruit over winter and any that are looking tired, dried up and lacking vigour.

3. Do not worry if your citrus has defoliated quite a lot over winter – this is a sign of too much heat or lack of humidity rather than a disaster, and bare branches can quickly produce fresh leaves.

4. Citrus plants can take huge amounts of pruning, and the harder you cut, the greater the health and vigour of any remaining branches, so do not be timid. This is especially so of lemon trees that are very vigorous.

5. All citrus plants produce their fruit on shoots grown the previous year. The more curving and woody a branch is, the more likely it is to produce fruit.

6. Although the fruits are very decorative and can remain on a mature plant for months, it is advisable to remove most from young plants as they take up a lot of energy. When the fruit reaches its expected colour it usually means that it is ripe, although fruit can stay on a tree for up to a year after ripening. In any event it is a good idea to pick any ripe fruit, as removing ripe fruit will stimulate flower production.

7. The most important thing for any citrus plant is good drainage. They hate sitting in waterlogged soil so mix at least one third in volume of horticultural grit in with the potting compost. It is also a good idea to stand the pots on blocks of some kind to avoid the pot sitting in a puddle after watering. In winter they can be allowed to completely dry out between watering but in the growing season they will need a good soak once a week, ideally with rainwater.

8. Feed weekly with liquid seaweed whilst outside but do not feed them once they go indoors for winter until you see new growth appear in spring.

YOU WILL NEED

Secateurs

Water

Seaweed feed

STRAWBERRIES IN A POT

As a child, strawberries from the garden were always the highlight of my July birthday tea – not least because they were such a brief seasonal treat. Nowadays we have strawberries available every day of the year but, trust me, none you can buy will ever taste as good as those you grow at home, eaten in season, whilst still warm from the summer sun.

Fortunately strawberries are easy to grow and are very happy in a container of any kind, including hanging baskets.

METHOD

1. Commercial varieties are grown primarily for appearance, fragrance and their ability to take the rigours of travel, with taste coming a long way down the list, so choose a variety that you cannot buy, that may not store at all well but which tastes magnificent. I recommend 'Gariguette', 'Cambridge Favourite' or 'Florence'.

2. Strawberries are thirsty and greedy plants and respond very well to rich soil as long as it drains well, so ideally add some garden compost or loam to your peat-free potting mix. Mix some grit or perlite in too to improve drainage and put crocks in the bottom of the container to ensure the holes do not get clogged up.

3. Resist the temptation to put too many plants in a small container – you will get more fruit from large, healthy plants that are not competing too much for water and nutrients. When planting outside in a bed I allow at least 10in/25cm between plants so a 1.3gal/5L pot, for example, should be right for no more than 3 plants.

4. Keep them well watered and put in a sunny place. When the flowers appear, feed weekly with liquid seaweed and put straw or cardboard under the fruits to stop them getting dirty.

5. Birds love strawberries and will eat them before they are properly ripe, so as soon as you see any redness in the fruits they will need protecting with a net.

6. When the fruit have finished, cut all the old foliage right back. This will discourage mould and pests and improve ventilation. New leaves will be growing beneath them and quickly become established.

7. Strawberries accumulate viral diseases and start to produce less and less fruit so need replacing with new plants – in fresh compost – every 3 or 4 years.

YOU WILL NEED

Strawberry plants
(1 per 12in/30cm)

Peat-free potting compost

Garden compost or loam

Horticultural grit/perlite

Crocks

Container

Water

Seaweed feed

Straw or cardboard

Net

BLUEBERRIES

Blueberries are delicious and largely trouble free if they have the right conditions. They naturally grow in acidic soil, so unless you live in an area that visibly favours rhododendrons, pines, heathers and camellias, they will need growing in a container with ericaceous potting compost.

Although some varieties – such as 'Sunshine Blue' or 'Bluecrop' – are self fertile, having two or more plants to pollinate each other will greatly improve cropping.

There are a number of varieties, some which lend themselves to training as standards, on a straight stem, and other more compact bushes, such as 'North Country', more suited to limited space but which will still produce a mass of fruits.

METHOD

1. Mix the ericaceous compost with some perlite or horticultural grit to improve drainage. If you have some leaf mould add about 25% in volume.

2. Fill your pot to about one third of its depth then place the blueberry, still in its container, in it and fill more compost around it. Gently lift the blueberry and pot out, remove the plant and slip into the space vacated.

3. Water well. It is important to water regularly and not to let them dry out, especially in spring and summer when the buds and fruits are forming. Wherever possible use rainwater, as tap water is likely to be too alkaline for them over a sustained period. Mulch every spring with composted bracken or pine needles.

4. Feed them weekly with an ericaceous liquid feed, but do not overfeed as this will only encourage shoots at the expense of fruits.

5. As fruit is ripening throw a net over the whole plant, as you will struggle to beat the birds to the delicious fruits.

6. Position the bushes in a sunny spot for at least half the day. This will help ripen not only the fruit but also the new wood. The better this wood ripens, the better the fruit next year.

7. Pruning should be done to leave a framework carrying the previous summer's growth that will bear the coming year's fruits. The best time to do this is between Christmas and the end of February. Remove all dead or very spindly growth and cut back last year's fruiting stems by about a third to retain shape and limit growth.

YOU WILL NEED

Peat-free ericaceous compost

Perlite or horticultural grit

Leaf mould (optional)

2 blueberry plants

2 containers

Crocks

Water

Net

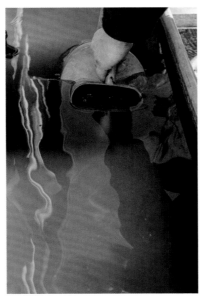

RASPBERRIES

A bowl of fresh raspberries, at room temperature (and, heaven forfend, not chilled), with single cream and perhaps a little sugar for texture, is pretty close to heaven. But to have raspberries really fresh and really good you need to eat them the same day – and ideally the same hour – they are picked. As it happens they are tough, long-lived, undemanding plants and so easy to grow.

There are two types of raspberry: summer and autumn. Summer raspberries fruit between the end of June and mid-August, and autumn raspberries overlap for a week or so in August and then, depending on the weather, can be picked well into October. Summer raspberries fruit on the previous summer's canes whereas autumn ones fruit on new growth.

I suggest that to start with, autumn-fruiting raspberries are the best choice. They are hardier, less likely to be eaten by birds (young blackbirds in particular, seem to find midsummer raspberries irresistible), so do not need netting and do not need permanent support and are much less complicated to prune.

METHOD

1. You can order bare-root raspberry varieties online or buy them already potted from garden centres. The best time to plant them is January to March.

2. Raspberries will grow on most soils but are happiest in a slightly acidic, sandy loam. They like coolish, damp weather and are happy in shade as well as being very hardy. You can grow them against a fence or trellis or leave them completely free-standing.

3. Although they like moist air and plenty of rainfall, raspberries hate sitting in cold wet soil, so if you have heavy ground, dig a wide trench mixed with plenty of organic material, backfill it and plant the raspberries shallowly, mounding the soil over them rather than burying them, which will avoid the risk of the plants standing over winter in a puddle of water.

4. Set the canes – little more than short sticks with some roots attached – vertically into the ground 18 to 24in/45 to 60cm apart, just covering them with soil and gently firming them with your foot so that they cannot be rocked by wind.

5. Water them in very well and mulch them thickly and widely. Raspberry roots are fibrous and very shallow so need room to spread laterally, and these roots like to be cool and slightly moist so a good mulch every spring is essential. Never use mushroom compost as this is too alkaline. Bark chippings work very well.

6. New growth will appear from late March and these are the shoots that will bear fruit. There will be a small crop in the first year but the canes will develop very quickly into multi-stemmed bushes. These will need temporary support – sticks and string – between August and November to stop them flopping.

7. Prune all the top growth down to the ground in the new year, ready to be replaced by the new shoots in spring.

YOU WILL NEED

Autumn-fruiting raspberry canes, such as 'Autumn Bliss', 'Polka', 'Glen Ample' or 'All Gold'

Weed-free strip of ground

Digging fork

Spade

Mulch

Water

Canes or sticks and garden string for support

APPLES

Familiarity has grown a degree of contempt but apples picked off your own tree when properly ripe are always better in every way than anything you can buy. This is mainly because if picked when ripe the sugars – and flavour – have developed fully, whereas commercial apples are often grown for their ability to take storage, handling and travel, with outward appearance sometimes more important than anything else.

Apples also make fine garden trees with exquisite blossom. They can be large enough for a swing or treehouse or trained to grow in almost any shape, including space-saving cordons, espaliers and step-overs.

All apples grow best with good drainage and as much sun as possible. They also dislike exposure to cold wind, so shelter will help greatly. So avoid wet ground, exposure to winds and deep shade when siting any kind of apple tree.

The rootstock – the roots and base of the trunk which is grafted to the stem just above ground level – dictates the size and vigour of the tree. It is indicated by a number, such as M106 or M9. The top part – the scion – gives the apple its name and dictates everything about the fruit.

So the same variety grown on three different rootstocks will look and taste the same but the trees may differ greatly in vigour, training and eventual size. Most retailers will have this information, which is vital to knowing how suitable the tree is for you and your garden.

No apple is reliably self-fertile, so each tree needs a pollinator to spread and receive pollen, and it is better to always plant at least two trees to be certain of pollination. However, for those near large orchards, or in the city with other apples nearby, you can get away with 'borrowing' other people's tree pollen.

METHOD

1. The best way to ensure a good start and long life for the tree is to dig a hole that is at least 3ft/1m wide but no more than one spade, or 8in/20cm deep. Break up the bottom of the hole but do not add any manure or compost.

2. Plant the tree in the centre of the hole so that the roots are only just below the surface and the soil firmed very well around them. Then stake it diagonally so that the support is facing the prevailing wind. This stake should be removed after 3 years.

3. Finally, water it very well and then mulch thickly with manure or compost. Keep the planting hole weed-free and mulched for at least 3 years.

YOU WILL NEED

Your choice of apple tree

Spade

Tree stake

Peat-free compost or manure

HARVESTING & STORING APPLES

However you grow your apples, the fruit should be treasured. Very early varieties must be eaten more or less as they ripen but any ripening from late September can be easily stored in a cool, dark place and should remain full of flavour well into the new year.

Never be tempted to store even slightly damaged fruit because they will not keep. Pick them very carefully, holding the apple in the palm of your hand and twisting gently so that it comes free in your hand. Then place rather than throw it into a basket. If it does not come away easily then leave it – whatever it looks like.

We have found that racks of some sort in a shed are ideal for storage. This will have ventilation and humidity as well as being cool. Ideally you want the temperature to be between 34° and 41°F/1° and 5°C and for the room to not get too dry, so a damp cellar or shed is ideal and undoubtedly the apples keep better if individually wrapped in paper.

Check your store often, discard any rotting fruit and eat the rest. If you're still wondering how to tell if an apple is ripe, cut one: the pips should be the colour of dark chocolate. You will get to know your apples and when best to eat or cook them over time.

PEARS

PLANT: LATE AUTUMN TO EARLY SPRING
HARVEST: LATE SUMMER TO AUTUMN
PRUNE: MID-SUMMER OR MID-WINTER

A ripe pear has sweet, slippery, silky flesh whose honeyed juices dribble down your chin. Pears are messy, sensual and indulgent and always a special treat.

But most commercial pears are grown for their durability and ability to take handling and are invariably sold unripe. So for the true luxury of a perfect pear the best place to go is your garden. This is because pears, unlike apples, ripen erratically on the tree, either falling unripe or rotting in situ. They have to be picked, stored and allowed to come to the point of perfect edible ripeness.

A standard pear tree will grow into a large tree which can live for hundreds of years, especially if grown on its own roots. However, modern trees are invariably grown on a quince rootstock which makes them more amenable to training as an espalier, cordon or fan, all of which will be productive, look good and fit into even a very small garden.

METHOD

1. Although they are tough trees – hardier than apples in most cases and more tolerant of slightly damper conditions – the fruit do need sun to ripen, and they grow best against a south or west-facing wall or fence.

2. They blossom before most apples in early April and can be affected by late frosts so again, the protection of a wall or location away from a frost pocket can help with fruit set.

3. Always harvest pears by carefully lifting the fruit until it is horizontal. If ready the stem of the pear will snap away from the tree. If not, lower it carefully and try again in a day or two. However, if it falls then the chances are that it will rot before it ripens and will definitely not store, so the pears should be checked daily from mid-September until the last one is harvested in mid-October.

4. Once off the tree they should be handled gently and stored in a cool, dark place to ripen. Check them regularly, and to avoid them all ripening at once I put a few at a time on a windowsill, to accelerate the process.

5. Pears ripen from the inside out so that the flesh immediately beneath the skin is the last to be ready. They should be checked for the perfect moment to eat them by carefully pressing at the flesh around the stalk for a slight yielding and then consumed within 48 hours to enjoy them at their sublime best.

YOU WILL NEED

2 pear trees, to pollinate each other. There are lots of varieties to choose from but I recommend 'Doyen du Comice', 'Beth', 'Williams Bon Chretien' and 'Concorde'. If you grow them as cordons you can fit half a dozen varieties along a 15ft/5m length of fence.

Wire to provide support if grown against a wall or fence, posts and canes or wire if a free-standing espalier

Care when harvesting

PEACHES
& NECTARINES

Growing nectarine trees (or peaches – which are essentially the same, with nectarines being a peach with a smooth skin) is not difficult. Given a sunny, sheltered spot and protection from spring frosts, they are an attractive, satisfying and delicious addition to any garden.

They can be grown in soil as long as it is rich, well drained and at least 18in/45cm deep, or in pots. Choose cultivars that ripen in mid or late summer for growing outside and a compact cultivar for growing in a pot.

METHOD

1. Choose a pot about twice the size of the one the plant arrives in. (It will need repotting in a few years' time as it grows.) Add crocks to the bottom to stop drainage holes from blocking, as good drainage is essential.

2. Add about a quarter of the grit in volume to the potting compost and mix thoroughly. If you have some sieved garden compost or soil improver add about a fifth in volume and mix this in too – but it is not essential. Put a layer of the compost mix in the bottom of the pot until the potted tree sits about 1 to 2in/3 to 5cm below the rim.

3. Remove the nectarine from its pot, and set it in the growing container. Backfill compost around the roots until the pot is full, leaving about 1.5in/4cm for watering and mulching.

4. Water well. The water should flow swiftly through the drainage holes in the bottom of the pot. It will need watering at least every other day between April and July and feeding with liquid seaweed weekly.

5. Place the potted tree in a sunny place – preferably against a south-facing wall – and lift it up on chocks so the water drains freely.

6. Nectarines (and peaches and apricots) all flower early in spring so are very vulnerable to spring frosts. Construct some kind of framework so you can put fleece in place against frosts between February and May. Remove this on warm, sunny days and take it away completely once the risk of frost has passed. Nectarines are self-fertile so will produce fruit from a single tree. However, they are pollinated by insects so it helps to take a soft brush and brush the pollen from one flower to another to ensure fruit forming.

YOU WILL NEED

Nectarine plant such as 'Early Rivers', 'Lord Napier' or 'Nectarella' (compact)

A large container

Crocks

Peat-free potting compost (preferably loam-based)

Horticultural grit

Garden compost or soil improver

Liquid seaweed

Water

Chocks to raise the bottom of the pot

Protection from frost (horticultural fleece or shade netting)

Secateurs

7. Peaches and nectarines fruit on young wood grown the previous year. Fruit is formed on round buds and new shoots on pointed ones, so always prune back to a pointed growth bud to encourage new shoots for next year's fruit. Pruning should be done in late spring and summer after the fruit has formed. However, compact varieties need little or no pruning, whereas those grown in the soil are best pruned as fans attached to wires against a warm fence or wall.

STRUCTURE
& DESIGN

DESIGN

Design, in the sense of distributing all the elements of the garden, both living and constructed, is as essential in a garden as it is in a room or building.

Obviously a garden is – and should be – as personal as your choice of food or the clothes you wear. How you design it will always be subjective and personal. But there are a few universal design features and tips that can be applied to almost any garden.

For example, it is really important to use the third dimension as much as possible, and the smaller a garden is, the more relevant that becomes. So walls, fences, trellises, trees, free-standing supports for climbers and tall plants are all essential tools to enrich and shape a design.

A good and interesting garden can be created simply by planting hedges interspaced with grass. That creates volume and structure and perhaps most importantly of all, the volume of space between plants. The manipulation of empty space is just as important as the planting and care of plant material, be it annuals or large trees.

Do not fight lines of desire. People will always take the most direct, easiest route even if it means stepping over the corner of a border or through a gap in a young hedge. Cater for this. Make utilitarian paths straight, smooth and easy for barrows and muddy feet. But if you want to encourage a slower, more meandering route, then block off any possible shortcuts, create curving paths and close off the sight lines so you have to follow the path to find out what it leads to.

Make borders wide and paths narrow. It is a common mistake to make a thin strip of border around the edge of a patch of lawn, but this only makes everything look meaner and pinched. Be generous. The smaller the garden, the more this is true and the more it should be filled, although lots of small plants and pots make a space cluttered whereas a few judiciously placed large ones always make a small space seem bigger.

Almost every garden can be subdivided in some way to make it seem bigger and have more substance and interest. Long thin gardens can be divided by hedges or walls to make two or three square spaces, each partially glimpsed and thus inviting you onwards rather than scanning the whole plot with one sweep of the eye.

A focal point will direct the gaze where you want it and provide a line of symmetry – even if the plot is asymmetrical. There are lots of ways of doing this. One of the simplest is to close off part of the garden with all but a gap. That gap then becomes the complete focus of attention. How you close it does not really matter – a hedge, wall, trellis, shrubs, bamboos, tall grasses, line of runner beans – the options are wide. But the effect is the same, like leaving an opened door into a room with a much more exciting and inviting glimpse as a result.

Simply framing a view can do the job. A pair of pots either side of a path will always be effective, especially if planted with a structural plant like topiary or small trees. If you lead the eye to a specific thing – a plant, chair or pot – then immediately you have created a whole new area of your garden, however small it may be.

Finally, accept that simplicity nearly always looks best. Choose a style and a palette and stick to it.

TREES

Trees can be bought and planted in all shapes and sizes and at all stages of their growth. Yes, there are giant oaks, chestnuts and beech, and anyone with even one of these in their garden is blessed, but there are also tiny yet exquisite Japanese maples growing all their lives in a pot and slender fastigiate trees with upright growth, both deciduous and evergreen, that are especially useful in a smaller garden that cannot accommodate the full canopy of a large spreading tree. Hawthorns, magnolias and crab apples have all the charm and presence of a large, mature tree and yet never grow very large.

Trees can weep, spread sideways, have a dense tangle of branches or be pruned to perfect spare shapes where the spaces between branches sculpt the air. Trees can be pleached and coppiced, espaliered or cordoned and, if you have the space, left to grow gloriously as they wish to be. Trees can flower and carry edible fruit or nuts or decorative berries. Trees can have rich autumn colour or sparkling new spring foliage. Trees can drop their leaves each year, providing an electric green energy as they regrow in spring, or be evergreen and create winter structure when the rest of the garden is stripped back to the frozen bone.

In short, there is a tree for every garden and every person.

Unless you are extremely rich or extremely impatient it always makes sense to plant trees small. My basic rule is that bare-root trees should be small enough to be lifted by one strong person, and trees in containers should be able to be carried by two people. In fact, I could lift and carry most of the trees in my garden with one hand when I planted them and some are now 45ft/15m tall with trunks as thick as a barrel.

Do not be put off by the seemingly inhuman timescale of tree growth. Yes, an oak may take 300 years to reach full maturity and there are yews growing a few miles from my own garden that are reckoned to be 3,000 years old, but half the pleasure of planting any tree is seeing it grow rather than waiting for it to become a 'proper' tree. All gardening is fundamentally about growing things, nurturing them and sharing their slow evolution into maturity.

When choosing a tree, it can seem that the choice is bewildering. But as with all plants, you can make the process of selection simpler and more effective. Look around your immediate neighbourhood and see if there are any trees that you particularly like the look of and which seem to be growing healthily (and if they look healthy they almost certainly are healthy). This will inform you what is best adapted for your soil and area and therefore what will thrive in your own garden.

TRAINING TREES

Many trees can be pruned and trained to grow laterally in two dimensions. The process of training a decorative tree, such as lime or hornbeam, in tiers is known as pleaching. Limes are ideal for pleaching because they grow fast and respond robustly to pruning. The new stems of limes have especially vibrant bark that glows in winter sunshine and then is easy to cut and train.

Fruit trees trained in parallel tiers are known as espaliers and are particularly good for apples and pears, although I have seen espalier gooseberries and even rosemary.

Whereas espaliers can begin their side shoots just above ground level, pleached trees are invariably grown on a trunk, usually about 6ft/1.8m high. This makes an excellent 'hedge on stilts' and visual barrier as well as wind break – and I think looks really good. The process of training is fun too.

METHOD

1. You will need to construct a supporting framework. Metal posts set in concrete and parallel rows of wires on tensioners is the long-term ideal but I have always used wooden posts reaching to the height of the top row and bean sticks or bamboos tied in as the horizontal support. Leave 24in/60cm between each tier.

2. Trees should be planted against each post and secured to them. They should not be pruned for the first year. Pruning is best done in January or February, when all the leaves have fallen and the tree is dormant.

3. The first thing is to reduce all shoots growing at right angles to the line of the pleaching, cutting right back to the trunk.

4. Then cut back all vertical shoots, leaving 1 to 2 inches of growth with a few healthy buds. Be aware that the final vertical shoot at the end of a branch might be suitable for bending down and tying into position to complete the horizontal growth.

YOU WILL NEED

Strong 8ft/2.4m posts

Lateral support (wire, bamboo canes or straight bean sticks)

2- to 3-year-old trees (limes are best, and do not be tempted to get them too big – it is easier to train new growth rather than try to bend existing branches to fit the support)

Plenty of strong twine

Secateurs

5. All that should be left are the horizontal shoots between each tree. Do not be tempted to have multiple side shoots. I have to be absolutely ruthless and cut away everything other than the 3 or 4 chosen lateral branches which, through lack of competition, will grow very quickly.

6. Tie-in the permanent lateral branches. I use tarred twine and tie every 6in/15cm or so, so they are absolutely secure.

7. Always train upwards if possible, as bending or training a branch down will restrict its growth. By the same token, when training a branch laterally, leave the final 6in/15cm growing upwards to encourage it to grow fast. When it has reached its eventual length (which in theory is half the distance between two trees, although in practice one side may grow more strongly than the other) then it can be pruned to length and tied firmly into place.

8. This harsh pruning stimulates vigorous new growth and by April it is sprouting new leaves from each knobbly cut, followed in May by the new stems.

PLANTING A TREE

Whatever type of tree you choose, you should give it the best possible start by planting it with care.

Do not plant into very wet ground or ground that is frozen. If it is a deciduous tree then the best time to plant is when it is dormant, between the middle of October and the middle of February – although climate change means that an earlier planting is likely to give a tree a better chance of establishing rather than one in late winter. Evergreen trees are best planted in September or April.

Unless you want an instant effect with a new tree it is always best to plant them small. Smaller specimens always establish much quicker than bigger ones and are much cheaper.

METHOD

1. Dig a wide hole at least twice the spread of the roots or use a container just deep enough to cover the roots. If it is a bare-root tree (see page 340), soak it for at least half an hour and leave it in water right up to the moment of planting.

2. Loosen the bottom and sides of the hole with a fork to break any compaction and improve drainage. Do not add any compost or manure at this stage as the quicker the roots adapt to the soil and grow out away from the planting hole, the better.

3. Place the tree in the hole and if it is bare root, spread the roots so that the base of the trunk is an inch or so above soil level. Try not to plant too deeply as this can rot the trunk – make sure the first set of roots are just below the surface of the soil. If you are planting in a container, don't plant any deeper than the level of the compost.

4. Holding the tree in position, gradually add soil to cover the roots. Firm the soil with your heel so that the soil forms a slight cone with the tree at its centre. In all events avoid planting into a shallow compacted saucer as this can become too wet and weaken and rot the roots.

5. In principle, trees grown without a supporting stake are better able to resist wind damage but all bare-root trees more than 3ft/1m tall, or a pot-grown one that is more than 6ft/2m tall and therefore top-heavy, will need staking, especially if it is in an exposed position.

6. Bang a stake in at 45 degrees to the trunk, with the stake angled directly into the prevailing wind. Tie the tree to the stake with a tree tie so that the trunk does not rub against the stake. Remove the stake after 3 years, as by then the roots should have formed a sufficient anchor, and the sooner the stake is removed, the quicker the tree will adapt to wind.

7. Once planted, water your tree very thoroughly. When the water has fully drained, add a mulch of compost or bark chips. This will stop evaporation and work into the top 6in/15cm of soil, which is where most of any tree's feeding roots are.

8. For the first year, give it a soak regularly. This means weekly if the weather is dry and at least once a month. Top up the mulch every spring and keep it weed-free.

YOU WILL NEED

A spade

Fork

Tree stake (if needed)

Tree tie

Water

Compost or bark for mulching

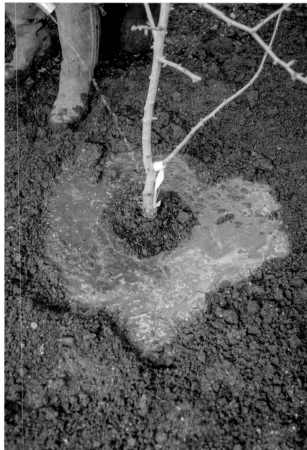

ACER IN A CONTAINER

Our perception of trees is hugely influenced by context. Knowing that the roots of a large oak or beech spread at least as wide as the canopy under the ground and have established an almost mystical symbiotic relationship with the soil via its fungi and bacteria is part of their mystique. Yet certain trees almost seem more like themselves in a pot. Think of olive, citrus, bay or cherry. All fulfil themselves in a pot and serve the gardener well. And in lieu of more space or soil, any tree in a pot is certainly better than no tree.

In fact, some trees look best in a pot, not least because they grow very slowly or never get very big. Acers, also known as Japanese maples, have an almost bonsai quality to them, and a beautiful pot is part of their attraction.

METHOD

1. Because a tree will last for years, it is worth taking some trouble in getting the growing environment as good as you can.

2. Acers hate sitting in wet soil so the compost has to be light and open. When you hold it, it should fall apart in your hand. A compost made from crushed pine bark mixed with grit or perlite and ideally some leaf mould would be perfect.

3. Be generous with the crocks and then put in a good layer of the compost. Sit the plant's roots on it so that the soil level of the plant is about 1in/3cm below the rim of the pot.

4. Holding it upright with one hand, steadily fill around the roots with the rest of the potting mix, pushing it down and around the roots with your fingers so that there are no air pockets and the tree is firm in the pot.

5. Water it well. The water should quickly run through the pot and out the bottom. Sitting the pot up on small chocks will reduce the risk of overwatering.

6. Acers hate deep shade so place the pot where it is in dappled shade with some sunshine and protected from strong wind.

7. Do not feed unless the plant looks tired, and then a foliar spray of liquid seaweed is best. Do this in the evening to avoid the leaves burning. In the main, there is more damage to be caused by overfeeding than underfeeding.

8. In very cold weather wrap the pot and the plant in horticultural fleece.

YOU WILL NEED

Japanese maple of choice, such as an Acer palmatum hybrid

Tree stake (if needed)

Bark-based potting compost

Grit or perlite

Leaf mould (if you have it)

A generous pot with good drainage holes. The pot should not be more than twice the size of the container that the tree is already growing in. A rim of about 4 to 6in/10 to 15cm of compost around the perimeter of the existing roots is ideal. Plastic is not suitable as it gets too hot in summer and too cold in winter.

Crocks

Water

Chocks to raise the bottom of the pot

Foliar spray

Liquid seaweed

Horticultural fleece

HEDGES

I love hedges. At their best they are magnificent living sculptures and at their worst, even the scruffiest, most uninspired hedge provides ideal nesting and cover for birds, insects and small mammals. Be they low, tall, narrow, wide, evergreen, deciduous, tightly clipped or loose and baggy, hedges are often the best thing in any garden.

I have always thought it significant that the word 'garden' derives from the Saxon word that simultaneously means an enclosure, yard or hedge. The whole psychology of creating domestic spaces is integrally bound with hedges, and whilst there are fascinating and beautiful completely unenclosed 'prairie' gardens, there are many more where hedges play an integral and sublime role.

Perhaps the most creative aspect of good hedges is related to what the Japanese call 'Ma'. This is an awareness of and manipulation of the beauty and significance of the space between things – and hedges can do this brilliantly well in any garden. Not only do they create garden 'rooms' but they also lead the eye by exact sizing of the width of an opening in a hedge or the height of a hedge in relation to the trees or border plants near it. This is an abstract but powerful design influence.

Hedges are always related to human proportions. The most important measurement in any garden is the height of the people that use it. Everything else relates back to this. So a hedge that is taller than you creates an enclosed space even though there are miles of sky above. I think that hedge height is critical and often got wrong. It must be proportionate to the space that it is creating and to what you want the eye to do. In other words it is a vital aesthetic decision, down to the last inch. As a rule it is better to be too high than too low as, counterintuitive as it might seem, height makes all spaces seem bigger, whereas a hedge that is squat and scant diminishes everything around it. Think how a small room seems so much more spacious if it has a high ceiling.

Walls can do this but walls do not have the volume of a hedge or the adaptability to swoop, curve or billow with elegance – let alone explode with a flurry of sparrows as you pass. A hedge, for all its fresh-cut crispness, retains the anarchy of growth and change which is the pulse beneath the surface of even the most rigidly controlled garden.

Hedges are extremely practical too. They baffle the wind far better than any fence or wall, filtering and sluicing it through its mesh of branches, and they create microclimates that can transform the range of plants that a garden can contain. Their shade is usually benign and protective and, not least, they provide the privacy that every garden must have if it is to be fully enjoyed.

CUTTING HEDGES

Hedges want to be a row of trees, and hedge trimming is just another form of pruning. It obeys the seasonal rules of pruning so that cutting in summer restricts vertical growth but encourages lateral shoots, making the hedge denser. Cutting in winter, when the leaves have all fallen, will encourage strong vertical growth from lower down, filling gaps. This will work even if it means cutting a deciduous hedge right to the ground.

It follows that if you have a healthy, thick hedge, the best time to cut it is after the birds have finished nesting in August. If you have a hedge that is gappy or thin, leave it till winter and then cut it back harder.

Hedges do not have to be four-square. A cloud hedge looks great, and hedges can just as easily snake and bend as march in a straight line. As a rule most hedges are too low. Just as a high ceiling tends to improve the proportions of a room, so high hedges make a garden seem bigger.

METHOD

1. Straight-sided hedges (as opposed to rounded ones) are best, with sides that gently slope, so that the base is wider than the top. This is called a batter. If you cut the sides dead straight then the top of the hedge, which always gets more light and therefore grows strongest, will shade out the bottom. Once this starts to happen, it gets progressively worse, but a slight batter lets light get at the bottom half of the hedge. This in turn means that it maintains its thickness and density right to the ground.

2. Start from the bottom and trim the sides hard, following the gentle slope up to the top. Leave the top uncut until it has reached the height you want to keep it at and then trim it off. To establish a dead straight line you can use bamboo canes with string levelled with a spirit level, but once the hedge is established it is easy to do by eye.

3. Try and keep young hedges narrow – this will create a core of thick growth. The more you trim the sides of a young hedge, the denser it will grow.

4. Established hedges have a tendency to gradually get wider with the inside of the hedge bare, so cut hard and every few years give a winter prune as well as a summer one to reestablish good density.

5. Summer hedge prunings, which are soft and leafy, can be mown and added to the compost heap. Winter ones are best shredded or burnt.

6. Evergreen hedges, such as yew, should be cut in late summer or early autumn to stay crisp through to the following summer. Some hedges such as privet, box and hawthorn will need cutting 2 or even 3 times a year to stay trim, but be mindful of disturbing nesting birds.

YOU WILL NEED

Sharp shears (Japanese are best)

Battery-operated hedgecutter

Rake

Barrow or trug

PLANTING A HEDGE

When planting any hedge it is important to remember that you are effectively planting a line of trees that could live for hundreds of years. This means that any preparation before planting will be a small investment for such longevity, by encouraging a large, wide root network.

Also remember that most hedges grow to at least 3ft/1m wide, however hard you cut them back each year. So allow room for the incongruously small plants to grow – which they will do surprisingly quickly.

It will take a few years for your hedge to look like its proper self, but the best thing you can do for hedging plants to grow fast and strong is to plant them well, so they have the best possible start in life.

Deciduous hedges should ideally be planted between the middle of October and Christmas, but certainly by the end of February. Evergreen hedges are best planted in April in colder areas and September in a mild, sheltered garden. As with most planting, avoid waterlogged or frozen soils.

METHOD

1. Dig the site of the hedge, removing all weeds and large stones. This is essential, as once perennial weeds are growing within the roots of the hedge, they can never be removed.

2. If you have bare-root plants give them a soak before planting and do not expose them to the air, which will dry the tiny feeding roots very quickly. Keep them in water, lifting each one when ready to plant.

3. Use a board or a string line and dig a trench to the depth of a spade and at least 1.5ft/.5m wide. Using a fork, break up the bottom of the trench, removing any compaction to make it easier for the roots to grow and improve drainage. Do not add compost or manure at this stage.

4. Dust the wet roots with a sprinkle of mycorrhizal powder to encourage better uptake of nutrients in the early stages of the hedges' growth. This helps but is not essential.

5. Place the plants at regular intervals of about 10in/25cm for hawthorn or box, 12 to 16in/30 to 40cm for hornbeam and beech and at least 24in/60cm for yew. Do not be tempted to plant closer than this, as the wider they are spaced, the stronger each plant will grow.

6. Plant deep enough to cover the roots but do not bury the stem. If anything, the base of the stem should sit on a shallow ridge – this is particularly true if you have very heavy soil.

7. Back fill the soil carefully, firming in the roots with your feet.

8. Water them in thoroughly, which will settle the soil firmly around the roots. Then mulch generously. Garden compost is ideal but bark mulch will do almost as good a job. Top this up for at least the first 3 years – mulch makes a huge difference to a hedge's growth in its first 5 years or so as it keeps the water in and weeds out. Keep your hedge well watered in dry weather for at least the first year.

YOU WILL NEED

Spade

Fork

Hedging plants, preferably small – 12 to 18in/30 to 45cm is ideal

Mycorrhizal powder (not essential)

Water

Compost or bark for mulching

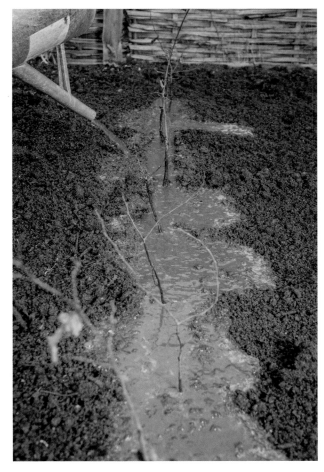

TOPIARY

Topiary can be formal and symmetrical, with cones, balls and pyramids, flowingly artistic as in Japanese Niwaki and cloud pruning, fun and kitsch – think topiary teddy bears and Disney characters – or a combination of all of these things, as exemplified by the wonderful Levens Hall in Cumbria.

But whatever your taste, topiary can be stylish, fun and surprisingly straightforward to create and maintain. Once grown, it gives maximum effect for minimum work.

Almost any woody plant can be topiarised although evergreen trees and shrubs are typically used. I use mainly yew and box, although box blight and box moth are making it increasingly unusable. If you are using box, it will need clipping twice a year, in June and September. Holly makes basic shapes well and privet is good but will need cutting at least three times a year. Phillyrea latifolia is a highly recommended alternative to box. I cut all my yew topiary once a year in August or September and this keeps it crisp through to the following May.

To get the best topiary from any plant it needs plenty of light. The less light it has, the thinner and less dense its growth.

Start as you mean to continue. Small shoots in the right place quickly become bigger, but a shoot in the wrong place, however healthy, will always be wrong.

Don't be frightened of cutting back hard. Gaps can be filled and mistakes rectified. Everything will regrow, and as with all pruning, the harder you cut back, the more vigorous the regrowth.

METHOD

1. Topiary is best created by training and growing a plant to a desired shape and then clipping it to hold it there, rather than 'finding' the shape in an overgrown bush, so always start with a strong, healthy plant that will grow well rather than one that already looks a little like the final object.

2. Remember that all vertical growth is much stronger than horizontal growth and tends to shade shoots below it. So all but the most established and biggest topiary should be wider at the base than the top.

3. The rules of pruning always apply: namely that cutting back hard will stimulate vigorous bushy growth and that leaving a leader (see page 340) will repress the growth beneath it.

4. Spread a sheet or tarpaulin under the bush to catch the clippings before starting, as this makes tidying up much easier.

5. If you are making a figurative shape of any kind, start training branches whilst they are still green and pliable by tying them to canes laterally or diagonally. Alternatively, but much more expensively, buy or make a 'former' or wire outline of the desired shape which the plant will grow through and which provides the skeleton to prune back to.

YOU WILL NEED

Sheet/tarpaulin to catch clippings

Battery-operated hedge trimmer

Sharp shears (Japanese are best and a joy to use)

Secateurs or hand clippers

Bamboo canes

Strong twine (NOT wire)

Rake

6. I have found that a lightweight battery-operated hedge trimmer or very sharp shears are best. I then follow this up with secateurs or clippers to remove any (inevitable) overlooked growth. Whatever you use should be light and comfortable so you can concentrate on what you are doing rather than how you are doing it.

7. Start at the top and work in long fluid lines, following the curves of the piece. Go all over it once roughly, stand back and have a good look, and then go over it again to get the details right.

8. Growth is likely to be uneven for the first few years, so when making any kind of complicated shape remember not to get carried away with cutting, in case you forget to leave growing shoots where appropriate to create the necessary growth to cut into in a year or two.

LAWNS

I cannot say that I share the need for a perfect lawn. If an area of grass is green and pleasant to sit or lie on, then it is good enough, and I do not object to the presence of a few daisies, dandelions or some moss.

An expanse of green will harmoniously link any of the colours that border it. Lawns make the perfect balance between the business of borders, trees and hedges.

The secret of a good-enough lawn is to put your time and energy into creating healthy grass rather than fighting all the perceived 'problems' like daisies, moss, ants, worm casts, moles, plantains, dandelions and fairy rings. Nine times out of ten if the grass is healthy then everything else will look after itself. Certainly there is never any need to use chemicals of any kind.

The best grass likes lots of water, lots of sunshine and very well drained soil. Moss, for example, is always a symptom of poor drainage, made worse by shade. Unfortunately even the best-prepared soil becomes compacted by matted roots and footfall. Even little feet running about on grass will compact it, let alone bikes, games of football and heavy boots pushing wheelbarrows. So regular aeration to reduce compaction and improve drainage is essential.

In northern Europe it is never necessary to water a lawn other than when it is first sown or laid as turf. However dry and badly burnt it looks, an established lawn will always recover.

When it comes to mowing, the most harm that you can do is to cut your lawn too short. The grass will be a lot healthier if allowed to grow to at least 1in/1 to 3cm and preferably a bit longer. Also, do not take too much off in one go. A light trim that evens the grasses to the same length will make a dramatic difference – and be much quicker than a less frequent scalping. If you do cut lightly, a mulching mower works well and saves the need for collection and will return organic material back into the soil.

I know that many people find grass cuttings a problem rather than a useful addition to the compost heap. Left in a heap they will quickly turn into a foul-smelling brown sludge that has no resemblance to sweet-smelling compost. This is because they have a very high ratio of nitrogen to carbon (about 50:50), and good compost needs to have the balance strongly in favour of carbon. This can easily be altered by mixing the mown grass with dried stems or other drier garden waste, crumpled-up brown cardboard, leaves or straw. The important thing is to mix all this up thoroughly rather than building a heap in layers. This lets more air in and stops wedges of wet grass accumulating. Do this and the mown grass becomes a positive benefit rather than a problem.

AUTUMN LAWN CARE

Every lawn, however carefully tended, enters autumn worn and compacted. Increasingly climate change means that a summer lawn is starved of water too. But however bad it looks by the end of summer, a little autumnal care will restore it to full health for next year.

METHOD

1. Start by raking your lawn with a spring-tine wire rake. This is quite hard work but will remove a surprising amount of thatch and moss, which can be put on the compost heap. Thatch consists of dead grasses, which is completely natural, and moss and other debris caught in the lawn. Moss is always a sign of poor drainage, usually combined with shade. Thatch can build up and prevent water from getting to grass roots so it's good to get it out. Do not worry about opening up bare patches – if larger than a dinner plate, a little grass seed can be sprinkled on, but otherwise patches will infill naturally.

2. For moss to thrive it must have two of the following three conditions: poor drainage, shade and water. For grass to thrive it must have good drainage, sun and water. Almost every lawn suffers from poor drainage by the end of summer as a result of compaction caused by ordinary foot traffic. The easiest way to deal with this is to aerate it.

3. If your lawn is reasonably small, a fork will do the trick perfectly well. Thrust it in as deep as possible every 9 to 12in/22 to 30cm. The more you wiggle the tines about, the better the drainage will be.

4. For a larger lawn, you can hire aerating machines that remove small plugs of soil. When you have finished, brush these plugs or loose soil across the surface to disperse them, and you may also like to brush in some sharp sand which will help improve drainage.

5. Don't worry if the lawn looks like a disaster zone after this treatment – it will quickly recover in time to face whatever winter can offer and start next spring in the best possible condition.

YOU WILL NEED

A wire rake

Garden fork

Sharp sand

Grass seed (if you have large bare patches)

WILDLIFE

WILDLIFE

There is much talk nowadays about 'rewilding', but this has come to mean a sliding scale, from the long-term experiment instigated in the Netherlands by the ecologist Frans Vera to observing what happens when we do not intervene at all, to patches of long grass or a few brambles on a roundabout. But what is not in dispute is that a healthy, sustainable garden depends upon a rich and varied ecosystem that is nurtured by the gardener.

The endlessly fascinating element of this is to create a haven for wildlife whilst also creating and maintaining a beautiful and productive garden – and it can most certainly be done!

The first thing is to avoid all chemicals – all pesticides, fungicides or herbicides. Not only are they indiscriminately harmful and long-lasting, they are also usually ineffective and ridiculously expensive.

There are three essential elements that any garden, however big or small, can introduce that will create the best environment for the full chain of life from bacteria to apex predators.

The first is to have some water, preferably as a pond, with plants both in and around the water. But even a very small pond will bring in dragonflies, frogs and toads, increased bird and bat activity and potentially grass snakes, and provide a drinking place for mammals such as hedgehogs.

Some long grass is also essential. This provides cover for insects but also small mammals, invertebrates and reptiles. Ideally you will have grass of varying lengths to provide a wide range of habitats, but 10.75 square feet/1 square metre of long grass will make all the difference.

As well as grass, the most active predatory insects, such as lacewings, hoverflies, ladybirds and parasitic wasps – which will keep damaging insects under control far better than any insecticide – can be encouraged by planting a few essentials such as dill, angelica, marigolds, calendula and cosmos. All are good and potentially beautiful plants that can be enjoyed by you as much as them.

You must also have plants that provide pollen and nectar to support butterflies and pollinating insects such as honeybees. Some of these are the same for lacewings and hoverflies, but essentially the secret is to have a range of plants with a range of flower shapes for as long as possible throughout the year, rather than one tremendous display in the summer months.

After the indiscriminate use of pesticides, nothing is more detrimental to wildlife than officious tidiness. Leave fallen leaves, windfall fruit, rotting wood, piles of twigs, patches of weeds, perennials overwintering in the border, grass growing in the cracks, moss on the stone. These are all important habitats and there is no reason why they cannot be gently tweaked to look beautiful as well as be useful.

MAKING A
WILDLIFE POND

Choose a site that gets direct sunlight for at least half the day. Try and avoid any overhanging trees if possible and allow room around the pond for future planting.

Do not worry if you only have enough space for a small pond; a pond 3 feet/1 metre in diameter will enrich your garden with wildlife almost as well as one five times as big. However, even a small hole takes quite a few barrowloads of soil to excavate, so plan what you will do with the waste soil – ideally incorporate it into the garden.

METHOD

1. Mark out the pond using string and canes, or a hosepipe. Allow for marginal plants by including shallow shelves around the perimeter. Aquatic plants such as water lilies need deeper water, so aim to include a section that is at least 3ft/1m deep.

2. Check that the edges are all level. Use a spirit level and be exact because water will instantly expose any inaccuracy. If the site is sloping then you will have to build up one side. Avoid steep slopes falling down into or away from the edge of the pond.

3. When you are satisfied with the shape and size, remove any stones or roots and then firm and smooth the soil. If you are using a rigid liner this can then be fitted into the hole and the soil backfilled around the edges. If you are using a flexible liner, line the surface of the soil with a geotextile underlay or carpeting underfelt. Whatever you use, the purpose is the same: to protect the lining from being punctured.

4. Calculate the size of the liner needed by measuring the longest distances along the length and breadth of the pond and add twice the maximum depth for both measurements. So a pond 10 feet x 6 feet/3m x 1.8m at its widest points and 2.75 feet/0.8m at its deepest will need a liner at least 15 feet x 11 feet/4.6m x 3.4m. Invest in the thickest, best-quality liner you can afford. They are expensive but last a long time, and replacing a cheap liner is an expensive and messy business.

5. Open the liner out and leave it in the sun for an hour. This will soften it up and make it easier to fit. Stretch it gently over the pool and let it ease itself into all the contours, gathering folds where possible to avoid creases. Do not start to fill it until you are happy that it has as few wrinkles as possible. Weigh down the excess liner securely with bricks or stones.

6. Fill up with water, pulling any creases free. The water will stretch the liner as it fills, ensuring a tight fit.

7. Finally, trim the liner, leaving at least 20in/50cm free all the way round, and then add stones, soil and plants to hide the liner and create a natural-looking pond.

YOU WILL NEED

Spade

Wheelbarrow

Spirit level

Wooden pegs (baton)

Club hammer

Geotextile lining or carpeting underfelt

Butyl or Epalyn liner

Bricks or stone to weigh down liner

Hose

MARGINAL PLANTS IN A POND

Marginal plants provide the link between water and earth that is visually pleasing for people, and unbroken cover for wildlife around a pond's edge.

Most marginal plants are equally happy submerged in a few inches of water (but always with their roots on the bottom rather than floating), squelching around in a bog or even growing in the heavy soil of a damp border. The unifying factor is that they have all evolved to have their roots in wet soil, but most will survive for months out of the water as long as they do not dry out completely.

These include some beautiful plants and give great scope to seamlessly integrate the planting of a pond with its surroundings. Most ponds are lined and have a stone edging of some kind, and marginals are very good for hiding that join – and it should always be hidden if at all possible. Of course, if you have a pond lined with puddled clay then the marginals can stretch from dry land to permanent water in one seamless flow.

As well as looking good, marginal plants provide excellent cover and habitat both above ground and below the surface of the water for insects, smaller mammals and aquatic life.

METHOD

1. Marginal plants should be planted in aquatic baskets (essentially pots with mesh sides) and placed in shallow water so that the pot sits on the bottom but the surface is only just submerged. The roots will grow through the mesh and into the detritus that inevitably collects on top of the pond's liner.

2. Pond water has almost all the nutrients that plants need, so do not use ordinary potting compost. Not only is this unnecessary, it will also add too many nutrients to the water and encourage the growth of algae. You can buy aquatic compost, which is very sandy and heavy, from any garden centre. Ordinary garden soil that is not enriched with compost of any kind is also perfectly good.

3. Remember to use a large basket for tall plants like rushes or the flag iris, otherwise they become top-heavy and can blow over unless they are rooted directly into mud. In fact, in my experience the lovely yellow flag iris will almost certainly root itself and multiply quickly, so will need dividing every few years if it is not to become a thug.

YOU WILL NEED

Your selection of marginal plants

Aquatic planting baskets

Special aquatic potting compost or garden soil

RECOMMENDED MARGINAL PLANTS

Flowering rush	Arrowhead	Purple loosestrife
Sweet flag	Pickerel weed	Skunk cabbage
Club rush	Dotted loosestrife	Asian skunk cabbage
Umbrella papyrus	Japanese water iris	Marsh marigold
Corkscrew rush	Japanese iris	Water mint
Water plantain	Yellow flag iris	Water forget-me-not

LONG GRASS

Whilst a perfectly maintained striped lawn looks good, adds balance and harmony to planting, is ideal for children to play on and will always have a place in gardens, it is a desert for insects and thus for the chain of life that is linked inextricably to them.

There are ten times more species and fifty times more individuals in long grass than grass that is mown once a week. So if you want to encourage more insects into your garden then there is no better or easier way to do it than by simply not mowing your lawn. If you wish to officially make this into a 'wildflower' meadow then that can look as beautiful as any herbaceous border, but the flowers in it make very little difference to the quality or quantity of wildlife. Grass and the length of it is the key to a healthy and varied insect population.

This does not mean that you have to abandon all the virtues of a lawn, nor give all your garden over exclusively to encouraging wildlife. You can have long grass, encourage maximum wildlife and have a beautiful, well-kept garden.

The answer is simply to grow an area of long grass. It does not have to be big to make a significant impact to the quantity and diversity of the insect population of your garden. It could just be a patch 3 feet/1 metre square or a narrow strip at the edge of a mown area. I have let hitherto tightly mown areas grow long but have kept paths mown through them. I think this looks great and is practical both to keep a footfall from crushing the long grass and for walking and wheeling barrows around. Whatever suits your lifestyle and your space, some – any – long grass will make a difference.

However big the area, you must follow the seasonal cycle of a hay meadow. Do not cut the grass at all (other than paths) until the grasses have flowered and set seed, which will not be before the end of June.

Then cut the grass any time between July and September. Obviously this cannot be done with an ordinary lawnmower, but you can hire suitable equipment if it is a large area and just use a pair of shears for a smaller space.

You must then rake it all up and compost the mowings. If your compost bin is too small, just make a heap of the grass in a corner and let it quietly compost down – becoming another haven for insect life as it does so. If you fail to do this and leave grass clippings on the surface after cutting they will rot down and fertilise the grass, which results in the stronger coarser grasses like ryegrass dominating and taking over. For a healthy insect population, diversity is important, with as many different grasses growing as possible.

After this initial cut you can then mow the grass regularly just like a normal lawn until autumn or let it grow long again before giving it a second cut any time before Christmas.

TAMEFLOWER MEADOW

SOW: LATE SUMMER OR EARLY SPRING
FLOWER: SPRING TO SUMMER
MOW: LATE SUMMER TO LATE WINTER

This is not strictly speaking a wildflower meadow – although wildflowers will be part of it. It is grass with as many flowers as possible – wild and tame – added to it and encouraged to thrive in that grassy environment.

It takes years to make a flower-filled meadow – and many have endured for hundreds of years – but we have lost 98% of UK meadow sites since 1945 and with them all the incredible diversity of meadow plants such as buttercups, ox-eye daisies, knapweed and yellow rattle. These support a rich insect, butterfly and invertebrate ecosystem that in turn supports birds and mammals, as well as sequestering carbon as effectively as the rainforest.

However, the garden version – which has planted bulbs and herbaceous perennials mixed in with wild flower seed – looks wonderful and has all the benefits for wildlife within the very limited space of the average backyard. A patchwork of millions of tiny meadows in back gardens is both a beautiful idea and goes someway to repairing the ecological vandalism that modern agriculture has wrought.

It really does not matter if you convert your entire garden or make just a square metre or verge to a path. The benefit to insect life in particular, as well as the conservation of wild flower species, is immediate and long lasting.

METHOD

1. Cut the area you wish to develop as a meadow as short as possible. Scalp it so the blades are scraping soil. Then rake it vigorously with a wire rake to scratch out as much moss and grass as possible, exposing lots of bare soil. It will – it should – look terrible!

2. You are doing this because wildflower seeds need soil to germinate. At the same time almost all the grass you have so abused will recover and grow back.

3. It is essential to sow yellow rattle. This is an annual with a flower composed of pale yellow bells of petals hanging off a central stem. These then become translucent seed heads and as the seeds within mature, they dry and rattle in the wind – hence the name. But the really important thing about yellow rattle is that it is semi-parasitic on grass and will quite aggressively restrict its growth. So any area of grass that has yellow rattle growing in it will behave as though the soil has been impoverished and give more delicate flowers a chance to compete.

4. Then sow the chosen mix for your particular soil. You can buy online the right combination of grasses and flowers for damp soil, shade, clay, chalk, peat, mountain – almost any conceivable garden situation.

YOU WILL NEED

Mower (or shears if small area)

Wire rake

Yellow rattle seed

Wildflower mixture appropriate to your plot

Spring bulbs

Water

5. Tread or roll it in so that the seed is firmly in contact with the soil.

6. Water it and do not let it dry out completely.

7. Add any spring-flowering bulbs such as daffodils, tulips, fritillaries, camassias, alliums and crocuses. Perennials such as hardy geraniums, Japanese irises and knapweed can be planted into the grass.

8. Do not cut it until July and preferably August. Then, when you do, cut it as short as possible and gather up every last scrap of grass. It can then be mown as lawn until late autumn so it goes into winter short.

9. It will change every year and you may have to reseed the yellow rattle if the grass becomes too dominant. Some years will be better than others. But it will be constantly alive with insects and constantly fascinating and beautiful.

SPRING POLLINATOR CONTAINER

PLANT: EARLY SPRING OR AUTUMN
FLOWER: MARCH TO JUNE

Pollinating insect numbers are declining across the board. Hornets, earwigs, ladybirds and hoverflies are all down in number. If these do not sound like conventional pollinators then think again. Hornets – and wasps – pollinate as well as eat a huge amount of otherwise damaging insects. Earwigs don't exist just to nibble your dahlias but eat fruit aphids and move from flower to flower pollinating as they go. Ladybirds move from flower to flower in search of greenfly and gather and redistribute pollen on their travels. Hoverflies love all kinds of garden umbellifers (the carrot family of plants) but the 250 different British species are also really significant pollinators of wildflowers. There are around a thousand species of beetle in Britain that are important pollinators, especially of umbellifers, with open, flat flowers with a strong scent, as beetles are attracted primarily by scent.

Bees are just about holding their own, which, considering how much attention there has been over the past few years in promoting bee numbers, is not good enough. Honeybees tend to get the most and best press although arguably the solitary bees are just as important as pollinators. Of the 270 species of bee in the UK – including honeybees and bumblebees – over 250 are solitary species.

For pollinators such as honeybees, with short tongues, you need accessible flowers. These are best found in those that are broad and open, essentially from the daisy family, or clustered in small florets such as alliums (edible and ornamental onions), marjoram, clover or lavender. Bumblebees, with their longer tongues, love foxgloves, thistles, borage and broad beans.

There is a misconception that you need swathes of meadow or large flowering borders to attract pollinating insects, or at least sufficient numbers to make a significant difference. This is not the case. A modest container with a few plants chosen for their attraction to pollinators is effective, significant and fascinating.

METHOD

1. Put crocks in the bottom of the container, having first ensured it has good drainage holes, and half fill with compost.

2. Plant your largest plant – the barberry or hellebore – in the centre and fill around the root ball with compost.

3. Around the outside fit primroses, bugle and lungwort.

4. If you prepare this in autumn, add early crocus bulbs. Bees love the flowers when they appear in February.

5. Water well and place in a sunny spot.

6. When the flowers have finished in late spring the plants can be removed and planted into the garden. The container can then be reused for summer pollinator plants.

YOU WILL NEED

Crocks

A generous container or a number of smaller ones

Peat-free potting compost

Early-flowering plants such as wallflowers, primroses, bugle, hellebores, lungwort, barberry and crocus

Water

SUMMER POLLINATOR CONTAINER

PLANT: SPRING
FLOWER: EARLY SUMMER TO AUTUMN

There are two important considerations when choosing flowers specifically to attract pollinating insects.

The first is to have a range of plants, catering for different kinds of insects' lengths of tongue and feeding practices. Honeybees for example have very short tongues so need open, flat flowers whereas bumblebees have much longer tongues and can reach into trumpet-shaped blooms. Many insects such as wasps and lacewings are drawn to umbrella-shaped flower heads like carrot, dill or angelica, and butterflies love sedums. Insects such as wasps and lacewings are drawn to tightly packed groups of tiny flowers like those on verbena bonariensis, or like the big flat plates of flowers on dill or angelica, and butterflies love landing on sedum flower heads.

The second requirement is to have as extended a flowering season as possible. Rather than one brilliant display for a few weeks, try and have something flowering from early summer into autumn.

As with all displays in a container, it is a good idea to have a central plant that has height and heft – in this case lavender or nepeta, both of which are shrubs that insects adore – fillers like sedum and verbena and a spiller like the nasturtiums.

METHOD

1. Having first ensured it has good drainage holes, put crocks in the bottom of the container and half fill with the compost that has had grit mixed in to about one third of its volume. Drainage is important for the plants in this pot so the grit is essential.

2. Plant your largest plant – in this case the lavender or catmint – in the centre.

3. Add the sedum (which is brilliant for butterflies in late summer), some marigold plants and the verbena (also good for later in summer), and plant the nasturtium right on the edge so it can spill down outside the pot. Don't worry if there seems to be little room for the plants' roots to grow – these are plants that will be happy in cramped and limited conditions for the summer.

4. Finally, sprinkle California poppy seeds on any remaining bare compost.

5. Water well and put in the sunniest spot you have. The pot will need watering at least once a week.

YOU WILL NEED

A generous container or a number of smaller ones

Crocks

Peat-free potting compost

Grit

Plants such as sedum, marigolds, lavender or catmint, verbena bonariensis, nasturtium or thyme

California poppy seeds

Water

BUG HOTEL

I hate the word 'bug' to describe insects because it has pejorative associations, and in any event is designed to provide cover for a wide range of creatures including small mammals, woodlice, spiders and amphibians as well as insects. But it has stuck so I will stick with it.

The whole aim is to create a varied range of tunnels, nooks, crannies and crevices that are warm and safe for small creatures to over-winter in. Some will be actually hibernating whilst others will be protecting themselves from the worst of the weather. They need to be able to get in and out easily, without predators doing the same.

Whatever you use – and the point is to improvise – keep it varied. Ladybirds like straw or hay, lacewings like corrugated cardboard, toads and frogs will love the dark gaps under tiles whilst solitary bees like tunnels. You might even get a hedgehog to hibernate if you have an old flower pot or space beneath a pallet.

METHOD

1. A frame makes the hotel more resilient and easy to handle but you can assemble your materials as a free-standing pile. In this case, place in a sunny, undisturbed, dry corner so that it remains as warm and dry as possible during the winter months.

2. The framework does not have to be fixed. Old pallets are ideal because they are slatted but boards will work with bricks or blocks of wood as spacers to create tiers.

3. Divide the hotel into blocks of material or divided areas and fill each section with a different material. If you have logs, drill into them to create tunnels for nesting bees, stack twigs and sticks and hollow stems of plants like fennel or alliums. Ideally the stems will have one end closed but if they are completely hollow, bees will build their own back wall.

4. Stones and tiles at the centre of the hotel will provide the kind of cool, damp environment that toads and frogs need.

5. Bark, leaves and decaying wood are ideal for woodlice and beetles.

6. Toilet roll tubes stuffed with straw or grass are good for larger invertebrates, and thin stems make a safe haven for tiny insects. Vary the arrangement and have as much variety of size and texture as possible.

7. Fill every nook and cranny, and if it is within a fixed frame, hang it well up off the ground to stop disturbance or worse by visiting dogs, foxes or squirrels. If it is ground-based, make sure children, bikes, dogs or clumsy feet cannot knock into it and then leave well alone.

YOU WILL NEED

Any materials that will create a patchwork of spaces, including:

Hollow plant stems

Bamboo

Sticks

Corrugated cardboard

Logs

Fir cones

Straw

Roofing tiles

Drill plus different bit sizes

BUTTERFLIES & MOTHS

Butterflies are declining rapidly in the British countryside. Their habitats are destroyed, the numbers pitifully low, and another natural treasure is sacrificed at the altar of modern agriculture and food policy.

But although it may be too late to reclaim their natural habitats in arable farmland, gardens remain a rich and productive source of nectar for adult butterflies and foliage for their caterpillars.

You really do not need a big garden to encourage butterflies, and even a very small plot can enjoy their beautiful, gentle embellishment with a few judiciously chosen plants. To encourage butterflies into your garden, plant blocks of flower so they can feed without having to travel too far, and plant flowers of similar heights together as butterflies have difficulty landing on flowers with taller plants in front of them. Deadhead favourites like buddleja regularly, to keep flowering prolonged. Do not use any pesticides or insecticides. They kill butterflies – along with many vital pollinating insects.

Above all, butterflies like hedgerows and wild flowers that are rich in nectar, and plants such as buddleja, honeysuckle, sedums, lavender, michaelmas daisy, and valerian are heavily dependent on butterflies for pollination.

If you have a privet hedge, leave part of it untrimmed so that it will flower – butterflies love it. Orange tips particularly like honesty which is one of my favourite spring flowers. Butterflies also love feeding on overripe juicy fruit, so leave fallen plums and pears on the ground in late summer and autumn, after wasps have finished their feeding.

Butterflies are easy to love, wafting through the garden like flying flowers. They are beautiful and precious but moths are essential. There are only fifty-nine species of butterfly in Britain, but there are over 2,600 species of British moth and they are hugely important pollinators. Amongst other garden plants, they will be especially attracted to campions, pinks, sweet william, evening primrose, honeysuckles, tobacco plants and knapweeds.

The size and shape of moths is much more varied than that of butterflies. Some are dramatically large like the hawkmoths, whereas others are so tiny that they look like flies.

But in fact the difference between butterflies and moths is surprisingly superficial. Butterflies all fly by day and tend to be brightly coloured and rest with their wings pressed behind their backs whereas moths have plump, hairy bodies and wrap their wings around them. But both lay eggs that hatch into caterpillars, which having fed and changed skins several times, pupate into a chrysalis from which the adult duly emerges.

Although their caterpillars can munch through a huge amount of foliage, moths perform a really useful role in pollinating certain groups of flowers that have evolved to attract insects at night, when the competition from other plants is radically reduced. So night-scented plants such as jasmine, honeysuckle, evening primrose and night-scented stock depend upon moths, and you should include some in your garden to increase the richness of insect life – as well as to give a huge amount of pleasure to the gardener.

BIRDS

The number and diversity of birds in your garden is as good a measure of its health as anything else. If a garden can attract and support lots of bird life, it must also be rich in the insects and seeds that they need to sustain them, which in turn implies a rich and varied ecology in your own backyard.

Every bird, from the blood-hungry peregrine to the insect-consuming tiny goldcrest, must have food to eat. The more available it is, the more birds you will have. So do nothing to interrupt or block the food chain. Remember that every predator needs prey, so greenfly might be attacking your roses but they are also essential for blue tits. Slugs and snails are a nuisance but without any in your garden you will have fewer song thrushes. Caterpillars might seem to be preparing to munch their way through your entire garden but a single family of nesting blue tits will devour up to a thousand caterpillars a day.

There is certainly never a good reason to use pesticides in any garden, and I would add to that herbicides and fungicides too. The richer and more varied your ecosystem, the better the range of creatures you will have right up the chain, including birds.

Tidiness is anathema to healthy wildlife and especially birds. Keep weeds, seeds, berries and nuts so birds can feed off them. Rotten wood and bark is perfect for a host of insect food for many birds, and piles of wood and leaves are essential. The kind of immaculate front garden with its bare winter soil ready for ordered rows of annuals in spring, its concrete paths sprayed with weedkiller and hedges clipped within an inch of their lives is a bird desert. By all means have your winter hedges trimmed tightly and neatly but do not cut them at all between February and August when birds are breeding. Birds also love scratching mulch and leaf litter – so leave it there for them to find their food.

A garden for birds must have cover. It is astonishing how much birdlife will be added to a small garden by the presence of a selection of deciduous and evergreen shrubs, a hedge or two and a small tree. This will provide nesting places, singing posts and protection from predators. Any hedge is good but deciduous ones are probably best, with hawthorn, beech and hornbeam ideal. Whilst hedges and trees provide the best nesting situations for all birds, bird boxes will help and are essential in a new garden.

There has to be some tolerance and a little horticultural compromise. Birds eat ripening fruit and vegetables, scratch up carefully spread mulch and nip the buds of some spring-flowering plants. Some birds are easier to love than others. But encourage as many birds as you can, of all kinds, into your garden. Everyone and everything, including you, will benefit enormously.

FEEDING BIRDS

I love watching the birds feed at the table outside our kitchen window. They are incredibly beautiful, absolutely fascinating and give me a real sense of contributing to the health of the whole ecosystem of the garden.

Winter is a much better time to see garden birds than summer because there is so much less foliage for them to hide amongst. The short days also mean that the birds are busier seeking out their food, whether in the soil, amongst the seed heads of your borders or on a bird table. Watching them at work is one of the great pleasures of the winter garden.

Although I do not feed birds in summer, starting in mid-October and continuing to mid-April, it is important to be as regular as possible with the supply once you do start, topping up daily, as the birds use up precious energy in coming to your bird table which is then wasted if it is bare. Also, keep a shallow dish of fresh drinking water, which they can also use to bathe in.

Put your bird table well out of reach of cats and dogs. Hanging mesh containers for nuts, fat and seeds will stop squirrels taking too much. Feed first thing in the morning and never leave any food lying around overnight on a table or the ground, as that will attract rats.

Occasionally a sparrowhawk will swoop in and take a sparrow or blackbird at the feeding station – but all birds, of all kinds, must be fed.

METHOD

1. Avoid any premixed seed mixes because they are often mainly composed of grain, which attracts pigeons, starlings and sparrows at the expense of other birds – many of whom will not eat grain.

2. Seeds, nuts and fat are best of all. Sunflower hearts (white) are best and better than the unhulled seeds (black). Peanuts (whole and crushed) are always good and fat balls or fat slabs are superb but will need a wire container to keep squirrels, rats and dogs at bay. Mealworms are high in protein and energy and much loved by blackbirds.

3. Leftover pastry, bread and rice always get eaten fast, and fruit is good, especially for blackbirds and thrushes. Grated cheese is popular, as well as cooked (but not raw) potatoes.

4. Avoid anything salty such as crisps, salted peanuts or bacon. I buy dried mealworms too, which robins, tits and wrens gobble up greedily. If in doubt, go for sunflower seeds and fat balls – preferably hanging so tits can land on them without being bullied away by more aggressive birds – which are invariably popular.

5. I find that an old log with lots of cracks and crevices means that smaller birds can extract every last bit of seed from the fissures that bigger, more thuggish ones like pigeons and starlings cannot reach.

YOU WILL NEED

Sunflower hearts

Peanuts

Fat balls

Mealworms

Hanging containers for peanuts and fat balls

Shallow container for drinking and bathing water

Water

Small seed

HOUSEPLANTS

HOUSEPLANTS

We know that houseplants improve our mental and physical well-being. In a strange way, plants effectively humanise an otherwise rather dull room.

There is also no need to be competitive about the rarity or difficulty of any particular plant. The most common and indestructible plant can be equally effective in enhancing our well-being and give just as much pleasure as one that is rare and takes great skill and experience to grow.

The pandemic increased this trend as, confined to their homes, people were desperate for greenery and the simple relationship with living plants. I confess that I have been a very late adopter to houseplants, only coming to appreciate them in the past few years. However I now get huge pleasure from them, both in the house and the greenhouse where succulents and cacti can get the bright year-round light they like best, combined with protection from the cold and especially the rain.

However well lit, no room is ever as bright as outside so plants that need good light should have as much of it as you can possibly give them. By the same token you can use the way that light falls noticeably as you move away from a window by placing shade-loving plants in the middle of a room, even if it is superficially well lit by windows.

All houseplants, regardless of their vast range and diversity, will share certain healthy characteristics, and you should be watchful for these. Leaves of any kind should not wilt. (Wilting may be due to water shortage but it may also be indicative of root damage.) Very few leaves should have spots or streaks, especially if accompanied by poor structure. Most pests will appear on the undersides of leaves first so check these regularly, even if there is nothing immediately apparent on the upper surfaces.

Every now and then take the plant out of its pot and check the roots and compost for any pests or root damage. If in the process you notice the roots are tightly wound around and compacted then it is time to repot.

Overwatering is the most common cause of death in houseplants. When you buy any plant give it a good drink by soaking in a sink for ten minutes, then let it drain completely. Thereafter avoid overwatering, particularly in winter when it is not actively growing. Once a week is almost always enough and less in winter. However, humidity is important at all times of year for many houseplants and a daily mist is always a good thing.

No plant likes sudden changes in temperature. Avoid south-facing windows that can get very hot even in winter and do not place plants above a radiator by a cold window that is on a timer. I have found that a north-facing window in a room with underfloor heating is as good as it gets for happy houseplants in my own house.

CACTI

Cacti need minimal care, but what care they do need is specific. They are expert at losing as little water as possible in extreme heat and drought as they have evolved a thick skin and leaves which have been reduced to spines. They also store water – the giant saguaro in the Arizonian desert can store up to 1,585 gallons/6,000 litres and go without rain for months. Although they cope well with drought they are generally very hardy, and as long as they have well-drained soil and as much bright sunlight as possible they will cope with cold and even freezing conditions. A south-facing windowsill in an unheated room is ideal.

There are also epiphytic cacti that live in subtropical and tropical forests, attaching themselves to trees and stone. As a result these prefer rather shady conditions and should never be exposed to direct sunlight, otherwise the stems (which look like leaves) will be scorched. They need a minimum temperature of 50°F/10°C and to flower in their true colours must be kept above 59°F/15°C. The most common epiphytic cacti are Christmas cacti (Schlumbergera), which flower in December, and Hatoria, which flower in Spring.

When you buy cacti they will be in thin plastic pots. It is a good idea to repot them both to check the roots and to ensure they have the right growing conditions.

POTTING DESERT CACTI

METHOD

1. Carefully remove the plant from its pot by wrapping bubble wrap or cardboard around the spines or wearing very thick gloves. Gently tease out any encircling roots.

2. All desert cacti need lime-free compost with plenty of grit mixed in. (This is why it is not a good idea to add builders' sand which often has lime in it.)

3. Choose a pot that is not too big – .39in/1cm extra around the edge of the pot is plenty. Put a layer of your compost mix in the bottom of the pot, place the roots in it so that they are just below the surface of the pot and gently fill around the edges. Add a layer of grit to the surface to improve drainage and stop any damp compost splashing onto the spines.

4. Keep the cacti cool between November and March and do not water them at all. This cool, dry period is necessary for the creation of flower buds. Then gradually increase the heat and water for a month until they are getting as much daylight as possible and they are much more likely to flower. To avoid over-alkalinity through the lime from tap water, it is best to use rainwater.

YOU WILL NEED

Cacti

Bubble wrap, cardboard and/or thick gloves

Peat-free potting compost

Grit or washed sand (NOT builders' sand)

Perlite or vermiculite

Pots with plenty of drainage holes (terracotta is ideal and handsome)

SUCCULENTS

Succulents have evolved to be tough, very adaptable plants which makes them ideal as houseplants.

All succulents have developed various ways of storing water that they can then draw upon at times of drought. Because of the way that they control their acidity and carbon dioxide absorption they also do best when there is a notable difference between day and night-time temperatures.

The one thing that succulents cannot cope with is too much water so to ensure any succulent does not become waterlogged you should use a very gritty compost mix, and they should be allowed to dry out completely before watering. This will vary from plant to plant and at different times of year but it is always better to water too little than too much.

If you have not grown succulents before then echeverias and aeoniums are a good place to start. There are scores of varieties to choose from. Echeverias are hardier but aeoniums can be planted out in summer months, growing happily in free-draining garden soil.

METHOD

1. Many succulents will take from cuttings but they do need special treatment. The best time to do this is in spring but it can be done at any time of year as long as the cuttings are kept warm and dry.

2. For aeoniums, cut a side stem, removing any lower leaves so you have at least 2in/5cm of stalk. With echeverias pluck a leaf from near the base of the plant so that it comes away cleanly and intact.

3. In both cases leave them in a warm, dry place for at least a week so that the cut end naturally scars over. This will stop water loss and rot entering, which will kill it.

4. Once the cut surface is fully scarred, bury the aeonium cutting in 1 to 2in/2.5 to 5cm of a 50:50 mix of grit or perlite and compost – although pure perlite works well too – and put it somewhere bright and warm but out of direct midday sun and leave it to form new roots. For the echeveria, bury just the base of the leaf, propping it up with a cocktail stick if necessary.

5. Water them in and then subsequently only water when the compost is mostly dry – no more than once a week. Ensure it doesn't ever sit wet as it will rot the cutting.

6. When you see obvious new signs of growth or roots from the bottom of the pot, plant it on into a very gritty, peat-free compost mix.

YOU WILL NEED

Healthy parent plant, such as aeonium or echeveria

Small pots with good drainage holes

Perlite or grit

Potting compost

Water

LEAFY HOUSEPLANTS

The majority of plants that will thrive indoors within the average room are those that stem from jungle conditions where the light levels are low or can cope in any deep shade like many ferns. The result is a rich green frondescence that can create a stunning indoor garden in its own right.

All plants are sensitive to light to some degree and few will last long in the deepest shade. Natural light is much more powerful than even the brightest household bulbs so the amount of light from windows in any room will greatly influence growth and health.

The other vital factor is moisture. Many houseplants can be allowed to dry out completely before watering but many also need humid air as well as water to their roots. A good rule of thumb is that if the air is too humid for soft furnishings then it is good for green, leafy houseplants. Cushions and swooping green leaves do not live happily together.

METHOD

1. The most common reason that houseplants show signs of distress or die is overwatering. The main sign of plants needing water is that they are drooping, despite being a healthy colour. If in doubt, leave them for a week.

2. When you do water, it is best to take each plant and soak it in a basin for 5 minutes before draining it completely. However, this is not always practical, so water each plant until the tray beneath it fills. Then empty the tray so it is not sitting in water. In other words, soak, saturate, drain. Then leave it until the compost looks and feels very dry before repeating.

3. However, that is only the half of it. These are plants that need much more humidity than all but a bathroom can normally provide. So get a good plant mister and spray the air around the leaves at least once daily. Twice is better, especially in winter when we all tend to have warmer, less well-ventilated rooms. The aim is to wet the air rather than the plants – although that will inevitably happen to a certain extent – so the finer the spray, the better.

RECOMMENDED HOUSEPLANTS

For draughty, dark spaces like hallways:

Aspidistra, button fern, ivy, rubber plant, kentia palm, Swiss cheese plant, Chinese evergreen

For bathrooms (especially in shade):

Spider plant, rabbit's foot fern, maidenhair fern, staghorn fern, Boston fern, bird's nest fern, purple shamrock

For light shade (light from east/west-facing window):

Monstera, philodendron, rubber plant, kentia palm, bamboo palm, pilea, snake plant, rabbit's foot fern, caladiums, fiddle leaf fig, weeping fig, dragon tree, rattlesnake plant, fishtail palm, sago palm and many more

ORCHIDS

Orchids have something of a reputation for being demanding but in fact some are very easy and most are not too difficult, if you get the basics right. The easiest to grow, and certainly the ones to start out with, are moth orchids.

These originate from the Philippines and love heat. Ideally they should be kept between 59° and 68°F/15° and 20°C at night and 68° and 86°F/20° and 30°C during the day. This is much warmer than most houses in the winter months so I keep mine rather cooler than this and they seem to be fine. However, they stop growing when the temperature goes over 86°F/30°C, so in summer they do better set back from a hot window.

They need light to trigger flowering, but they can scorch, so never put them on a south-facing windowsill – a north- or east-facing one is ideal, or set them back in a bright room.

Light is necessary to the roots as well as the foliage so they are always sold and grown in clear pots. They are epiphytic plants and grow anchored on the surface of trees with the roots exposed. This is why, although they like to be humid, they hate sitting in damp compost. The large bark chips provide anchorage and perfect drainage but minimal nutrition.

REPOTTING PHALEANOPSIS ORCHIDS

METHOD

1. When you see the roots spilling out of the pot, it is a signal that it is time to repot. Remove the plant from its container and gently untangle the roots, trying not to damage them in the process. Cut off any shrivelled or damaged sections and shorten the remaining healthy white roots to about 6in/15cm.

2. Put the plant back in the same pot if it will fit, but if not, only go up to a slightly bigger size. Use very coarse pine bark chippings – they are sold as special orchid potting material. Hold the plant in position and fit the bark chippings around the roots so that it is really firm.

3. The best way to water orchids is to soak them once a week (ideally with rainwater) and to sit the pot in a saucer on damp pebbles so they do not dry out completely. Water and mist in the morning so they are not damp during the cooler nights.

4. Each flower spike can bear over a dozen flowers and will last for months. But once it is spent – and has not produced any new flowers for a week or two – cut back the spike to the first node. This will stimulate a fresh side shoot which in turn will develop flowers.

YOU WILL NEED

A clear plastic pot

Scissors or secateurs

Special orchid potting bark chips

Rainwater

CARNIVOROUS PLANTS

I grow a number of carnivorous plants, including venus flytraps and sundews, but I think my favourite are the sarracenias, or pitcher plants, as they make fascinating and beautiful houseplants. Their needs are few but specific. They will not tolerate any alkalinity so need an ericaceous growing medium. They are true bog plants so must never dry out, and they like bright sunshine but will tolerate shade. They seem unaffected by extreme heat and will tolerate temperatures in winter down to 23°F/-5°C.

METHOD

1. All pitcher plants will need old leaves removed either in autumn or early spring. These should be cut right back at the base if they are at all fading and brown. This seems radical but they very quickly produce new foliage in spring. Keep removing old leaf 'pitchers' throughout summer, and new leaves will grow until winter and their dormant period.

2. If the roots are completely filling their pots then they can be divided and repotted in early spring.

3. Take the plant out of the pots, remove any faded leaves and check the roots. At this point you can divide plants that are too large for their pots by gently pulling the roots apart.

4. Mix up a potting medium made with 30% volume of grit or perlite. They have evolved to take all their nutrients from the insects that they catch and digest in their pitchers so need no nutrients from the roots. Therefore do not use ordinary potting compost as it can kill them. I have found homemade leaf mould to work well, as does composted bracken or very fine pine bark. Do not put them into too large a pot – its purpose is primarily to support and hold it, not to provide nourishment or moisture, so .39in/1cm of potting mix under and around the roots is plenty.

5. Water them with rainwater and then stand the pots in a shallow tray or dish. Keep this topped up with rainwater, although I found in drought when we ran out of rainwater, a few weeks of tap water did no noticeable harm.

6. Pitcher plants need a dormant cold period of at least 6 weeks in which the temperature is ideally between freezing and 54°F/12°C so a centrally heated room will be too warm. During this cool, dormant period they will need less water although should not dry out. Then in spring they will respond to warmer weather by starting to produce new leaves and will grow rapidly.

7. I leave the flowers until they fade – I think they look great – but young plants will establish more quickly if you remove the flowers and let the plant develop more pitchers.

YOU WILL NEED

Sharp secateurs or scissors

Perlite or grit

Proprietary carnivorous potting mix OR for homemade, leaf mould or fine pine bark or composted bracken

Pots

Rainwater

A tray or shallow container of some kind

PRUNING

Any cutting back, from deadheading a rose to coppicing a large tree, is a form of pruning. It can be a very creative, enjoyable aspect of gardening, but understanding how plants react to being cut back is essential before you begin to hack away.

For example, cutting back the leader (see page 340) on any plant will encourage subsequent sideshoots to thrive and therefore create bushier growth.

Some plants flower on new growth (such as most roses and late-flowering clematis) and some on shoots made the previous summer (like lilac, philadelphus or spring-flowering clematis). It is important to know which is the case to avoid the risk of cutting off flowering stems.

The first rule of all pruning is to always cut back to something. This might be a leaf if deadheading or the main trunk of a tree. But never cut in the middle of a stem or branch.

Always start with removing anything that is clearly dead or damaged. If any branches are rubbing against each other, remove one of them, otherwise a wound will form which is liable to become an entry point for infection or fungal problems. Plenty of light and air between branches will increase ventilation and sun exposure to ripen any flowers, fruit or new growth. Keep standing back and checking that it looks good to your eye.

Remember that the lower branches never shift up a tree and the inner section never moves out – all growth is always from the outer perimeter of a plant, not the base. Therefore a good-looking, healthy branch in the wrong place always has to go, whilst a mere leafy sprout in the right place must be nurtured so it will (surprisingly quickly) become a branch in exactly the right place.

Any removal of foliage will reduce a plant's ability to feed its roots via photosynthesis so will potentially slow down growth. It is therefore best to do it in the tree's dormant season – when it has no leaves – unless you are deliberately pruning in summer to restrict growth. It is also a good rule of thumb to avoid removing more than one third of its branches in any one year. However, it is a very common technique to control shrubs such as hydrangea or currant bushes by removing a third of their growth completely every year, cutting right to the base of the plant. This means that they completely renew themselves every three years without being weakened in any way.

When removing anything thicker than your wrist, always make an undercut about 1in/3cm or so deep and 1 to 2in/3 to 6cm away from the trunk or adjoining branch. This will stop it tearing. When you have removed the branch, cut the stub back at a slight angle so water drains from it.

Do not seal cuts with any kind of paint, however big. This only seals in moisture and encourages rot and fungal problems. Allow them to heal naturally and form a protective callous.

Finally, always use very sharp tools and something that can make the cut comfortably within its capability. If you have to force a cut, it is likely to damage the tree and probably yourself. Nowadays there are superb Japanese saws of all sizes that make pruning much easier and I use them even for quite small branches.

SUMMER PRUNING

Summer pruning is done in July and August when the plant is in full leaf and when, if a fruit tree, it is carrying all its ripening fruits. It is done specifically to restrict and curtail growth, whereas winter pruning stimulates vigorous subsequent regrowth.

Pruning is especially applicable to fruit trees that are trained as espalier, fans or cordons, to restrict their growth and to keep within the shape they are being trained to. It is also a chance to remove shoots that are obscuring the ripening fruit from direct sunlight.

In winter I prune my espalier pears to encourage new shoots, and the harder I cut them back, the stronger the growth will be the following summer. But in summer I reduce all new growth upright from the fruiting spurs down to a healthy couple of spurs (which will produce next year's fruits) and any other growth that goes outside the limitations of the three parallel rows of the espalier.

This applies to fan-trained, step-over and cordon fruit too, as well as any large apple or pear trees that have become too crowded and overgrown.

The result is a streamlined, less shaggy version of itself with plenty of light and air reaching the ripening fruit.

METHOD

1. Remove any new shoots that are growing beyond the range of the desired final shape or growth – e.g., beyond the end of a horizontal layer of an espalier or the diagonal shoots of a fan.

2. Vertical shoots will always grow stronger and longer than horizontal ones so cut these back to the lowest pair of leaves (usually about 2 to 5in/6 to 12cm), being careful not to remove any ripening fruits.

3. Tie in any new growth you want to keep, leaving the final few inches of any new horizontal shoots turning up slightly until they have reached the desired length – as their desire to grow vertically will speed up their growth before you tie it down to the final horizontal position.

4. Finally, check that all the remaining growth is securely tied in to the supporting wires, canes or trellis.

YOU WILL NEED

Secateurs

Loppers

Sharp pruning saw for larger branches

Soft twine for tying in new growth

WINTER PRUNING

Pruning a deciduous tree or shrub when it has lost its leaves, between November and the end of February, means that you can clearly see the branches, distinguish new growth from old, easily see where branches are crowded, damaged or rubbing against each other, and identify any potential disease such as canker.

Cutting back in winter has the effect of stimulating vigorous regrowth in spring. So if you want to reinvigorate a hedge that is thin and gappy, you should cut it back hard in winter and it will grow back thicker and bushier. However, if you want to keep it trim and neat, then cutting in summer will restrict growth.

This can be used to good effect when training fruit trees or stimulating shrubs that have decorative stems.

Do not winter prune plums, apricots, peaches or cherries. These should be pruned in late spring and only if absolutely necessary.

METHOD

1. The first job in pruning in winter is to remove any damaged or crowded growth. Aim to have no two branches or shoots touching or rubbing against each other.

2. Then remove any dead, damaged or diseased growth, cutting back into healthy wood. As with all pruning, always cut back to something. So do not leave a stub or stem but cut just above a bud, spur, branch or the trunk. Ideally the cut should be at a slight angle but do not obsess over this.

3. Having taken this remedial action, take a look and assess whether you want to increase growth in any particular direction. If so, you must counter-intuitively cut back harder here, removing any weak shoots so that stronger regrowth is stimulated. This is particularly applicable if you are growing espalier, cordon or fan-trained fruits. However, it also applies to small trees and shrubs whose shape is part of their aesthetic appeal.

4. Fruit will not be produced on new shoots, so if you do not need the extra growth for the tree's structure, cut back any wispy young growth to older, knobbly wood (the side shoots).

5. If you have established fruit trees, trained or otherwise, the fruit will develop and ripen better if there is light and air between them, so remove any crowded side shoots so they are spaced reasonably evenly. This will also encourage good airflow and thus reduce fungal problems.

6. After pruning one plant, it is a good idea to clean tools in soapy water, with alcohol or anti-bacterial spray, before moving to the next plant, to prevent cross-contamination if any disease is present.

YOU WILL NEED

Secateurs

Loppers

Sharp pruning saw

PROPAGATION

"Propagation" is one of those slightly intimidating terms that seems designed to measure your horticultural chops – it is as though there is a lurking exam paper that comes in tow. It can seem daunting compared to the ease of buying a ready-raised plant and popping it into the ground the same day.

But there is no need to be anxious about any kind of propagation, be it by seed, cuttings or division. Some plants propagate more readily than others but there is no mystique to it. It is immensely satisfying to raise a plant yourself and imbues the plant with much more meaning than one bought off the shelf. It also means that you can start to garden with larger quantities of plants, which changes completely the way that you can create and design your borders – and saves a fortune in the process.

Herbaceous plants can be divided either from those already growing in your garden or new plants. In fact, a good tip is to buy the largest herbaceous plant available, grow it for a year in your garden to see if you like it and it likes your garden and then subdivide it right down to as many pieces as possible. This is much cheaper than buying lots of smaller plants.

Seed sowing will dominate spring but continues through to early September. After that there is too little light to make it worthwhile sowing seed before the days start to lengthen in mid-January.

By midsummer, cuttings start to become a really useful and important way of creating lots of new plants, initially with softwood cuttings and then, from August through to October, semi-ripe ones, followed by hardwood cuttings between November and February.

One of the great luxuries in my own garden is a well-equipped potting shed with a greenhouse and cold frames at hand. But it is a luxury rather than a necessity. For many years I did all my propagating on a trestle table outside the back door, protecting delicate seedlings on windowsills, and raised many hundreds of plants every year.

You will need to have some potting compost to hand and have a bag of perlite or horticultural grit at all times. Young seedlings need an open texture for their delicate roots, and perlite, mixed in with potting compost, is excellent for this as well as stopping waterlogging. Cuttings need to go in a very free-draining mix, and often pure perlite works perfectly.

Plastic seed trays and pots are essential. Buy stout ones and reuse them for as long as possible to cut down plastic waste.

You will also need a watering can with a fine rose so you can water young seedlings without crushing them under the weight of water.

If you have a greenhouse or a wide windowsill, I strongly recommend buying a propagator of some kind, even if it is only a clear cover to go over a seed tray. If it can be heated, so much the better. Heated mats are terrific and not too expensive but make all the difference. Gentle bottom heat is the key, whereas a radiator blasting out might be too hot and dry.

However you go about it, once you start to propagate and see some success then you will be hooked.

HARDWOOD CUTTINGS

Hardwood cuttings are taken from current season's growth that has matured sufficiently to develop a strong woody section at the base. These are always taken in autumn and winter and usually after the leaves have fallen. They are slow to form roots but very slow to die, so mostly need no protection at all other than good drainage, and can be placed directly outside into a slit trench (see below) with some sand or grit in the bottom. They are ideal for soft fruit, roses, and indeed almost any deciduous shrub or tree, and like all cuttings will produce a replica of the parent.

METHOD

1. Select and cut straight lengths of new growth at least 6in/15cm long and twice that if available. Make sure that you have all the cut ends together so you keep them the right way up.

2. Cut each stem into lengths 4 to 8in/10 to 20cm, cutting straight across the bottom and angling the cut at the top. This ensures that they remain the right way up and protects the upper cut surface from collecting moisture.

3. If you are growing the cuttings in pots, fill with a mixture of potting compost and sand, grit or perlite and bury each cutting by at least two-thirds of its length. Leaving just a couple of centimetres showing is fine. You should get at least 4 cuttings to each pot. Water them and place outside in a sheltered but unprotected place where they will be undisturbed for at least 6 months.

4. If growing them outside, make a slit trench with a spade by inserting the spade to its full depth and pulling the soil back so one side is straight and the other angled towards you. Half fill this slit with grit or sand and line the cuttings along the straight side about 4in/10cm apart so the majority of each length is underground. Close the trench and bury the cuttings to at least two-thirds of their length by pushing the angled side up against them. Water them.

5. However you raise the cuttings, they will take at least 6 months to form roots and I always leave mine for 12 months. (If by then there is no new foliage then it has not and will not form roots.) Those with new foliage can then be carefully lifted and either repotted individually or planted out directly where they are to grow.

YOU WILL NEED

Secateurs

Potting compost or 3ft/1m strip of bare soil outside

Sharp sand, horticultural grit or perlite to improve drainage

Water

Spade

Label

SEMI-RIPE CUTTINGS

Taking cuttings is an easy and rewarding way of making new plants for free. They also have the advantage of being exactly the same as the parent plant in flower and leaf colour, growth habit and size, which is often not true of plants grown from seed.

You can take cuttings from any woody shrub, but herbs such as rosemary, lavender and sage also make ideal cutting material.

The best time to do this is from July through October when the new shoots have matured a little but are still fresh. These are generally referred to as semi-ripe cuttings.

METHOD

1. Choose healthy, strong, straight growth for cutting material that is free from any flowers or flower buds. Cut stems about 6in/15cm long with a stub of older wood at the base. Each stem makes one cutting.

2. Once you have taken material from the plant and placed it in the polythene bag, go and pot it up immediately. The cuttings are effectively dying from the second you cut them until they develop new roots, so the quicker you can aid that process, the more likely you are to have success.

3. Mix your potting compost half and half with perlite, and fill a pot with this mixture. Cuttings need water and oxygen for the new roots to form, but too much water inhibits oxygen, so very good drainage is essential and perlite (or vermiculite) both retains sufficient moisture and improves drainage.

4. Strip off all lower leaves so that only a couple of centimetres of foliage remain, with the rest of the stem bare. Cut the bare stem cleanly with a sharp knife just below the point where leaves grow from (a 'node') and bury it 1 to 2in/3 to 6cm deep in the very free-draining compost. It is best to place the cuttings around the edge of a pot, and you can always get at least four and often more in one container.

5. Water it well and then place a polythene bag over the pot, supported by a slim stick (ice lolly or floristry sticks work well) in each corner so the bag is held clear of the cuttings. Seal the bag so it forms a clear bubble over the pot. This will trap moisture and greatly increase the chance of the cuttings surviving until they have grown new roots. It should only need watering every 3 or 4 days, but only if the compost has dried out.

YOU WILL NEED

Healthy donor plant with strong new growth

Pair of sharp secateurs or scissors

Penknife

Polythene bag (ziplock is ideal)

Peat-free compost

Perlite (vermiculite, horticultural grit or sand will do)

Small (3in/7.5cm is ideal) pot

Slim canes or lolly sticks

Watering can

GOOD PLANTS FOR THIS TYPE OF CUTTING:

Box

Yew

Hydrangeas (with a little bit of wood from last year)

Philadelphus

Ceanothus

Viburnum

Bay

Lavender

Sage

6. Put the pot somewhere warm and bright but shaded from the hottest sun. You will know that the roots have formed when you see fresh new growth. At that point the cuttings can be removed from the pot and potted on individually before planting out next spring.

SOWING SEEDS

Seed sowing is easy. All we can do is give them the best opportunity to do what they do best. So do not obsess over the niceties. Get some peat-free compost, scatter seed, cover, water, put somewhere warm and they will grow. Job done.

Having said that, good gardening is as much about detail, and the difference between success and failure often hangs upon very fine margins. So here are my secrets of seed success.

Use fresh seed wherever possible. Some seeds – notably legumes – stay viable for years, and others, such as field poppies, have evolved to stay dormant for scores of years until triggered into germination by exposure to light. But fresh seed that is not more than two years old is more likely to germinate and grow than old seed.

Sow thinly. With tiny seeds this is all but impossible. However, it is worth taking trouble over this, not least because you will only end up throwing away half the emerging seedlings if they are too close together. But the main reason is so that each seedling has room to develop good roots with minimal competition.

Larger, heavier seeds such as beetroot or French beans are best sown into modules or small pots as these will then be transplanted directly to the garden. Occasionally I sow in clusters in modules – this works well for beetroot, rocket or other leafy greens – and only thin each cluster lightly, transplanting them outside in small clumps rather than as individual plants. But on the whole the aim from the outset is to produce strong individual seedlings.

Water thoroughly but not too much – I water mine once a day in the morning – and give maximum light as soon as the seedlings emerge. If you only have a windowsill then turn regularly so the seedlings get equal and even light.

What garden plants are best grown from seed? Almost all vegetables. Many herbs, including shrubby ones like rosemary, sage and thyme as well as the annuals like parsley, dill or coriander, grow very well from seed and give an opportunity to raise plants in the kind of quantity that would otherwise be very expensive.

All annuals, tender and hardy, are best raised from seed including climbers such as cup and saucer vine and of course sweet peas. Biennials such as foxgloves, wallflowers, sweet rocket, teasels and evening primrose can be sown in spring and they will germinate, develop roots and leaves and then flower the next spring and summer.

Whatever you grow, there is one thing I can guarantee. There is little else as satisfying in life – let alone in the garden – as seeing a beautiful plant in full flower or harvest that you have nurtured from seed. In that simple process is contained all the wonder and joy of gardening.

COMPOST

Making garden compost is by far the best way to improve the health and fertility of your garden. Think of compost like a starter for sourdough. It feeds the soil, recharging and stimulating its complex biome, which in turn feeds your plants.

Garden compost suggests a rotting process – but that is not what happens in your compost heap. In fact the transformation from odds and ends of kitchen waste, dried stems, dead-headed flowers and the thousand other possible components, from wood chips to grass cuttings, is done mostly by digestion by billions of bacteria, fungi, nematodes and protozoa, along with slugs, beetles and brandlings – the red worms that are only found in compost and dung heaps.

The secret of making good compost is to create the ideal conditions for these organisms – and they will do all the work for you.

METHOD

1. If you have the space, you can make a 'slow' compost heap by putting all your composting material in a long low mound and simply leaving it for 18 months to 2 years, by which time the compost will be ready. The down side to this 'slow' method is that it takes up time and space.

2. It is much quicker and much more economical with space to make compost in containers of some kind. I use bays made from pallets and scaffolding boards, but dustbins work well – although ideally you need three: one for ready compost, one with maturing compost and one to fill with new material.

3. If you only have small, incremental amounts of waste material, gather it up in a bucket or plastic trug before adding it to the heap.

4. Shredding, cutting, chopping up or even mowing waste increases the surface area and dramatically speeds up the composting process as well as using less space.

5. Compost is primarily composed of nitrogen and carbon. Nitrogen typically comes from lush, green material, and carbon from dry or woody stems. Too much carbon and the composting process will be very slow, whereas too much nitrogen (as with fresh grass cuttings) and it becomes anaerobic and an evil-smelling sludge. So for every load of freshly cut grass, you should mix it with the same volume of straw, cardboard, sawdust or shredded dry garden waste such as old flower stems.

6. Turning adds oxygen, which is the ingredient that bacteria depend on, and bacteria are the most important element in any compost heap. Once every 4 weeks is ideal but if the heap has cooled and is clearly not ready, turn it again.

7. Water is also important for both bacteria and fungi to do their work. If you have the right mix of brown to green material, it is easy to find that your heap becomes rather dry. Keep it moist, putting a sprinkler onto it if need be. If it becomes sodden, it is a sign that you do not have enough carbon in the mix. It should be damp until the very last stages.

8. It is ready when it is a sweet-smelling, brown crumbly material that is pleasant to handle. There is no set time that compost should take. Every batch is different but as a rule allow 3 to 6 months in summer and 6 to 9 months in winter.

9. Once the compost is ready, it is best spread as a mulch about 1 to 2in/3 to 5cm thick on the surface of the ground. More than that is unnecessary. Worms and weather will quickly incorporate it into the soil.

YOU WILL NEED

Kitchen waste (excluding fats, meat or cooked carbohydrates)

All garden waste, including all annual weeds and the top growth of perennial weeds. The roots of bindweed, couch grass or ground elder are best burnt and the ashes added to the heap.

Cardboard (best torn or scrunched-up rather than added in layers)

Hair, wool, straw, bracken

LEAF MOULD

Once fallen, whatever their colour, all deciduous leaves are ready to be converted into leaf mould. I love leaf mould. It is ideal for mulching all woodland plants and when added to any soil it helps improve its structure. It also improves any potting compost it is added to.

Unlike good garden compost, which needs turning regularly to spur the bacterial digestion which is the predominant action in its conversion from raw material to the final product, leaf mould is almost entirely made by fungal activity and does not need heat or oxygen for this to happen perfectly efficiently. The only really important factor in converting a fallen leaf to leaf mould within one season is moisture, as dry leaves take much longer to break down.

METHOD

1. Leaves are easier to collect when dry but will need damping down to speed up the conversion process. Damp leaves bypass that process but are almost impossible to shred/mow. My own preferred technique is to brush or rake the leaves into long rows and then mow them. Mowing leaves into small pieces makes them rot down faster and take up much less storage space.

2. After being mown, they go into a large chicken-wire container and are kept wet. In a dry year this means thoroughly hosing them layer by layer. However you do it, avoid burying dry leaves within the heap. Increasing the surface area increases the effect of rainfall in keeping them damp, so a large, low rectangular bay is better than a tall, slim one. I appreciate that most gardens are not large enough to have a permanent large wire bay for leaf mould. In this case the answer is to put the leaves in a black binbag, leaving the top turned but not tied. Make sure the leaves are really wet, and punch a few holes in the side of the bag to drain excess water. They will rot down very well and can be stored behind a shed or tucked away in any corner to quietly convert from leaf to mould. This should be soft and crumbly and can be put directly on the soil as mulch or sieved for use as potting compost.

3. Leaf mould is slightly acidic so is good for rhododendrons, camellias, sarracenias, blueberries and other ericaceous plants as well as being ideal for bulbs like lilies.

YOU WILL NEED

Wire rake

Brush

Barrow

Ideally a mower

A storage bay made from chicken wire or old pallets

Bin bags

WEEDS

Gardeners should have mixed feelings about weeds. On the one hand weeds infiltrate your chosen plants and sometimes submerge them. They can be hard to remove, infuriatingly robust and prolific, and seem to stand as evidence of your own lack of horticultural skill and effort.

But on the other hand a weed is a plant hero, an adaptor and survivor coping with any weather and outperforming all those around it.

The greater fecundity of your weed population, the healthier and better conditioned is your soil. So if you take on a new garden and it is filled with weeds, be thankful the soil that they are growing in is good. Secondly, the greater the diversity and range of weed types that you have growing uninvited, the greater the range of chosen plants of your choice that you will eventually be able to grow.

The type and limitations of the weeds growing are a useful indicator of the nature and condition of your soil:

Very acidic soil will produce lots of sorrel and plantain but no charlock or poppy, which need an alkaline soil.

Chickweed is a good indicator of a neutral pH.

Nettles, ground elder, fat hen and chickweed all point to a soil high in nitrogen and often follow a fresh application of manure.

Docks indicate a deep, rich but rather heavy soil.

Creeping buttercup, horsetail and silverweed point to a damp soil with poor drainage.

You also need some weeds in your garden because flowering weeds are an important part of a garden's self-sustaining biodiversity. Many weed flowers are important as food sources for predators such as wasps and hoverflies, which in turn feed off pests such as aphids. Finches eat thistle seeds; blackbirds and other songbirds love chickweed; goldfinches eat dandelions and so on. This means that spraying with weedkiller is not any kind of option because it inevitably damages the food chain that surely will damage your garden – let alone the whole ecosystem.

So do not try to eradicate all weeds from the garden. This will not only save you a lot of time and energy but will also greatly enhance the wildlife that feed off them in one form or another. A clump of nettles or the odd thistle, dandelion or ramble of chickweed here and there do more good than harm.

However, for all their undervalued virtues, weeds must also be controlled to some extent.

The first thing is to identify whether they are annual or perennial and this will determine your specific approach. Annual weeds tend to be easy to pull from the ground and are prolific seeders. They die away each year, with the seeds creating new plants the following year. Perennial weeds are usually hard to pull from the ground and generally have an extensive root system or tap root which help them survive winter. This can create an issue if left for a long time.

A thick mulch will help enormously with all weeds. It will not suppress the tough perennial ones like bindweed or horsetail, but it will weaken them and make them easier to pull out.

Weeds are survivors. They are spread by birds, human feet and wind and creep underground. So try and weed little and often, removing the worst offenders as you see them, and accept that weeding is a constant task, the gardening equivalent of washing up, which, if you get on top of it, is not so arduous.

ANNUAL WEEDS

Annual weeds germinate, grow, flower, set seed and die all within the same growing season which, in the UK, is between February and November. To do so much in such a short time means that these weeds tend to have two characteristics. The first is that they are adaptable and grow fast and strong in most conditions. They cope with most weather, most soil and most situations. The second is that they tend to be very prolific with seed, with some plants like groundsel or chickweed each producing thousands of seeds.

The good thing about annual weeds is that most do not have strong roots and are easy to pull up or hoe. Also, if you can stop them setting seed, then they will soon die back and not reappear.

So the first control of annual weeds is to stop them seeding. The best way to do this is to pull them up by hand in a flower border or to hoe them whilst they are still young in the straight rows of a veg plot.

If you grow vegetables then a hoe is essential, and one of the main reasons vegetables should be grown in rows or grids is so you can differentiate between emerging crops and unwanted weeds. The secret of hoeing is to do it little and often, never letting weeds become dominant. The ideal is to hoe in the morning of a dry day. Leave the hoed weeds on the surface of the soil and they will dry out during the day. They can then be raked up and put on the compost heap in the evening.

If you have a very weed-infested bit of ground you want to cultivate and the weeds have not yet gone to seed, then a good tip is to hoe the weeds off, removing as much growth as you can, and then dig the whole thing over. This will not get rid of the perennial weeds but will allow you to grow a crop of fast-growing and weed-suppressing vegetables like potatoes, beans or squashes or sow a green manure (a sacrificial crop which is dug into the soil to add nutrients).

A hoe is too crude a weapon for a border, as the risk of damaging herbaceous perennials and of accidentally removing emerging flower seedlings is too great. The answer is to get down on your knees and carefully remove every scrap of weed with your fingers and a hand fork. By doing this you really get to know your soil, your plants, the seedlings and the herbaceous perennials coming through and you improve an area dramatically. The old adage 'one year's seeding means seven years' weeding' is pretty much accurate. If you cannot pull or hoe them, then cut the tops off as soon as they flower until such a time as you can get at them properly.

When sowing any new crop, from a new lawn to a row of radish, it is always a good idea to prepare the ground and then leave it fallow for a few weeks. Many annual weeds are triggered into germination by soil disturbance and exposure to light so will now quickly germinate. These can then be hoed off, leaving the field clear for your sown seeds to germinate and establish without competition for water and nutrients for a few extra weeks.

ANNUAL WEEDS

Shepherd's purse

Chickweed

Groundsel

Prickly sowthistle

Fat hen

Caper spurge

Petty spurge

Goosegrass

Himalaya balsam

Knotgrass

Shepherd's needle

PERENNIAL WEEDS

Perennial weeds, such as nettle, bindweed, ground elder, couch grass and thistle, survive for more than two growing seasons – sometimes for very much longer. Dock seeds can apparently lie dormant in the soil for up to ninety years, waiting for the soil to be disturbed before germinating.

Whilst nettles and thistles spread by seed, weeds such as couch grass, bindweed and ground elder have extensive rhizomes. These rhizomes produce new plants which, in turn, have their own extensive rhizomatous root system. On top of that, the rhizomes tend to be very brittle so snap when you try and dig them up, and even the smallest section left in the ground will produce a new plant. This makes them difficult to truly eradicate.

Difficult – but not impossible. The answer is to systematically dig out every scrap of root. Whilst the top part of the plant can go on the compost heap – and usefully so, for most weeds make the most of whatever nutrients are available in the soil to create healthy plants. If you compost them, then some of that goodness will be recycled back into the soil – and the plants which you choose to grow, the non-weeds, can benefit from it.

But perennial roots should always be burnt or disposed of via your town or borough. If you do burn them, the ash can go on the garden or compost heap. The important thing is to be thorough. Far better to properly weed 10.75 square feet/1 square metre than to half-heartedly do ten times that amount, leaving bits of root in the ground.

There are also weeds like horsetail, horseradish and Japanese knotweed with roots of enormous depth and resilience. Horsetail can go down 7.5 feet/2.5 metres and knotweed be as tough as steel hawsers. They are a problem to which there is no easy answer. Repeated cutting will weaken them, and I have a patch of ground elder that has not spread in twenty years because I mow it every week. But it is still there.

Certain weeds like ground elder, bindweed and couch grass have a habit of winding in amongst the roots of plants you wish to keep, so have a safe haven from the most diligent of weeding. The way to deal with this is to dig up the infested plant and wash the roots thoroughly under a tap or power hose, blasting out every scrap of the weed's root. Before you replant it, dig over the planting site with obsessive meticulousness to remove every tiny scrap of root.

Some border plants become weeds because they do so well and out-compete their less robust neighbours. This is true of the allium 'Purple Sensation' and the chocolate-coloured foliage of purple loosestrife, Lysimachia ciliata 'Firecracker', both in our Jewel Garden, or the shuttlecock fern that is now rapidly spreading uncontrollably in my Damp Garden, all of which started out as carefully nurtured treasures but which have become rampantly dominant. A weed, by definition, is always a robust, healthy plant.

COMMON PERENNIAL WEEDS

Very difficult
(will take long-term strategy
or inspired acceptance)

Japanese knotweed

Horsetail

Lesser celandine

Take very seriously
(dig up every scrap of root and burn)

Ground elder

Bind weed

Creeping buttercup

Couch grass

Work at
(dig up as and when you can)

Broad-leaved dock

Nettles

Spear thistle

Creeping thistle

Burdock

Handsome but intrusive

Daisy

Greater celandine

Teasel

Rosebay willowherb

Common hogweed (pictured above)

PESTS

A garden is never a strictly natural environment. We cram masses of delicious soft foliage in the shape of lettuces, hostas or young seedlings into a small space and then wonder why every slug and snail in the vicinity hungrily fall upon them. Grow row after row of brassicas in an allotment or garden and of course cabbage white butterflies will home in on them like heat-seeking missiles. Gardens are immensely attractive to all wildlife – including that which we do not particularly want.

Throughout the twentieth century most gardeners prized themselves on their knowledge and ability to control and destroy any living thing that impacted upon their prize plants, be they floral, structural or edible. All insects were branded 'pests' and were ruthlessly – and vainly – suppressed with liberal doses of pesticides. It was ignorant and doomed to failure but it was an approach supported vociferously by the horticultural establishment and promoted by the chemical companies that made huge profits as a result – not least because their products were ineffective so therefore needed applying again and again.

The organic approach to gardening has always aimed at a holistic self-setting and self-adjusting balance. Aside from the balance of nutrients and uptake that every plant micro-manages in its subtle and complex relationship with the ecosystem of the soil, for every pest there is a predator, and every predator must have its prey. One of the absurdities of the chemical regime was (and all too often still is) that by killing all prey you also remove all predators. When, as inevitably happens, the next wave of 'pests' emerge, such as aphids or caterpillars, there is no natural control, which means that you need even more chemicals – and so the absurd wheel turns and turns.

But being righteous about organic versus chemical horticulture does not solve the problems of one's cherished plants being eaten, destroyed or infected. The answer is to attract predators before they are needed, and apart from providing the plants they like, it also means accepting some prey. Birds eat caterpillars and aphids, frogs and toads eat slugs, beetles eat slugs, and ladybirds eat aphids. No caterpillars mean no blue tits to eat them. No aphids mean no ladybirds – and so on.

So you have to accept some collateral damage in order to have a healthy and resident predatory population. I admit that this can be irritating – for example, moles periodically ravage my garden, and cabbage white caterpillars can rip through cabbages over the course of just one weekend. But by and large these are small worries and you can never isolate one particular problem. Everything is connected to everything. So a garden with some water, long grass, cover for birds, insects and small mammals, as well as plenty of plants for pollinators and butterflies will always be far more effective at controlling inevitable outbreaks of so-called 'pests' on your plants.

The other vital fact is also the health of the plants themselves. A healthy plant is the least likely to be attacked. Health does not just mean visible size and looks. Very often a smaller plant is healthier than one that has been forced into extra growth by overfeeding or mollycoddling. The healthiest plants are those that have adapted best to their situation, whatever that might be.

So grow plants hard from the very beginning so they adapt to your garden from the outset. Have a wide range of habitats. Avoid monoculture. Never resort to pesticides. Accept a little damage for the sake of a resident predatory population, and always see the bigger picture. Every garden is a holistic entity and every garden is connected to the wider ecosystem, so care for your back garden just as you would like us to care for the planet.

Slugs and snails are top of every gardener's hate-list but they have a role clearing up dead and decaying material. The healthier a plant is, the less likely they are to select it for dinner. Avoid nitrogen feed which will encourage lots of green, soft growth that is especially attractive to slugs and snails as well as sap-sucking creatures.

Vine weevils are second only to slugs and snails as a horticultural hate figure, particularly to plants in containers. Adults eat the edge of leaves but the larvae eat roots and so do more harm. The adults are almost all female and will each lay over a hundred eggs in the soil around the host plant from late July. The larvae will then feed on the host's roots until the following spring when they pupate.

The best way to deal with adults is to look for them with a torch at night and pick them off, and before buying any plant in a container, take it out of the pot and check carefully for adults in spring and larvae in late summer.

Like slugs and snails, aphids love fresh new growth. But they are an important source of food for a wide range of predators, so encourage ladybirds, blue tits, lacewings and hoverflies.

Box tree caterpillars are the greenish-yellow larvae of a moth and after hatching they can completely defoliate a box plant as well as eating bark, which will kill a branch or shoot. There are no wholly effective treatments but physically picking off the female moths at night before they can lay their eggs is effective – if extreme.

The bright red lily beetle can ravage members of the lily family – primarily lilies and fritillaries – and are increasing every year. To date, the only control is to pick them off by hand and dispose of them.

The caterpillar of the cabbage white butterfly lays its eggs on the underside of the leaves of all brassicas, which then hatch into the yellow and black or pale green caterpillars who feed voraciously on the leaves. The best cure is prevention: cover the plants with a fine net when you plant them out.

Finally, some creatures are unfairly blamed but do relatively little harm. Ants make powdery cones of soil on lawns and they can make nests in the base of pots but do not feed on plant material. Earwigs do much more good than harm, and woodlice prefer rotting wood to plant roots – although if these are too wet and the pot is not disturbed they may have a nibble.

DISEASE

On a show bench, a gold medal–winning plant will be, to all intents and purposes, the perfect example of its kind. It will be flawless and certainly not showing any sign of attack or disease. But although it is easy to see this as the yardstick by which to measure our garden efforts at growing the same plant, in practice this is delusionary. It would be like comparing a Crufts-winning poodle posing in perfect pom-pommed array to a labradoodle just returned from an exhilarating and particularly muddy walk. One looks unblemished but the other – muddy, dishevelled and perhaps carrying the odd scar or wound – is radiant with lusty life.

So many of your plants, like mine, will be afflicted not just by pests but also disease. This is most likely to be viral or fungal. Most plants will barely notice this and many will recover from quite bad attacks. However some will inevitably be lost and sometimes this can be devastating.

Viral, fungal and bacterial diseases can be spread by animals, insects, rain and humans. The most common spread of viruses is when sap is passed from one plant to another. This normally occurs when aphids move from one host to another or when a plant is cut for pruning and then the infected pruning implement cuts another plant. So frequent washing of secateurs and shears is good practice.

But in the end the most important thing is not how to treat disease of any kind, let alone prevent it – which is doomed to failure – but how to prevent it from becoming too a big problem.

I often have anxious questions about plants that have some signs of disease or malformation – blotches on leaves, perhaps a gall or bit of dieback – yet in every other respect are performing without a glitch, producing leaves, flowers and, if relevant, fruit, exactly as desired. In other words they are exceptionally healthy despite having a minor affliction that is actually not troubling them at all.

Good tool hygiene is important, and ventilation achieved by pruning and positioning of plants is often decisive. But in the end the most important thing is to focus on raising healthy, robust plants which will heal and thrive despite the inevitable afflictions that will befall them. This means caring and tending for them with attention, timing and some knowledge but also growing everything as unprotected as possible so that it has to adapt from the very first. The better a plant can adapt to what will inevitably be problems of weather, soil, pests and disease, the healthier it will remain.

FUNGAL DISEASE

Fungal problems come in many guises but most result from warm, humid conditions with insufficient ventilation. Climate change, with the trend of warmer, wetter winters, has accentuated this, and I have noticed a big increase in fungal problems in my own garden over the past twenty years.

This is because fungus is much more prevalent on soft, sappy growth which, in turn, is more likely in warm, moist conditions.

Most fungi exist below the ground as mycelium that have wide-spreading filaments that feed on decomposing matter. So a 'fairy ring' in a lawn marks the extent of the mycelium growing outwards like the spokes of a bicycle wheel. The reason that the grass is greener and longer at the outer limit of the circle is that the fungus has used all the nutrients in the soil within the circle, whereas at the edge it excretes chemicals into the ground ahead to provide it with food and the grass temporarily responds by growing lusher. As to stopping or limiting it, nothing is more effective than reducing compaction and encouraging good drainage.

There are thousands of fungal diseases of plants but a few are very common in gardens:

Box blight has destroyed almost all my own box plants, with the fungus entering through pruning cuts in the humid warmth of late summer and spreading like wildfire along the lines of tightly clipped hedges. Only ventilation and refraining from pruning can save the plants – which means no box hedges or topiary.

Potato blight can reduce potato foliage to mush in 24 hours although the spores are waterborne, so the potatoes themselves will be protected if they have a good layer of dry earth over them for a few days – although the crop is often ruined. The same fungus attacks tomatoes with equally disastrous effect.

Roses have various fungal afflictions including rust, which shows itself with orange spores; blackspot, which manifests itself with spreading brown and black splodges on leaves, leading in bad cases to total defoliation; and powdery mildew which, unlike the previous two, is made worse in dry conditions. For all three (indeed all fungal problems) the best treatment is pruning to improve ventilation and limiting feeding to avoid too much soft growth.

Canker and scab in fruit trees are both caused by fungi that flourish where the drainage around the fruit tree's roots is poor and unpruned branches restrict airflow. But, whilst not ideal, it need not be a disaster. I have thirty-year-old espalier pear trees riddled with canker that have nevertheless produced excellent pears year after year.

Clematis wilt, where the whole of a large clematis will collapse and seemingly die in 24 hours, is caused by the fungus Calophoma clematidina entering into a damaged part of the stem. The best defence is to plant deeply with at least an inch of stem below soil level. The plant will then regrow healthily from this subterranean section.

Honey fungus can kill shrubs and trees including beech, holly, apples, magnolias, lilacs and acers. It manifests itself above ground by clumps of tawny toadstools appearing from early autumn at the base of trees or bushes. These toadstools are perfectly harmless but between the bark and wood, you will find white mats of mycelium, and around affected roots and just below the soil surface, you will find black, lace-like strands called rhizomorphs. It is these that spread the fungus from dead to neighbouring living, woody tissue.

But life depends upon fungi. In just one gram of soil – about a teaspoonful – you would expect to find around 10,000 species of fungi that are part of the indescribably complex synthesis that enables plants to grow healthily. Without fungi in your garden you would have no garden.

JOB CHART

	JANUARY	FEBRUARY	MARCH
Bulbs	Snowdrops and aconites flowering	Crocus, iris and first daffodils flowering	Plant lilies, plant crocosmia, plant and move snowdrops whilst still green
Annuals		Sow hardy annuals indoors	Sow tender annuals indoors
Perennials		Cut back all dead material from borders	Cut back all dead material from borders
Shrubs	Plant deciduous shrubs, prune roses	Plant deciduous shrubs, prune roses	Plant deciduous shrubs, prune buddleja
Climbers	Sow sweet peas indoors, plant climbing roses	Trim wisteria, sow sweet peas indoors, plant climbing roses	Prune late-flowering clematis, sow sweet peas indoors
Grasses		Cut back all deciduous grasses and clean up evergreen grasses	Cut back all deciduous grasses and clean up evergreen grasses
Ferns			
Vegetables	Sow chilies, onions under cover	Sow chilies, tomatoes, rocket, spinach under cover, sow broad beans outside, plant onion and shallot sets outside	Sow tomatoes, salad leaves, beetroot, chard, spinach, summer cabbage, kale, broccoli under cover, sow broad beans outside, plant onion and shallot sets outside, plant early potatoes outside, prick out tomatoes and chilies
Herbs	Protect Mediterranean herbs from rain and extreme cold	Sow parsley indoors	Sow parsley and coriander indoors
Fruit	Prune tree fruit such as apples and pears but NOT plums or cherries, prune autumn-fruiting raspberries, plant raspberries and all soft fruit bushes, prune grape vines	Prune tree fruit such as apples and pears but NOT plums or cherries, prune autumn-fruiting raspberries, plant raspberries and all soft fruit bushes	Prune gooseberries and redcurrants, protect peaches, nectarines and apricot blossom from frost, plant strawberries, harvest rhubarb
Trees, Hedges & Shrubs	Plant deciduous trees, shrubs or hedging plants, prune/train deciduous woody plants, cut back hard any straggly or thin hedging to encourage regrowth	Plant deciduous trees, shrubs or hedging plants, prune/train deciduous woody plants	
Lawns			Aerate, scarify and mow
Wildlife	Do not cut grass, feed birds plant trees and shrubs with berries, put up nest boxes	Do not cut grass, feed birds, plant perennials for pollinators, put up nest boxes	Do not cut grass, feed birds, plant perennials for pollinators
Houseplants	Water sparingly, mist daily, give midwinter clean of foliage	Water sparingly, mist daily	Give all plants a good soak, begin to feed weekly, repot and cut back pelargoniums, continue misting daily

JOB CHART

	APRIL	MAY	JUNE
Bulbs	Plant lilies, nerines, gladioli, eucomis, begonia, crocosmia. Tulips at best	Plant dahlias outside	Plant dahlias outside
Annuals		Sow hardy annuals direct outside, plant out tender annuals, sow biennials	Plant out tender annuals, sow biennials
Perennials	Plant and divide and replant herbaceous perennials	Stake tall perennials	Stake tall perennials, cut back some late-flowering perennials to extend season ('Chelsea Chop')
Shrubs	Prune hydrangeas		Prune early-flowering shrubs, prune early species roses
Climbers	Plant out sweet peas, sow tender annual climbers	Plant out sweet peas	Prune early-flowering clematis
Grasses		Plant and divide grasses	
Ferns	Plant any hardy fern	Unwrap and/or plant tree ferns	
Vegetables	Sow squashes, sweetcorn, French beans, courgettes, cucumber, radicchio under cover. Sow peas, broad beans, carrots, parsnips, all salad crops, beetroot, potatoes outside	Continue sowing salad crops outside, plant tomatoes, cucumber in greenhouses. Plant summer cabbage, kale, broccoli, chard, beetroot outside, prick out and pot on as necessary. Harden off indoor crops raised indoors before planting out	Continue sowing salad crops outside, harvest broad beans, salads, pot on chillies, cucumbers, plant tomatoes, squash, sweetcorn, French beans, courgettes, radicchio outside
Herbs	Sow basil indoors, sow dill, fennel outdoors. Plant any herbs outside in ground or pot	Sow parsley, plant out basil with tomatoes under cover	Plant basil outdoors
Fruit	Protect peaches, nectarines and apricot blossom from frost, prune citrus and figs, harvest rhubarb	Harvest rhubarb, repot citrus as needed	Harvest gooseberries, redcurrants, raspberries and strawberries, harvest rhubarb
Trees, Hedges & Shrubs	Plant evergreen trees, shrubs or hedging		
Lawns		Mow weekly	Mow weekly
Wildlife	Do not cut grass, sow wildflower seed, plant annuals for pollinators, feed birds, make and plant pond	Do not cut grass, leave patches of nettles and self-sown plants for insects, plant annuals for pollinators, make and plant pond	Do not cut grass, plant annuals for pollinators, make and plant pond
Houseplants	Watch for leaf burn as sun gets brighter and hotter, continue repotting watering and feeding regime, take aeonium cuttings	Many houseplants (especially cacti and succulents) can go outside after last frost for summer, take aeonium cuttings, keep dusting and cleaning evergreen leaves	Pinch out spent flowers on pelargoniums to encourage sideshoots and take cuttings, keep dusting and cleaning evergreen leaves

JOB CHART

	JULY	AUGUST	SEPTEMBER
Bulbs	Remove lily seed heads when flowering finished (but leave stems and foliage)	Deadhead dahlias daily	Plant all spring bulbs – crocus, daffodil, muscari, iris, alliums, hyacinth, fritillaries, camassias (but NOT tulips), deadhead dahlias daily, nerines, amarines and sternbergia flowering
Annuals	Sow biennials	Deadhead to extend season	Plant out biennials, sow hardy annuals for overwintering under cover, deadhead to extend season
Perennials	Deadhead regularly	Deadhead regularly	Deadhead regularly
Shrubs	Prune species roses		
Climbers	Prune rambling roses, prune wisteria	Prune rambling roses	
Grasses			
Ferns			
Vegetables	Continue sowing salad crops outside, harvest garlic, broad beans, peas, carrots, salads, chard, beetroot, summer cabbage, plant out any tender crops, harvest tomatoes, cucumbers indoors	Continue sowing salad crops outside, harvest all crops as ripe, indoors and out, plant winter cabbages, brussels sprouts, sow swede, turnip, rocket, chard, oriental greens for winter harvest	Plant garlic, cut back squash leaves to improve ripening, continue harvesting all crops as ready
Herbs		Sow parsley	Take semi-ripe cuttings from woody shrubs such as rosemary, lavender, thyme and sage
Fruit	Harvest peaches, apricots, nectarines, cherries, gooseberries, redcurrants, blackcurrants, raspberries and strawberries, thin apples and pears to two fruit per group. Summer prune all trained fruit and any overgrown fruit trees, prune plums and cherries (but only if necessary for shape and size)	Summer prune trained fruit, harvest peaches, apricots, nectarines, raspberries, strawberries, blueberries and blackcurrants	Harvest apples, pears, plums, raspberries and blueberries, plant strawberries, prune summer raspberries
Trees, Hedges & Shrubs		Trim hedges	Plant deciduous trees, shrubs or hedging plants, trim hedges
Lawns	Mow weekly	Mow weekly	Mow weekly, sow seed and/or lay turf
Wildlife	Cut long grass	Cut long grass, sow wildflower seed	Cut long grass, sow wildflower seed, plant bulbs, make bug hotel
Houseplants	Take pelargonium cuttings, keep dusting and cleaning evergreen leaves	Take pelargonium cuttings	Take pelargonium cuttings

JOB CHART

	OCTOBER	NOVEMBER	DECEMBER
Bulbs	Plant spring bulbs (except tulips), deadhead dahlias daily, nerines, amarines and sternbergia flowering	Plant tulips, lift dahlias and store	Plant tulips
Annuals	Plant out biennials, sow hardy annuals for overwintering under cover		
Perennials	Deadhead regularly	Cut back and tidy any growth needing support but leave freestanding growth for cover over winter	
Shrubs	Plant deciduous shrubs, prune straggly growth on roses	Plant deciduous shrubs	Plant deciduous shrubs
Climbers	Prune climbing roses, sow sweet peas to overwinter under cover	Prune climbing roses, plant climbing roses	Plant climbing roses
Grasses			
Ferns		Protect tree ferns from winter cold	
Vegetables	Plant garlic, pull up tomatoes, cucumbers, sweetcorn and all tender crops, plant out indoor-raised salad crops under cover for winter harvest	Plant garlic	Plant garlic
Herbs	Protect Mediterranean herbs from rain and extreme cold	Protect Mediterranean herbs from rain and extreme cold	Protect Mediterranean herbs from rain and extreme cold
Fruit	Harvest apples, pears, plums, raspberries, plant strawberries, plant fruit trees and bushes	Harvest apples, plant fruit trees and bushes	Plant fruit trees and bushes, mulch rhubarb when leaves have died back
Trees, Hedges & Shrubs	Plant or move deciduous trees, shrubs or hedging plants	Plant or move deciduous trees, shrubs or hedging plants	Plant deciduous trees, shrubs or hedging plants, prune/train deciduous woody plants
Lawns	Mow weekly, aerate, scarify, sow seed and/or lay turf		
Wildlife	Cut long grass but leave patches long at margins for winter cover, sow wildflower seed, plant bulbs, leave any dried stems, and piles of leaves, logs and twigs for winter cover, make bug hotel	Plant bulbs, feed birds, leave any dried stems and piles of leaves, logs and twigs for winter cover, plant trees and shrubs with berries	Feed birds, plant trees and shrubs with berries
Houseplants	Reduce watering, increase misting as central heating comes on	Reduce watering, increase misting as central heating comes on, move tender plants away from cold windows	Water sparingly, mist daily

SOIL CHART

	CLAY pH 6—7	CHALK / LIMESTONE pH 7—8.5
Pros	**Neutral pH.** Very fertile for most plants. Retains moisture	**Alkaline pH.** Quick to warm up, good drainage. Ideal for Mediterranean plants and many flowering shrubs
Cons	Heavy and sodden when wet and brick-like when dry	Dries out fast. No good for ericaceous plants.
Vegetables	Brassica, beans, peas, potatoes, lettuce, chard, spinach, squash	All brassicas, sweetcorn, spinach, asparagus, artichoke, chard, leeks, peas, beans, garlic
Herbs	Mint, parsley, borage, comfrey, dill, chives, fennel, lemon balm, basil	Rosemary, lavender, oregano, thyme, marjoram, sage, lemon verbena
Fruit	Strawberries, fig, plums, apricot, peach, crab apple, apples, pears, plums, blackcurrants	Cherries, crab apples, apples, pear, mulberry, fig
Trees	Hornbeam, birch, crab apple, holly, arbutus, oak, ash, horse chestnut, willow, alder	Yew, box, cherries, beech, hawthorn, gleditsia, ash
Shrubs	All roses, hydrangea, ribes, lilac, cotoneaster, cornus, amelanchier, hazel	Ceanothus, weigelia, philadelphus, deutzia, lilac, oleander, hazel, viburnum, euonymus, buddleja
Climbers	Roses, hydrangea, honeysuckle, wisteria	Clematis, honeysuckle, jasmine
Bulbs	Snowdrops, fritillaries, camassias, daffodils, snowflake, alliums, lilium regale	Crocus, iris, muscari, scilla, tulips, daffodils, alliums, lilium candidum and lilium henryii
Perennials	Hosta, thalictrums, rodgersia, aster, helenium, persicaria, pulmonaria	Geranium, hemerocallis, catmint, rudbeckia, penstemon, hollyhocks, sedum, lily of the valley
Annuals	Sweet peas, foxgloves, forget-me-nots, petunia	Cornflowers, sweet peas, alyssum, marigolds, sunflowers, wallflowers
Grasses	Miscanthus, panicum, pennisetum, hakinechloa, calamagrostis	Miscanthus, stipa, pennisetum, poa, festuca

	SAND pH 5.5–6.5	PEAT pH 3.5–5.5
Pros	**Neutral to acidic pH.** Fast drainage. Easy to work	**Very acidic pH.** Ideal for ericaceous plants
Cons	Dries out fast and loses nutrients.	Wet. No good for lime-loving plants and the brassica family.
Vegetables	Carrots, parsnips, turnips, asparagus, artichoke, garlic, onions	Radishes, chili, potatoes, rhubarb, cucumbers
Herbs	Rosemary, lavender, oregano, thyme, marjoram, sage, lemon verbena	Sorrel, basil, thyme, sweet cicely
Fruit	Blueberries, vines, raspberries, peaches, apricots, fig	Blueberries, currants, raspberries, gooseberries
Trees	Birch, pine, juniper, gleditsia, sweet chestnut, scarlet oak, acer, robinia, sorbus, magnolia	Pines, acer, firs, rowan, cedar, alder
Shrubs	Witch hazel, magnolia, viburnum, choisya, berberis, cotinus, forsythia, kerria, spiraea, buddleja	Azalea, rhododendron, erica, camellia, witch hazel, magnolia, heathers, bilberry, berberis, gardenia, pieris
Climbers	Wisteria, Virginia creeper, passion flower, jasmine	Virginia creeper, climbing hydrangea, ivy
Bulbs	Crocus, iris, ixia, daffodils, muscari, scilla, tulips, alliums, lilies	Lilies (especially the oriental hybrids)
Perennials	Sedum, ferns, verbena bonariensis, acanthus, anthemis, crocosmia, dianthus, echinops, catmint, echinacea	Japanese anemones, trillium, liriope, astilbe, dicentra, ajuga, meconopsis, ferns
Annuals	Foxgloves, antirrhinums, cosmos, coreopsis, zinnia	Foxgloves
Grasses	Miscanthus, stipa, agrostis, deschampsia, festuca, leymus	Phormium

GLOSSARY

Aerate Make holes in turf to reduce compaction and improve drainage.

Alkaline Soil or compost that has a pH value of 7 or above (6–7 is neutral). Certain plants such as many flowering shrubs, brassicas, clematis and Mediterranean herbs thrive in alkaline soil.

Bare root Plants sold straight from the growing field and not in a pot. These tend to be cheaper, better quality and have a much wider range to choose from. However they need immediate planting or temporary storage in a container or holding trench in the ground.

Bud An unopened flower.

Bulb An underground storage organ containing the future flower and food for its development, such as daffodil, tulip, onion, lily and garlic.

Crocks Usually pieces of broken terracotta pots (but can be pebbles or polystyrene pieces) used to ensure drainage at the bottom of a pot before adding compost.

Cutting A section of plant material that will form roots if inserted into a suitable growing medium. Unlike seed, which can hybridise, all cuttings exactly replicate their parent.

Division The splitting of plants either by cutting into sections or pulling or tearing apart so that each section has roots and at least one shoot. These can then be individually raised as separate plants.

Drill A shallow groove drawn in prepared soil in which to sow seeds.

Ericaceous Soil or compost that has a pH value of 6 or below (6–7 is neutral). Plants such as rhododendrons, azaleas, camellias and blueberries need ericaceous soil to thrive.

Garden compost Garden and kitchen waste that has biodegraded through bacterial action to make an organic feed and soil improver.

Germinate The process by which a seed develops shoots and roots.

Graft A section of vegetation (usually woody) inserted into another woody plant so that they form a union and grow as one. The added section is called the scion and the receiving section the stock. Most commercial roses are propagated this way.

Horticultural grit Finely graded stone used to improve drainage in potting compost.

Humus Soil that has a high organic content and is thus very fertile.

Leader The dominant shoot in any woody plant both growing vertically and at the end of each branch. Leaders suppress shoots beneath them and become dominant but rarely carry flowers or fruit.

Leaf mould Fallen leaves that have biodegraded, primarily through fungal action, to form a soil and compost improver and mulch.

Mulch A layer of organic material such as garden compost or bark chips laid over bare soil to suppress weed germination, retain moisture and improve the soil structure and fertility.

Node The point at which leaves or buds emerge from a stem.

Pan A shallow terracotta container, usually used for small bulbs or alpine plants.

Perlite A white mineral that is quarried, heated to high temperatures so that it expands hugely and is then broken into fine particles. Used as an addition to potting compost to improve soil structure, drainage and water retention.

Pinch out To remove the growing tip (or leader) of plants such as sweet peas, pelargoniums, cosmos or fuchsias in order to encourage sideshoots that bear the flowers.

Plug/Module A tray of cells in plastic or silicone. These are available in various sizes and good for raising or growing on individual seedlings with uniform root space.

Potting compost A growing medium for raising plants for future planting or permanent display. Ingredients can include coir, various bark, bracken and neighborhood waste but as of 2024 not peat which, in any event, should never be purchased or used, as its extraction is environmentally catastrophic.

Potting on Transferring a young plant to a bigger container when its roots begin to outgrow the current space. Part of the process of encouraging steady, unstressed growth.

Pricking out Transferring young seedlings after germination and the development of true leaves from a seed tray to plugs or pots.

Propagate Raising plants vegetatively by seed, cuttings, division or bulb.

Rhizome Horizontal fleshy roots that store food and produce shoots for new growth. Bearded iris, ginger, bamboos, water lilies and many ferns have rhizomes.

Rootstock Most fruit trees are grown by grafting the named variety onto a general rootstock, usually a few inches above ground level. Whilst the graft (the top part) determines the details of the leaves, flowers and fruit, the rootstock determines the size and characteristics of the growth. This means, for example, the same apple can be grown on trees that vary from dwarf to medium to large 27ft/9m specimens. Different rootstocks will be suitable for different soil types and growing situations as well as for size.

Scarify Scratching the surface of grass with a wire rake to remove moss and dead grass (thatch) to allow more light, moisture and air to reach healthy new grass and thus repair wear and tear.

Seed leaf The first leaf that every seed produces and which is formed by the seed itself rather than by roots. All seed leaves are similar, being smooth edged and propellor-like.

Seed tray A shallow container, usually plastic, in which you sprinkle seeds over a layer of potting compost so they can germinate and develop into seedlings.

Seedling A very young plant, emerged from a seed. In the case of an annual, this stage may only refer to a few weeks whereas an oak tree can be a seedling for a number of years. Although seedlings have the foliage of the mature plant, they do not produce flowers.

Side shoot A lateral growth from a stem, often bearing flowers.

Thin Reducing the density of emerging seedlings to allow even spacing and reduce competition of nutrition and water.

Tilth Soil that has been dug, weeded, raked and prepared to a fine and even consistency ready for sowing seed.

Transpiration Water taken up via the roots and stem of plants and lost from the leaves, stems and flowers via evaporation. This accounts for the vast majority of all moisture taken up by plant roots.

True leaf The second and subsequent leaves to grow on a seedling after the seed leaf. True leaves have all the characteristics of the parent plant and are thus identifiable.

Tuber A fleshy underground storage organ enabling plants to survive winter and grow again in spring when new leaves can photosynthesise. Unlike bulbs, they do not have a single plant that regrows but produce numerous eyes or shoots. Potatoes, dahlias and Jerusalem artichokes grow from tubers.

Vermiculite A tawny, beige mineral that, when heated to high temperatures, expands greatly and is used, like perlite, to improve soil structure, water retention and drainage. Whilst perlite takes years to biodegrade, vermiculite breaks down more quickly so tends to be used with seed compost rather than potting compost.

Vernalise To expose seed to a period of cold, either outside or in a fridge or freezer to simulate winter. As the seed subsequently warms up, it thinks it is spring so is triggered into germination.

ACKNOWLEDGMENTS

All books are a collaborative venture to some extent but in my experience at least, none more so than this one.

Marsha Arnold created her superb images, often in freezing cold, ably assisted by Chris Athanasiou, Paul Musso and, behind the scenes, Sam Hardwick. It was an unfailing pleasure to work with them.

At Ebury Albert DePetrillo has masterminded and calmly nurtured this project from inception, with Nell Warner and Charlotte Macdonald handling the often complex and seemingly disjointed material with good humour and efficiency. The designer Dave Brown has exactly captured the freshness and accessibility we all vaguely spoke of – as well as tolerating our endless inputs and alterations along the way.

My agent Alexandra Henderson has been a constant support in every way and detail, which I have come to take as read, but I hope never for granted.

My in-house team of Polly James and my son Adam have worked tirelessly and cheerfully, organising all the shoots, sourcing unlikely props at the last minute and plants out of season, liaising with all parties as well as contributing a huge amount to the details of the layout and design. Their contribution has been invaluable.

Caroline Danby, Jamieson McNabb and Rob Jones have kept the wheels of the garden turning and looking its best self when too often I have been bound to a desk or a TV camera.

Finally, my wife, Sarah, encourages, supports and inspires everything good that I might do. For that which falls short, I alone take responsibility.

INDEX